Springer Series: FOCUS ON WOMEN

Violet Franks, Ph.D., Series Editor
Confronting the major psychological, medical, and social issues of today and tomorrow. Focus on Women provides a wide range of books on the changing concerns of women.

THE BATTERED WOMAN SYNDROME (1984)
Lenore E. Walker, Ed.D.
WOMEN THERAPISTS WORKING WITH WOMEN: New Theory and Process of Feminist Therapy (1984)
Claire M. Brody, Ph.D., Editor
WOMEN'S THERAPY GROUPS: Paradigms of Feminist Treatment (1987)
Claire M. Brody, Ph.D., Editor
WOMEN AND DEPRESSION: A Lifespan Perspective (1987)
Ruth Formanek, Ph.D., and Anita Gurian, Ph.D., Editors
TRANSITIONS IN A WOMAN'S LIFE: Major Life Events in Developmental Context (1989)
Ramona T. Mercer, R.N., Ph.D., F.A.A.N., Elizabeth G. Nichols, D.N.S., F.A.A.N., Glen C. Doyle, Ed.D., R.N.
NEW DIRECTIONS IN FEMINIST PSYCHOLOGY: Practice, Theory, and Research (1992)
Joan C. Chrisler, Ph.D., and Doris Howard, Ph.D., Editors
THE EMPLOYED MOTHER AND THE FAMILY CONTEXT (1993)
Judith Frankel, Ph.D., Editor
WOMEN AND ANGER (1993)
Sandra P. Thomas, Ph.D., R.N., Editor
TREATING ABUSE IN FAMILIES: A Feminist and Community Approach (1994)
Elaine Leeder, M.S.W., C.S.W., M.P.H., Ph.D.
WOMEN AND SUICIDAL BEHAVIOR (1995)
Silvia Sara Canetto, Ph.D., and David Lester, Ph.D., Editors
BECOMING A MOTHER: Research on Maternal Role Identity from Rubin to the Present (1995)
Ramona T. Mercer, R.N., Ph.D., F.A.A.N.
WOMEN, FEMINISM, AND AGING (1998)
Colette V. Browne, Dr.P.H.
WOMEN'S HEALTH NEEDS IN PATIENT EDUCATION (1999)
Barbara K. Redman, Ph.D., R.N., F.A.A.N.
AGING MOTHERS AND THEIR DAUGHTERS: A Study of Mixed Emotions (2001)
Karen L. Fingerman, Ph.D.

Karen L. Fingerman, PhD, is Assistant Professor of Human Development and Family Studies and Faculty Affiliate with the Gerontology Center at Pennsylvania State University. She has conducted research and published numerous scholarly articles on positive and negative emotions in social relationships. Her work has examined mothers and daughters, grandparents and grandchildren, friends, acquaintances, and peripheral social ties. The National Institute on Aging has funded her recent work on problematic social ties across the life span and the Brookdale Foundation has funded her recent work on parent/child ties in adulthood. She received the Springer Award for Early Career Achievement in Research on Adult Development and Aging from Division 20 of the American Psychological Association in 1998 and the Margret Baltes Award for Early Career Achievement in Behavioral and Social Gerontology from the Gerontological Society of America in 1999.

Aging Mothers and Their Adult Daughters

A Study in Mixed Emotions

Karen L. Fingerman, PhD

Springer Series: Focus on Women

Springer Publishing Company, Inc.
536 Broadway
New York, NY 10012-3955

Acquisitions Editor: Bill Tucker
Production Editor: Pamela Lankas
Cover design by Susan Hauley

01 02 03 04 05 / 5 4 3 2 1

Library of Congress Cataloging-in-Publication Data

Fingerman, Karen L.
Aging mothers and their adult daughters : a study in mixed emotions / Karen L. Fingerman, author.
p. cm. — (Springer series, focus on women)
Includes bibliographical references and index.
ISBN 0-8261-1379-6
1. Parent and adult child. 2. Mothers and daughters. 3. Aging parents. 4. Family life surveys. I. Title II. Series.
HQ755.86 .F56 2000
306.874'3—dc21 00-063518
CIP

Printed in Canada

This book is dedicated to John A. Yeazell, who brings a physicist's perspective to the social sciences. He taught me that, as in quantum mechanics, when you seek to understand mothers and daughters, you must look at many aspects of the relationship.

Contents

■ Four: Mothers' and Daughters' Reactions to Problems

Acknowledgments

I wish to thank a number of individuals who contributed to this book in different ways. This research began when I was a student at the University of Michigan. Eric Bermann and Joseph Veroff cochaired my dissertation with patience, wisdom, and a generosity of time and spirit that is deeply appreciated. Funding for this study was provided by: The Society for the Psychological Study of Social Issues, Sigma Xi Society, American Psychological Association Dissertation Award, and Rackham Graduate School of Studies, University of Michigan. I am grateful that so many sources saw much promise in this work. In recent years, my work has been funded by the National Institutes on Aging and the Brookdale Foundation.

In the years that followed completion of my dissertation, Lillian Troll took over as an informal mentor. She has been an avid supporter throughout my career. In particular, her comments on a draft of this book provided the final impetus for its fruition.

Although I alone am responsible for the findings presented, I received help from many sources. Numerous students provided assistance with literature review, coding, and organization of the tables. I am grateful to Krista Etters, Kira Birditt, Elizabeth Van Citters, Elizabeth Hay, and Claire Kamp for their input. Anastasia Snyder prepared the table in the Introduction. Linda Burton, Catherine Cohan, Ann Crouter, Janis Jacobs, Eva Lefkowitz, Susan McHale,

Warner Schaie, Sherry Willis, and Steven Zarit, my colleagues at Pennsylvania State University, have broadened my intellectual perspective considerably. The Transcoop working group on Intergenerational Ambivalence sponsored by the Humboldt Foundation and organized by Kurt Luescher and Karl Pillemer provided insight into the complexities of emotions in parent/offspring ties. In addition, I have benefitted immeasurably from the guidance of colleagues in the field, including Toni Antonucci, Victoria Bedford, Laura Carstensen, Rosemary Blieszner, Dorothy Field, Colleen Johnson, Frieder Lang, Karen Rook, Alexis Walker, and Susan Whitbourne.

I also wish to thank those individuals who assisted in the preparation of this book. Danielle Swiontek and Jeremy Wood read drafts of chapters. Rhonda Fingerman and Donna Ballock gave input and help in proofreading drafts of this book. My husband suggested the title; his humor and advice were available to me at all stages of this project. I am particularly grateful to Bill Tucker and the staff at Springer Publishing for their patience in seeing this book through to completion. Seeking tenure and writing a book appear to be incompatible goals; I thank Springer Publishing for allowing me time to pursue the former.

Finally, on a personal note, a book on family ties in adulthood would not be complete without family. I am grateful to mine, particularly to my mother and her daughters.

Introduction

Among the myriad of advances that occurred during the twentieth century, increased longevity may have had the greatest impact on individuals' lives. The average life expectancy at the start of the twentieth century hovered between 40 and 50 years, but by the end of the century it had nearly doubled. With increased years of life, intergenerational relationships, in particular, have changed in tenor. Parents and offspring now have the advantage and disadvantage of negotiating their relationships over much longer periods of time than was previously the case. At the turn of the twentieth century, nearly a quarter of children lost at least one parent by the age of 15 (Hagestad, 1982). At the start of the twenty-first century, most individuals experience many decades in which both their parents are alive and in good health.

Social and technological advances over the past 200 years have also changed the qualities of ties between parents and offspring. Economic advances permit freedom from the family farm. Indeed, families are no longer bound to a single geographic region. Some grown offspring relocate to where their specialized job skills are needed. Many healthy, retired older adults find themselves with financial security in later life, requiring little or no support from their grown offspring. Thus, we might expect parents and grown offspring to care little for one another and to have little contact in the modern world. In actuality, most parents and adult offspring maintain relationships characterized by warm regard, frequent contact, and mutual exchanges of help and assistance (Davey & Eggebeen, 1998). Indeed, the parent/offspring relationship in modern America is based more on emotional affection than on economic or cultural imperatives. Parents and offspring keep in touch because they enjoy one another.

This is not to say that all ties between parents and offspring are the same. Certain relationships are more emotionally intense than others. Structural factors such as geographic location and gender play a key role in defining the nature of parent/offspring ties. Parents and offspring residing in the same geographic area often share strong affinities for their relationship. Mothers and daughters report deeper emotions, positive and negative, in their intergenerational relationships than do fathers and sons. These two features of parent/offspring ties, proximity and gender, are discussed here. This book focuses specifically on one distinct intergenerational relationship, namely, mothers and daughters who live in proximity.

Throughout this book, discussion focuses on parents and their biological or adopted children. This book does not deal with stepmothers in later life, despite the increasing prevalence of this type of parent/child tie (Fine, Coleman, & Ganong, 1998; Ganong & Coleman, 1999). It would be inappropriate to consider stepparents and parents interchangeable. Instead, in a small study of this type, it is important to focus on one group of individuals. In making a decision about which group to examine, I considered the cohort of older women in the 1990s. Divorce rates were not as high among elderly parents as they are at present, and therefore, middle-aged daughters are less likely to have been raised by stepparents than is the case for present cohorts of children. Thus, discussion here focuses primarily on mothers who are married to their daughters' fathers or who are widowed. Although this approach limits the scope of this book, this group includes many of today's older women and their offspring. Of course, it will be important to consider stepparents and their stepchildren in future cohorts if we desire to understand family ties.

GEOGRAPHIC DISTANCE AND PARENT/OFFSPRING TIES

Technological and economic advances of the past 200 years have made it possible for parents and offspring to go their separate ways.

Yet, surprisingly, families are not widely dispersed around the country. Of course, many offspring do move away from parents when they reach adulthood. Alternately, some well-off parents relocate to sunny locations after retirement and leave behind offspring who remained in the area. Notwithstanding, the majority of older parents live in proximity to at least one of their grown children. In a national study of intergenerational ties, researchers reported that 50% of parents lived within 5 miles of their closest child. For those parents who had more than one child, 50% reported that their second child also lived within 35 miles. Indeed, 75% of parents reported that their closest child lived within 35 miles of their own home (Lin & Rogerson, 1995). Other studies have found even greater proportions of parents who reside within an hour's drive of one of their offspring (Rossi & Rossi, 1990; Shanas, 1979). Thus, most older adults have close relationships with at least one of their children.

Of course, the pattern is not the same with regard to offspring's distance from parents. Most grown offspring do not live near their parents (Sweet, Bumpass, & Vaugn, 1988). To understand why this is the case, imagine a family with four grown offspring. One of these offspring might live near their parents, but the others do not. This is not to say that few offspring live near their parents. Indeed, as can be seen in Table I.1, data from a national survey indicates that a sizeable proportion of offspring remain near their parents, particularly near their mothers in adulthood. When offspring do move away,

TABLE I.1 Distance Adults Live from Their Parents*

	Lives within 50 miles of		Lives in home with	
Offspring	**Mother**	**Father**	**Mother**	**Father**
All	42.9	30.8	3.4	2.4
Men	42.8	31.8	4.1	2.8
Women	43.0	30.1	2.9	2.1
Black	45.8	32.6	2.6	2.1
White	42.2	30.4	3.6	2.5
25–34	56.5	45.4	5.8	5.2
35–44	44.1	33.2	2.3	1.7
45–54	32.7	16.8	2.5	.6

*Weighted percentages (N= 7095), data from the National Survey of Families and Households.

aging parents may follow, relocating to be close them, particularly if these parents incur health problems (Lin & Rogerson, 1995). As will be discussed, these rates decline as offspring grow older, but the decline reflects parents' mortality more than geographic mobility.

This book deals with parents and offspring who reside near one another. Thus, a large number of offspring are excluded from the purview of discussion. It is not clear how distant offspring differ from their more proximate counterparts. Some studies have found that offspring who move away from their parents in young adulthood do so for educational or career opportunities, rather than for reasons stemming from their relationships with their parents (Lin & Rogerson, 1995). Theorists have argued, however, that offspring with deeply problematic relationships with parents choose to move away from them (Bedford & Blieszner, 1997). Still other researchers have suggested geographic distance serves as a buffer in this relationship. When parents and offspring do not live in proximity, offspring get along better with their parents because day-to-day problems do not arise (Climo, 1992). Finally, geographic distance itself may generate tensions if parents and offspring wish they resided in closer proximity, particularly when crises arise (Halpern, 1994).

Nonetheless, geographic distance does seem to have some consistent effects on the parent/offspring tie. When parents are asked to describe a child who is particularly important in their lives, they tend to name a child who lives nearby (Aldous, Klaus, & Klein, 1998). Indeed, this pattern carries down the generational ladder. Grandparents feel closer to the children of children who reside nearby (Fingerman, 1998a). Offspring who live near parents are more likely to be called upon to care for those parents when the need arises than are their distant siblings (Brody, Hoffman, Kleban, & Schoonover, 1989).

The important issue here is frequency of contact rather than the actual distance of residence. Parents and adult offspring who reside near one another have more opportunities to get together than do parents and offspring who reside at a distance. Proximity permits a degree of intimacy and participation in one another's day-to-day life that is more difficult when distances are greater. Frequent contact can foster emotional intensity. Parents and offspring who have more contact have more opportunities to build an affectionate relationship and to feel upset with the other party (Luescher & Pillemer, 1998;

Mares, 1995). When crises arise at the end of life, offspring who reside near their parents are more likely to intervene with the types of hands on, intensive caregiving that creates stress in this relationship (Connidis, Rosenthal, & McMullin, 1996). By focusing on mothers and daughters who reside in proximity, this book deals with those parent/offspring ties that are most likely to have an impact on each party's well-being in the second half of life.

GENDER DIFFERENCES IN PARENT/OFFSPRING TIES

Gender also plays a key role in the emotional qualities of parent/child ties. Regardless of where they live, women are more likely to maintain strong ties to their parents and their children than are men. In fact, the strength of the mother/daughter bond distinguishes it from other social ties. Marital partners divorce when disparities arise, friendships dissolve when life situations change, and family members become estranged in the face of conflict (Bedford & Blieszner, 1997; Blieszner & Adams, 1995; Gottman, 1998). Few relationships endure with the strength of the mother/daughter tie throughout life.

Demographic, psychological, and social structural factors render unique qualities to women's intergenerational ties. Their shared "femaleness" contributes to the nature of their ties. Women share a disadvantaged status in society. Poverty, educational deprivation, and poor health care forge ties between mothers and daughters. Women are more likely to require assistance with daily tasks, emotional problems, and financial needs than are men; they often receive this assistance from their mothers or their daughters. Yet, as will be discussed in this book, even women who are well off retain strong bonds to their mothers and daughters.

The maternal role appears to have special psychological salience for women. Throughout life, mothers tend to be more invested in their children than are fathers. Indeed, in old age, women are likely to consider one of their children to be the most important person in their life. Older women were socialized from an early age to view themselves as mothers, and the maternal identity enhances their investment in their children. Moreover, older women's greater value for offspring partially stems from demographics. Longevity is not evenly distributed by gender, and women outlive men. As a result, most women are widowed in old age, whereas most men are not. Moreover, divorce rates began to climb nearly 50 years ago and remain high. Women are unlikely to remarry in the second half of life. As a result, women who lack a partner turn to their children, and particularly to their daughters for solace and support.

Gender differences are also evident with regard to filial ties to parents. Daughters, more often than sons, retain intimate ties to their families of origin throughout adulthood. As increasing numbers of women find themselves divorced or single at midlife as well, they turn to their mothers for help with finances, comfort, and child care. More importantly, women are socialized to value their families and to invest in generations above and below them. From childhood on, girls are taught to remain close to their mothers, while boys are encouraged to establish independence from their parents (Chodorow, 1994).

Mothers and daughters also share the burdens and joys of family work throughout adulthood (Fingerman, 2000). Men establish their primary ties to their wives when they marry (Troll, 1988). By contrast, women tend to bring their husbands into the orbit of their own family constellation when they marry. Thus, the mother/daughter tie is important not only to the participants involved, but to the larger kinship network in which it is embedded. Given the central role of the mother/daughter tie in family functioning, the emotional complexities of this relationship may provide insights into the family as a whole. Mothers and daughters who maintain stronger ties may foster closer ties to other kin. By contrast, when mothers and daughters are upset with one another, their feelings may taint family gatherings and other relationships.

I do not wish to imply that the phenomena described in this book are biologically determined or that all women's relationships follow specific patterns. Rather, for a variety of reasons, these patterns are more often found in intergenerational ties involving women than in intergenerational ties involving men. Of course, some men maintain a deep intimacy with their parents, but women are more likely to do so. Thus, descriptions of mother/daughter relationships should be taken as descriptions of intergenerational relationships based on strong emotional bonds, rather than ties that are inherently linked to sex.

Specifically, this book focuses on the mother/daughter tie during an under-researched period of the life span, when daughters are grown and have entered midlife, but their mothers remain healthy. Most people spend the majority of their adult years in relatively good health. Yet, the majority of research on mother/daughter ties in late life has focused on mothers who have experienced dramatic declines in health. By considering the mother/daughter tie when both parties are healthy, we gain insights into the more normal patterns of their relationship. Moreover, to truly understand the stresses that daughters incur when they provide care for their mothers, we must know about the stresses that they incurred before they began to provide care.

The book consists of four sections. The first section provides an overview of the mother/daughter tie in late life. The mother/daughter tie is a relationship that women value greatly throughout life, but it takes on unique characteristics when daughters enter midlife and mothers enter old age. The second section of the book describes the positive qualities of the mother/daughter relationships. Mothers and daughters perceive distinct benefits from their relationships and enjoy the other party in specific ways. The third section deals with the difficulties that women encounter in their relationships with their mothers and daughters in the second half of life. As was mentioned, studies addressing tensions between aging mothers and their daughters have often focused on the caregiving context. Yet, women report difficulties in this relationship before the mother incurs health declines. The third section of this book introduces a framework for understanding these tensions called the "developmental schism" framework. This section then provides descriptions of the tensions that mothers and daughters in this study have experienced. The final section deals with mothers' and daughters' reactions to the problems that they encounter and includes a conclusion integrating mothers' and daughters experiences in their relationships. There has been little attention to a theoretical framework that might explain the mother/daughter tie in late life. In this book, each section includes a chapter involving literature review and theory and at least one chapter involving reports from this study of mothers and daughters.

This book deals with the complexities of mothers' and daughters' relationships when mothers have begun to age, but are still healthy, active, and independent. Intergenerational bonds between women tend to be particularly strong at this stage of life. Yet, women also report feeling anxious, frustrated, guilty, and even angry in their relationships with their mothers and daughters. By understanding the emotions that women experience and how they handle those emotions, we will gain greater insight into how relationships can endure throughout a lifetime.

■ one

AGING MOTHERS AND ADULT DAUGHTERS

■ 1
Complexities of the Mother/Daughter Tie

I think one of the things I've noticed lately is that she's getting older. I feel like I have to watch over her a lot. I'm always kind of amazed at how vulnerable she seems. She's getting older. I think it definitely annoys me because I feel . . . I get fearful, not really angry at her. I'm just fearful for her safety and her continued independence. So, what ends up happening is I get angry. I think, 'How can you walk down and go shopping?' It's like she's not paying attention to what's going on around her. Someone could so easily come up to her and knock her over and take her purse, or harm her in some way. . . . Like I said, her vulnerability irritates me, but I don't think she's that conscious of it. I get angry at myself for being that way. I mean she's not scared. I don't want to impose those fears on her. I'm always amazed at how independent she is.

—Brenda, 38-year-old daughter

Over the past 10 years, I've interviewed hundreds of women about their relationships with their mothers and daughters. When I began my work, other researchers had already documented the strengths of the mother/daughter tie, but few researchers had considered the intricacies of negative emotions in this relationship. In one of my first studies, a middle-aged daughter summed up her experiences, "If my mother were my husband, I would have divorced her years ago." Yet, despite these negative feelings, this daughter did not spend less time with, feel less affection for, or do fewer tasks for her mother. The strength of the mother/daughter tie is perplexing. How much tension exists between older mothers and daughters? What causes problems? How do mothers and daughters deal with difficulties in their relationship in later life? Do they communicate their feelings to the other party? Do mothers view the relationship differently than their daughters do? Why do positive feelings in this particular relationship endure in the face of negative feelings? These questions are particularly intriguing when daughters are grown and mothers are healthy. These women could presumably dissolve their relationships, but they do not. Instead, most mothers and daughters are strongly invested in their ties.

When daughters enter midlife, their relationships with their mothers are amorphous. The parameters of the mother/daughter relationship are well defined when daughters are young; the relationship revolves around nurturing and socializing the child. When both parties are adults, however, it is unclear whose needs take precedence. Social norms concerning ties between parents and offspring in adulthood are vague. Early patterns of interaction where mothers give advice to daughters are no longer relevant when daughters acquire skills that surpass those of their mothers. In late life, both parties experience feelings that were not previously a part of their repertoire. Daughters begin to worry about their mothers. Mothers come to view their offspring as the legacy that will outlive them. These changes introduce new emotions in the mother/daughter tie.

This study came to light out of a concern for understanding how aging mothers and daughters relate to one another when both parties are in good health. Prior to this research, gerontological literature equated stress between mothers and daughters in late life with the mother's physical or mental decline. Researchers had written a great deal about the caregiving roles but they seemed to assume that stress between mothers and daughters arises in late life when mothers suffer health declines or cognitive impairments. Yet, ambivalence between mothers and daughters is evident long before the mother's health declines. Equating problems between mothers and daughters in late life with health problems is a bit like studying a diabetic adolescent and attributing all of her difficulties with her mother to the diabetes. The more intriguing issues involve mothers' and daughters' feelings for one another in the absence of an obvious external problem. That is where this study begins.

EMOTIONAL COMPLEXITIES IN MOTHER/DAUGHTER RELATIONSHIPS

This book focuses on 48 pairs of mothers and daughters who participated in an in-depth study of their relationships. All of the mothers were over the age of 70 and described themselves as being in good health. Their adult daughters lived within a 30-mile drive and saw them on a frequent basis. Additional information about the study is provided in the second chapter. Here, two pairs of mothers and daughters illustrate the complexity and diversity in this relationship at midlife.

Intimacy and Demands

Lois[1], a 70-year-old mother, has been married to her husband for nearly 50 years. She has two grown children, a daughter and a son. She is active in her community. She provides care for her son's preschool aged child 3 days a week and, therefore, describes herself as employed parttime. Her daughter Roberta participated in this study. Roberta is 40 years old and is also married. She has two children of her own, both of whom are in school. Roberta works part time outside the home, but does so while her children are in school and does not rely on her mother for childcare. Roberta and Lois are in frequent contact, they visit at least 2 or 3 times a week and they talk on the phone everyday. Their contact and the different demands in their life add to the complexities of their relationship.

As part of the study, mothers and daughters described the pleasurable and the disagreeable aspects of their relationships. Lois indicated that her visits with Roberta were always a source of pleasure. In fact, when asked to describe the most recent time she had had an enjoyable visit with Roberta, Lois referred to a conversation that she had had on the telephone that morning:

> Most every time I encounter her is a pleasure and I think we had kind of a nice visit this morning on the telephone. I passed along some news about a mutual friend. We discussed the problems of the mutual friend, but it was pleasant. She was interested and was very supportive. I felt really good.

The simplicity of Lois's pleasure is a common theme between mothers and daughters in late life. Many older mothers described benefits derived from simply talking with their daughters or being in their daughter's presence. Almost any discussion, any activity, any form of sharing is marked by pleasant feelings (Fingerman, 2000a).

Roberta, on the other hand, described the warmth she felt from her mother's positive regard for her specifically. Roberta also described a telephone conversation with her mother, but in this case, she referred to her mother's shared investment in the family and more importantly, her mother's investment in her.

> I would choose the phone call I got today. She called this afternoon just to thank me for picking up my nephew at their house. She takes care of him 3 days a week. One of the things that I'm most appreciative of her is the caretaking she does for the children. And she called to tell me that I was a saint. It was really nice to hear her say that. It's not everyday that she calls you a saint.

Roberta's pleasure from her mother's praise is a theme that also arises repeatedly in middle-aged women's descriptions of their ties to their mothers. Although many aspects of the relationship change as daughters enter midlife, certain emotional qualities remain constant (Fingerman, 1997b). In particular, mothers continue to influence the way their daughters feel about themselves. Years after daughters are grown, daughters feel guilty and ashamed when their mothers criticize them and feel happy when their mothers are proud of them. Indeed, women find it difficult to balance their desire to please their mothers while dealing with the inconveniences that arise in their relationships.

Roberta, in particular, felt that the frequent phone calls she and her mother have become a source of irritation at times. Roberta is a busy woman with a husband, two active school-aged children, and a job to maintain. When asked to describe a recent time when she was annoyed with her mother, Roberta complained:

> The day last week when she called me five times. By the last call, I was pretty frustrated. She just wanted to say, "Hi" and talk. She had different things to say throughout the day. She's always planning. My nephew's birthday is coming up, and she was trying to plan for that. Then, she was upset with an interaction she had with my sister-in-law and she called to ask my opinion about that. Later, she called to tell me how that situation had been resolved. By the last call, I was exhausted.

Although Roberta enjoyed a recent phone call when her mother praised her, she finds the persistence of her mother's calls demanding and fatiguing. Lois, in turn, experiences aggravation when her daughter is unavailable. When the interviewer asked Lois to describe a recent disagreeable visit, she responded:

> The last time was about a week ago when I called her to ask how she felt about my finding a substitute babysitter for her brother Donald's children for a few hours. She was in a bad mood. That's the only time we have any problems, when she gets tired. She gets unreasonable. She was completely negative about this babysitter, when I expected her to be supportive. I was kind of hurt. I thought to myself, 'Oh boy, this was not the time to call.' When it doesn't go well, I just sort of hang up. If she's feeling good, you can discuss almost any sort of problem with her.

Lois framed her aggravations with her daughter in terms of their generally positive interactions. She was hurt and disappointed that her daughter did not have time to help her with an important decision, but she noted that Roberta usually took the time to discuss her concerns and to show support.

A central issue in Lois' and Roberta's relationship involved their efforts to be a part of one another's lives. Lois valued Roberta a great deal, and Roberta valued Lois as well, but at times she found her mother's needs constraining. Many middle-aged daughters described the tensions they experienced between intimacy and demands. The flip side, a sense of being let down, occasionally appeared in mothers' descriptions of their relationships. Like Lois, most mothers tend to cast the problems in their relationships with their daughters in favorable terms. They recognize that irritations arise, but view their ties as positive in general.

Continuity in Mother/Daughter Roles

In addition to the tension between intimacy and intrusion, mothers and daughters described difficulties negotiating the changes that incur in late life against the background of continuity in their relationship. Many older mothers enjoy their daughters' newfound efforts to nurture them. For example, Esther, an 84-year-old widow described her pleasure in her daughter Julie's attention. Julie brought Esther a homemade cake for her eighty-fourth birthday. Esther was moved by Julie's efforts on her behalf. She punctuated her description of the visit by commenting, "She's a very loving daughter." It was clear that Esther not only enjoyed the cake, she took pride in Julie as a person, and saw Julie's generosity as the outcome of her own efforts as a mother.

Julie, a 42-year-old married accountant, had no children of her own. She also enjoyed her mother, but on different terms than a younger woman might. Young women rarely think about their mothers as individuals who have feelings of their own. When young adult daughters describe enjoyable aspects of their relationships with their mothers, their discussions focus on what their mothers do for them (Fingerman, 2000a). In midlife, many daughters come to see the unique strengths that their mothers possess. Julie commented:

> My mother has this wonderful ability to see the bright side in everything. I enjoy visiting with my mother because no matter what the situation is, she seems to figure out something funny to say about it. The most recent time, I was just there this week, and we went to a workshop talking about health care power of attorneys. The workshop was offered by the senior club, and it's a fairly serious topic. When we got home she made a joke about, well, she says, 'We all have old age. You know it's a disease we can't get away from.' And she'll make a joke like that, something that's funny. I almost always enjoy being around her. She makes me laugh.

Although neither Esther nor Julie explicitly mentioned that they took pleasure from the changes that they were experiencing in their relationship, the types of situations they described are uncommon in women's descriptions of the mother/daughter tie at other stages of life. In midlife, women take note of the fact that they must do more for their mothers than they did previously, and that they can benefit from their ties to their mothers as unique individuals (Fingerman, 1997a). Older women, in turn, bask in their daughters' attention.

Of course, the mother/daughter relationship does not arise anew in late life. Indeed, problems from the past relationship can taint the mother/daughter tie in late life. There are several ways in which the history mothers and daughters share may contribute to tensions in late life. In some rare cases, extreme problems persist from earlier stages of life into old age. Mothers and daughters in these instances may have severed their ties at some point in adulthood. A more common pattern involves the renewal of past problems when mothers and daughters confront new challenges in their relationship (Field, 1989; Steinman, 1979; Whitbeck, Hoyt, & Huck, 1994). Moreover, families establish ways of interacting in childhood, and they may find it difficult to break these patterns in adulthood. Thus, tensions may persist (Fingerman & Bermann, in press; Troll, 1996). For these reasons, older mothers and daughters report problems as well as pleasure from their efforts to deal with continuity and change in their relationship.

Esther's irritations with her daughter did not involve a specific encounter or visit. Instead, she was upset by a decision her daughter had made:

> Gee, I cannot think of something specific. The big thing was when she lived with her husband before she was married. I was really upset with her. The reason I got upset was that I was afraid she'd be hurt. It didn't matter to me what she did, but I really didn't want her to be hurt. I'm a little straitlaced. I didn't think it was right. I tried to talk to her about it, but she did it anyways. I cried about it.

Although Julie had been married for several years, Esther remembered the situation clearly and was still bothered. In fact, the situation arose 10 years previously when Esther was in her 70's and Julie was in her 30's. At some level, Esther still wanted to be a mother to Julie, to protect her, and to have Julie follow her advice. Julie described a more recent time when she perceived her mother as acting "motherly."

> She worries a lot. I feel annoyed and frustrated with her when she is overly concerned with us. Sometimes she's worried about my brother or my sister, sometimes she is worried about me. There are lots of times when she'll tell me she was talking to someone and she was worried about something. She tells me that she doesn't sleep well because she's worried about one of us. I wish I could help her to feel more at ease. I wish she did not feel like she still has to be our mother and take care of us.

Julie clearly has a sense of her mother as an older woman who deserves to be freed of worries and concerns. Indeed, Julie's role as nurturer of her own mother makes her wish that she could assuage her mother's concerns. Yet, Julie is frustrated that her mother cannot give up the maternal role. This sort of tension takes many forms as mothers and daughters enter late life.

The theme of continuity and change arises repeatedly in middle-aged women's descriptions of their mothers (Fingerman, 1997a). Middle-aged women are aware of their mother's aging, but they are also frustrated by their inability to stop the process that is taking place. In some cases, older mothers resent their daughters' efforts to protect them. They feel belittled and betrayed when their daughters do not allow them to act as mothers. In other cases, mothers react with gratitude. These interactions shape their relationship in new ways as both parties enter late life.

OVERVIEW OF COMPLEXITIES IN MOTHER/DAUGHTER TIES

The two mother/daughter pairs described in this chapter do not cover the full array of issues that mothers and daughters find pleasurable and problematic in their ties. Yet, these relationships introduce several themes that are evident across ties in late life. First, women's intergenerational relationships are marked by strong positive and strong negative feelings. Nearly every mother and daughter who participated in this study was able to think of a recent time when she had enjoyed the other party's company and a recent time when she was irritated with the other party. Mothers were consistently more positive about their relationships with their daughters than were their daughters. Yet, daughters desired to please their mothers. They felt hurt by their mother's criticism and derived pleasure from their mother's praise, even in midlife. The emotional valence of ties between mothers and daughters does not appear to diminish even after daughters are well established as adults in their own rights.

The types of issues that these four women discussed were common across mother/daughter pairs. Mothers and daughters derive pleasure from their shared investment in the family. The daughter's children, partner, siblings, and father are central players in the mother/daughter tie. Daughters were likely to feel torn by the competing pull of other social ties and work. Even when their mothers were still healthy, many daughters experienced demands they could not meet. Moreover, in general, mothers are more invested in their tie than are daughters, and this difference in investment can lead to tensions.

In many cases, the same situations that underlie pleasure also contribute to tensions. Mothers and daughters face the task of balancing their desire for intimacy against their needs for autonomy. They confront pleasant changes that bring the daughter into a more equal and nurturing position relative to the mother, yet also struggle to deal with the continuity and history of their relationship. The remainder of this book deals with these complexities in relationships between mothers and daughter as daughters enter midlife and mothers enter old age.

Specifically, this study addresses the rewards and costs that mothers and daughters incur in their relationships in old age. Mothers and daughters report mixed feelings about their relationships. There are three aspects to these feelings. First, the actual emotions that mothers and daughters experience for the other party contribute to the intensity of their bonds (Troll & Fingerman, 1996). A central focus of this study involved the types of feelings that mothers and daughters report for the other party. Anecdotally, it seems that mothers and daughters feel love, intimacy, pleasure, and yet also feel disappointed, irritated, hurt, frustrated, and betrayed by the other at times. A first step in this study was to document the degree to which mothers and daughters really do experience complex feelings for the other party.

Second, it is important to consider how mothers and daughters perceive their relationships. How do mothers and daughters describe the strengths and weaknesses of their relationships at this stage of life? The way in which people think about their relationships can have an impact on their behaviors in that relationship. Researchers interested in early childhood have found that mother/child ties are shaped in large part by the mother's beliefs about the child and their relationship (Goodnow, 1995; Moscovici, 1984), yet researchers have given little attention to this issue at the other end of life. Mothers and daughters do not experience benefits and costs from their relationship in an objective sense, but rather in a subjective sense. Each woman's beliefs about the other party is central in determining the nature of their relationship.

Finally, it is important to look at mothers' and daughters' behaviors in their relationship. Marital researchers have considered spouses' reactions to relationship problems as a key indicator of the marital relationship (Cohan & Bradbury, 1997; Gottman, 1979, 1998; Veroff, Young, & Coon, 1997). Yet, little is known about how mothers and daughters deal with difficulties that come up in their relationships. Indeed, researchers have rarely distinguished between problems and reactions to problems in this tie. Several studies have found that older parents and adult offspring report little conflict when they are asked to provide global ratings of their relationships (Umberson, 1992; Webster & Herzog, 1995). These low ratings may reflect a distinction between the *experience* of problems and the *expression* of problems. It is possible for a mother or daughter to be upset with the other party without telling her about the problem. The term "interpersonal tensions" is used throughout this book to refer to negative situations mothers and daughters encounter. These situations may take place without confrontation or even mutual recognition that a problem exists. In this manner, it is possible to consider mothers' and daughters' negative feelings as distinct from what they do to handle those feelings.

To fully understand ties between mothers and daughters in later life, we must consider the wide array of feelings and behaviors that contribute to these ties. Although mothers and daughters generally characterize their relationships as positive in late life, they also struggle to balance a variety of negative feelings in their relationships. The next chapter provides an overview of the mothers and daughters who participated in this study. Their relationships are strong, rich, and meaningful. Their ties are also clearly fraught with mixed emotions.

NOTE

[1]Names of women and minor details have been altered to protect the confidentiality of participants. In some instances, redundancies and grammatical errors were edited from direct quotations. In no case was the meaning of the quotation altered.

2
The Mothers and Daughters in This Study

I enjoy her interest in what I am doing, such as going to this literary discussion group for seniors. For years she thought I should do other reading, besides reading the newspaper as thoroughly as I do. She thinks that I shouldn't be solely interested in the world news. And now I am actually doing what I should do in my old age—I am reading books that are worthwhile reading. One really puts those things off, if you're busy with an awful lot of other things. In fact, I got her interested in reading one of the books that was supposed to be coming up in the future for my reading group. It's like we're sharing it. We have other subjects that we talk about. I sew for the grandchildren and we're always making plans for something that I should take on as a project. She wishes that I would have more time to do what I used to do as a grandmother. But those classes that I've been going to—art history and this discussion group—are taking a lot more of my time. She encourages me in it, and I'm happy for that. So, what I've failed to do for her as a result, she's not complaining about it. Although I think she would like me to help out more.

—Sarah, 75-year-old mother

> *I stopped over at her house after a doctor's appointment. I just wanted to stop in for a half an hour and visit with her. She had someplace to go. I had to get to work. But, I had to eat of course. I guess that's what you have to do when you're in your mother's home. And it had to be a balanced meal. It's real typical of my mother. She's very nurturing and it doesn't matter if she is out the door or has someplace to go. If you stop in, that is the most important thing that is going on right then. So, the message I got from that as I was growing up to is that her kids were her entire priority. And this Monday was a real typical example that it never, ever changes. She's very consistent about that. She would drop anything and do something for her kids. It seems really almost selfless.*
>
> *—Kathy, 36-year-old daughter*

Throughout the 1970s and 1980s, researchers focused considerable attention on proximity, affection, and patterns of assistance between parents and offspring. Most studies involved large surveys of men and women who provided ratings of different features of their intergenerational relationships using 7-point scales and standard measures (e.g., Atkinson, Kivett, & Campbell, 1986; Roberts, Richards, & Bengtson, 1991; Rossi & Rossi, 1990; Shanas, 1979; Umberson, 1989). This research provided important insights into parent/child relationships and highlighted the intensity of mother/daughter ties in comparison to other intergenerational ties. Yet, there remained a gap in our understanding of the complexities of mother/daughter relationships. Specifically, there was little information about how women experience these ties. Older women do not think of their lives in terms of the 7-point rating scales that are most convenient for social scientists. A few researchers began to use more qualitative or open-ended techniques to look at mother/daughter ties (e.g., Fischer, 1981, 1986; Suitor, 1987; Talbott, 1990). Yet, well into the 1990s, theorists continued to call for research using different methods to examine older families (Bengtson, Burton, & Rosenthal, 1996). This study addresses those concerns.

Rather than conduct a large study of hundreds of women, I chose to look at fewer women, but to use multiple methodologies to assess the mother/daughter tie. Each woman participated in an individual, face-to-face interview about her relationship with her mother or daughter. Each woman completed a lengthy questionnaire. Finally, mothers and daughters came together and completed a joint interview within 2 weeks of their initial individual interviews. A variety of approaches provided insights into the complexities of this relationship. The women completed some standard measures of intergenerational ties involving rating scales, but they also answered open-ended questions about their relationships, provided the endings to different stories about mothers and daughters, and were observed in their interactions with one another. These multiple approaches to assessing the mother/daughter tie provided unique insights into the emotional qualities of their relationships. This chapter focuses on the 96 women who participated in this study.

OVERVIEW OF THE SAMPLE

Forty-eight mothers over the age of 70 and their adult daughters provided information about their relationships. Mothers and daughters defined themselves and one another as independent, active, and healthy.[1] They resided in separate households, yet considered the other party a central member of their social world. Specifically, the daughters in this study lived within a 30-mile radius of their mothers. As was discussed, most older adults live near at least one of their grown offspring, and a daughter in close proximity tends to be one of the most important people in their lives (Aldous, Klaus, & Klein, 1985; Rossi & Rossi, 1990). A first step in designing this study involved decisions about the type of women who should be invited to participate.

Recruitment

Given the large literature that already existed on older women who require care from their daughters, only older women in good health were invited to participate in this study. To obtain such older women, recruitment took place through the mothers. A variety of sources provided access to healthy older women who might wish to participate including: senior exercise classes, church and synagogue groups, senior advocacy groups, enrichment courses offered to older individuals, the AARP, senior mentor programs, a local health clinic, and word of mouth. Participants were given a broad overview of the study during the recruitment process. Mothers learned about the types of issues covered in the study, including positive and negative aspects of the relationship. Most women who had daughters in the area were interested in the opportunity to share their relationship as part of this study. Each mother then supplied the name and telephone number of a daughter who resided nearby.

Surprisingly, there has been little research looking at pairs of mothers and daughters in late life. Often, only the mother's or the daughter's perspective on the relationship had been considered. Indeed, even when studies had considered both parties' perspectives, they had not brought the mothers and daughters together in one interview. This study is unique because both mothers and daughters alike provided information about their tie. In cases where a mother had several daughters who resided in the area, the mother selected one daughter to participate in this study. As will be discussed, mothers did not appear to select either most-favored or least-favored daughters to participate. All daughters who were contacted about the study agreed to participate, often citing their mothers' desire to be a part of the study as their motivation.

Individual Characteristics of the Women

The mothers who participated in this study ranged in age from 69 years, 9 months to 93 years, with a mean age of 76. The daughters ranged in age from 32 to 58 years with a mean age of 44. As is discussed in greater detail in Appendix A, a role relationship approach was used to set parameters for mothers and daughters in this study. As mentioned, a decision had been made to focus on healthy, older mothers and their daughters. The criterion of age 70 was used to define older mothers. This age limit was imposed in order to obtain a sample of women who had completed the transition to retirement if they had worked. Adults ages 60 to 70 are sometimes called the "young old" because they so closely resemble middle-aged adults. Although age is not a clear criterion for many indices in adulthood, most gerontologists would consider individuals over the age of 70 to fit the category of "older adults." In this study, women over the age of 70 in good health were asked to participate in the study, with no upper age limit. The ages of their daughters varied; the only criterion for the daughters was that they resided nearby. As a result, the ages of the women who were defined as mothers or as daughters in this study spanned more than a decade. Thus, the defining characteristics of the sample did not include the period in which these women grew up, but rather the nature of their relationships at present. The dyads included women who would be perceived as "old" by society, yet who remained physically fit, and their adult daughters.

These women were predominantly of European descent, although two of the dyads were African American. Table 2.1 provides informa-

TABLE 2.1 Characteristics of the Sample

Characteristics	Mothers (n = 48)	Daughters (n = 48)
Marital status		
Married/remarried	.38	.69
Remarried	.02	.15
Engaged/Living with other	.00	.04
Divorced	.04	.08
Widowed	.56	.02
Never married	.00	.02
Religion		
Protestant	.38	.29
Catholic	.21	.15
Jewish	.29	.33
Other	.13	.23
Years of education		
At least some high school	.10	.02
High School	.23	.04
Some college	.31	.15
College	.17	.42
Graduate School	.19	.38
Employment status		
Currently works for pay	.06	.73
Has worked for pay	.85	.23
Never worked for pay	.08	.06

tion describing the mothers and daughters involved in this study. The mothers and daughters appeared to be middle to upper-middle class based on their high education levels and the high education levels of their husbands. Complete information on socioeconomic status is not available (several mothers and daughters refused to answer questions pertaining to their income). Most mothers and daughters in this study were well educated for their respective generations, but daughters tended to be more highly educated than their mothers. Thirty-eight daughters had a college or graduate degree and seven more had additional technical training after high school. A third of mothers had a high school degree or less, a third had 1 or 2 years of training after high school, and a third of mothers had a college degree.

These women were also exceptional in terms of their involvement in activities outside their families. Most of the women who participated in the study had worked outside their homes for pay at some point in their lives. Most daughters were currently employed, whereas most of the mothers were not. Even after retiring, the mothers maintained busy schedules of travel, senior activities, and volunteer work. One challenge of the study involved pinning the mothers down to meet for an interview before they jaunted off to Africa or between charity drives for the homeless.

Mothers and daughters generally shared the same religion. Mothers and daughters defined themselves as Catholic, Protestant, Jewish, and agnostic/other in fairly equal numbers. Religious differences were not a pervasive theme in this study, but where such differences contributed to tension between mother and daughter, they are discussed.

There were differences in mothers' and daughters' family contexts. Daughters tended to have spouses or lovers, while their mothers did not. Nearly two thirds of the mothers were widowed or divorced. Forty daughters were either married or remarried, and of the eight unmarried daughters, two were engaged to be married and four of these women had lovers.

A final criterion placed mothers and daughters in a specific position in the family lineage. Although women in their 70s could still have a living parent, none of these mothers had living parents of their own. Therefore, this study focused on mother/daughter relationships at a stage when the mother is no longer an active daughter herself. Rather, the mothers in this study were likely to be widows whose closest relatives were their children. This discrepancy appeared to play a central role in shaping their relationships.

Health Status

Although mothers and daughters defined themselves as healthy prior to the start of the study, the interview included specific questions about their well-being. As can be seen in Table 2.2, the women who participated in this study were independent, fit, and energetic. Mothers reported having been sick more days than their daughters in the past year. Yet, the average number of days mothers claimed to have been ill, 13 days, is equivalent to the period of time that one bout of flu might incapacitate a young adult. Neither mothers nor daughters claimed that they cared for the other party on a frequent basis. In fact, over 90% of mothers and daughters reported

TABLE 2.2 Health Indices for Mothers and Daughters

Health indicators	Mothers	Daughters	Paired *t*-test
Number of days incapacitated this year	13.60 (25.30)	6.45 (11.60)	2.02*
Number of days in the hospital this year	6.89 (5.70)	4.56 (2.92)	1.74
Rated daily stress (1 = none, 5 = very stressful)	1.83 (0.88)	3.11 (1.06)	6.35***
Rated sufficiency of leisure time (1 = too little, 5 = more than enough)	3.17 (0.86)	2.30 (0.81)	5.39***
Provision of care for other (1 = weekly, 5 = almost never)	4.50 (0.92)	4.76 (0.69)	2.42*
Received care from other (1 = weekly, 5 = almost never)	4.84 (0.52)	4.60 (0.92)	1.71
CES-D/Depression Scale item average	1.39	1.31	–0.89
(1 = almost never, 4 = most of the time)	0.49	0.38	

* = $p < .05$, ** = $p < .01$, *** = $p < .005$.

caring for the other less than once a year, although daughters did claim to provide care for their mothers more often than their mothers claimed to care for them.

In addition, mothers and daughters provided ratings of their psychological distress over the past week. They completed the Center for Epidemiological Studies-Depression Scale (CES-D; Radloff, 1977; Radloff & Teri, 1986). Mothers and daughters rated their emotional well-being highly, and reported little psychological distress.

Daughters found their lives more stressful and claimed to have less leisure time than their mothers did. These issues are discussed in the next section with regard to the family context of mothers and daughters. In general, daughters incurred more demands from work and other social ties than did their mothers.

Limitations in This Sample

Later life is marked by variation. Most older women suffer from some sort of chronic illness such as arthritis, high blood pressure, heart disease, hearing loss, digestive difficulties, dental problems, or osteoporosis (National Center for Health Statistics, 2000). Many older adults begin to require daily assistance when they are in their mid-70's. Some older women suffer financial setbacks when their retirement savings are insufficient and they must live off meager social security payments. Yet, despite the increased rates of health problems in the population as a whole, a substantial proportion of older women remain healthy and active into their 80's.

Nonetheless, the women in this study were not representative of the American population of women over the age of 70 and their adult daughters. These relationships were "normal" only in the sense that implies an absence of pathology, not a statistical average. The mothers in this study were healthier, wealthier, and better educated than most women their age. Their relationships with their daughters provided a forum for investigating tensions in the absence of many factors which have been attributed to intergenerational tensions, including: economic dependency, educational disparities, poor health, cognitive decline, and emotional isolation. These women led advantaged lives relative to many older women.

In addition, it is not clear how the homogeneity of the sample shaped the types of responses that women provided. The majority of research on family ties in late life has focused on European Americans. The few studies that have included ethnic minority members have documented the strength of the mother/daughter tie across groups (e.g., Blieszner, Usita, & Mancini, 1996). Indeed, research examining African American families suggests that female lineages are particularly central in family life (Franklin, 1997; Spitze & Miner, 1992; Sudarkasa, 1997; Taylor, Jackson, & Chatters, 1997). Households are more likely to be organized around mother/daughter dyads in this community than in the European American community where marital dyads take precedence (Taylor et al., 1997). Even when generations do not reside in the same household, mothers and daughters are viewed as particularly important for family functioning and for individual social support in the African American community (Franklin, 1997). Yet, this study provides little insight into African American women's lives.

Moreover, this sample was distinct in that most of the older women had resided in the United States most of their lives. Some of the women in this study had immigrated to the United States when they were young, but all of them spoke English fluently and had experienced economic security in midlife and old age. Some researchers have suggested that linguistic difficulties may plague relationships between immigrant women and their daughters in late life if the mother came to the United States in adulthood (Usita, 1999).

In addition, the daughter's family contexts were remarkably homogeneous. Several daughters had been through one or more divorces, but nearly all of them were in stable relationships at the time of this study. Little information is available about the daughters' sexuality. This gap in information stems from concerns about asking older women questions about their sexuality. An initial decision was made to ask mothers and daughters the same questions. Although four of the daughters reported that they were in "romantic relationships," they did not spontaneously mention the gender of their partner during the course of the interviews. Therefore, we know little about the characteristics of the sample with regard to sexual orientation.

Despite these limitations, this study provides insights into mother/daughter relationships when women have advantages that mitigate the presence of external stresses. Such stresses have been associated with closer bonds between mothers and daughters who depend on one another for support, and also have been associated with increased tensions in this bond. These women were advantaged and elite relative to many women. Yet, they retained close ties and experienced tensions.

CHARACTERISTICS OF THE DYADS

In addition to individual characteristics of the mothers and daughters in this study, the sample was defined around several relationship characteristics. Mothers and their adult daughters resided in close proximity. These women were also in frequent contact. Ninety percent of mothers and daughters reported at least biweekly visits and weekly telephone calls. Visits between generations in this sample were somewhat higher than has been found in other studies. Other studies have found that 65 to 80% of parents report such frequent contact with one of their children (Field, Minkler, Falk, & Leino, 1993; Rossi & Rossi, 1990; Shanas, 1979).

The frequent face-to-face visits between mothers and daughters in this study precludes generalization to mother/daughter relationships where distance prevents such visits. In many cases, a daughter has moved across the country, while the mother remains behind; these women may be forced to accept once yearly or even biannual visits. Yet, mother/daughter ties with frequent contact do represent an important aspect of older women's lives. Visits with the most-seen child accounts for the majority of familial contact in later life (Cicirelli, 1983b; Field et al., 1993). The women who participated in this study had ample opportunity for unpleasant as well as pleasant interactions.

Some researchers have found that parents and offspring who are in frequent contact also report warm regard (Houser & Berkman, 1984; Lehr, 1984). This pattern suggests that the daughters in this study might have been their mother's favorites. Nonetheless, mothers did not appear to systematically select either "most favored" or "least favored" daughters to participate in this study. Rather, if more than one daughter resided in proximity, mothers selected a daughter they felt could most conveniently participate in the study. The mothers who participated in this research were busy with activities and they often cited scheduling the joint interview as a basis for selection of a particular daughter. For example, one mother with more than one daughter in the area commented, "Why don't you call Janet? If we need to meet for a second interview, Tuesday would probably work best for me. Susan's children take piano on Tuesdays and she won't be able to make it."

In general, mothers and daughters held their relationships in high esteem. As part of the study, mothers and daughters rated the degree to which they: understand one another, treat one another fairly, trust one another, respect one another, and feel strong affection for one another (Bengtson & Schrader, 1982). The total scale ranged from 5 to 25 and mothers' average ratings were 21.58 (SD = 2.84), whereas daughters' average ratings were 20.52 (SD = 2.52). Although mothers rated their relationship somewhat more highly than daughters did, both parties felt good about the tie.

THE CONTEXT OF THE MOTHER/DAUGHTER TIE

The mother/daughter relationship is embedded in the context of other relationships that help determine the relative importance of this tie. When women have few competing ties, they may value their relationship with their mother or daughter more. A single or divorced daughter might rely on her mother as a confidant or for help with child care. A widowed mother may turn to her daughter for advice or comfort. When women have many competing ties, they may have less available time for their mother or daughter. Middle-aged daughters with careers and children of their own may value their mothers, but consider their own children more central in their day-to-day lives. Active older mothers with many children and grandchildren and long-time friends in the area might be less invested in any particular daughter.

The individual interviews began with questions about mothers' and daughters' larger social network. Mothers and daughters provided information about their families, explained why they feel closer to some people than others, and answered questions about whom they rely on for social support.

Living Situations

In general, older mothers lived with fewer people in their households than did their daughters. As was mentioned, 29 mothers were either widowed or divorced. Thus, the majority of older mothers lived alone. The remaining older women resided with one other person, their current husbands. Mothers and daughters had a comparable number of children. On average, mothers had three children (*SD* = 1.83), with two offspring residing within a 50-mile radius, including the daughter participating in the study. None of the mothers lived with their offspring. By contrast, daughters tended to have several people in their households, including young children who depended on them. Nearly all middle-aged daughters lived with a spouse or lover. Daughters had an average of 2.45 (*SD* = 1.33) children. Three-fourths of these children lived with them full time. Many of the other children returned home for vacations during their college or postgraduate training.

In summary, on average, these mother/daughter dyads consisted of an elderly woman who did not work, but who was healthy and active in outside activities, and who, more often than not, came home to an empty house. The dyads also included a middle-aged woman who worked full-time, came home to a husband or lover, one or two children, and also faced demands from an additional adolescent or young adult offspring not residing with her. In other words, given the competing demands daughters faced, mothers had more available time and energy to devote to their daughters. Mothers were also more susceptible to loneliness, and thus, might be more motivated to seek out their daughters for company.

Allocating Time for the Mother/Daughter Tie

Although mothers and daughters reported frequent contact, they often discussed problems they had finding time in their schedules for this relationship. As was described in the prior chapter with regard to Lois and Roberta, demands from a mother or daughter can generate stress in this tie. Indeed, in nearly every dyad, at least one party brought up the difficulties they faced in maintaining contact. It was more common for daughters to experience these feelings, but mothers also mentioned complications in keeping this relationship active. Mothers' and daughters' descriptions of their efforts to find time to be together provides insights into the nature of their relationships.

Because these mothers were in good health, they had many activities that kept them away from their daughters. Clarissa, a 73-year-old widow, commented on the difficulties of coordinating her schedule with her daughter:

> You know, we talk on the phone and we can talk for a couple of hours on the phone. To me, it's as good as a visit. It's so sporadic that it's not like everyday or every week. In the summer time they get busy. I get busy. It could be 3 weeks before I talk to her. Usually I see her at one of her children's birthdays or something like that. So it's not just, "Hey, let's get together and have a chit chat." It's not that. Of course, sometimes I'll hop in the car and just pop out there and say, "Listen let's go up and have lunch," but that can't happen all the time.

Clarissa expressed a degree of confusion over how she and her daughter maintained their relationship. On the one hand, she felt that they got together over specific events like the children's birthday, on the other hand she wanted it clear that she was free to be spontaneous. In her initial reaction, she described long phone conversations that brought her great enjoyment. It is evident, however, that Clarissa's relationship with her daughter involves a fair degree of coordination and that their relationship must fit into other activities.

Mothers were generally aware that their daughters had greater demands on their time than they did. Several mothers mentioned that they wished they could spend more time with their daughters. Lucille, a 76-year-old mother, explained:

> There are, of course, times when we get together, but not as often as I might like because she's just a busy person. So am I, but not as busy as her. She came to get me on my birthday and took me out to lunch. We just visited and she had picked a place to go that I have never been before. Then, she had to get back to something at work quite soon, so she had me open my present in the car. We laughed about that because she was in such a hurry. She said, 'Well, we're running late. I don't have time to stop by at your house, so we'll just have you open your present on the way.'

Lucille was able to see the humor in her daughter's schedule, but Lily, an 83-year-old widow, felt hurt that her daughter could not find more time for her:

> It's so hard to explain our relationship. It really is. I love her dearly, but I feel like sometimes she should be a little bit more caring. Maybe she is, but she can't show it. She's always busy. We can't discuss anything. On the phone we hardly talk because she's always in a hurry. She always cuts me short. If I want to ask her something she'll slough me off. Let's say I'll call her up. She says, 'Mother, I'm on the other line, I'll call you back.' And she never gives me the time I feel like I should have with her. It's hard to explain this feeling a mother has for her daughter.

Lucille was exceptional to some degree. Few mothers expressed resentment of their daughters' schedules. Indeed, these mothers were themselves once middle-aged women with demands from work and children. For the most part, they understood their daughters' constraints and were grateful that their daughters took time for them.

When daughters discussed these issues, they tended to see the problem as more continuous in their relationships. For example, Laura, a 51-year-old daughter, commented:

> I'm from the branch of the family where we have quick visits and my mother is from the branch of the family that likes long visits. So, when I say, 'Not long,' I mean we got together for about 45 minutes or an hour, not just 5 minutes.

Laura went on to explain that part of the problem involved the contexts in which she and her mother got together. Laura's schedule did not allow her time to see her mother alone as often as her mother might like. Laura explained:

> And sometimes, they're here for a longer period of time, like around 3 hours with the entire family. Usually, when everybody leaves, my parents would be the last to leave. That's when my mother wants to sit down and visit with me alone, but that's when I least want to sit down and visit because I'm already tired.

Daughters also recognized that their mothers tried to understand their busy schedules. For example, when the interviewer asked Carol, Lucille's daughter, about their contact, Carol explained:

> If we're including phone conversations as visits—we probably do that more than once a week. I talk to her several times on the phone and we usually have nice conversations. She tries to call when I'm free. She knows or she asks if I'm busy or I ask her if she is busy, and we make arrangements to sit and talk on the phone like that. So, it's not that we get together at her house every week, but we do have a long conversation at least weekly.

Carol recognized that her mother attempted to be considerate of her time, but she was not aware of her mother's disappointment in her lack of availability. It was clear that daughters were more important in their mothers' lives than were mothers in the daughters' lives. As will be discussed, daughters and mothers struggle in their relationship in late life because mothers often would like more from their daughters than daughters are able or willing to provide.

The Salience of the Mother/Daughter Relationship

Additional questions in the first interview addressed the importance of the mother or the daughter to the other party. The distribution of responses can be found in Table 2.3. Mothers considered their

TABLE 2.3 Importance of Mother/Daughter Relationship

Importance	Mothers (n = 48)	Daughters (n = 48)	McNemar's Test exact p value
Ranked importance of other party			p = .0963*
Most important person in life	.23	.08	
Within the top 3	.52	.50	
Within the top 6	.15	.31	
Within the top 10	.10	.10	
Who get along with best			
Target (mother/daughter)	.48	.13	p = .0005
Who can talk to when upset			
Target (mother/daughter)	.54	.17	p = .0002
Who annoyed with most often			
Target (mother/daughter)	.08	.31	p = .0350

*McNemar's test calculated using 2 groups:
1 = top 1 or top 3 most important, 2 = among 6 or 10 most important.

daughters to be of central importance; 75% of mothers indicated the daughter was the most important person or among the three most important in her life. Despite the other demands in their lives, daughters also valued their mothers a great deal. Over half of daughters rated their mothers as being among the top three important people in their lives, although a substantial proportion of daughters considered their mothers to be less important than that.

Table 2.3 also shows the proportions of mothers and daughters who claimed that the other party served each of three important emotional functions in their lives. Mothers and daughters held different ideas about the emotional role of the other party in the relationship. Mothers tended to name their daughters when asked whom they got along with best or to whom they could speak when upset. By contrast, nearly a third of daughters named their mothers as the person who annoyed them most. Some mothers or daughters may have responded to what they perceived as the focus of this study by naming the other party. Indeed, participation in this study may have enhanced the salience of the mother/daughter tie. Yet, that enhancement is most evident in positive dimensions for mothers and in negative dimensions for daughters.

There are several reasons why mothers may place greater importance on their relationships with their daughters than do their daughters. Throughout life, parents tend to be more invested in their offspring than are their offspring in them. This discrepancy in investment is exacerbated in late life. Older adults narrow their social worlds, choosing to maintain contact only with those individuals whom they find emotionally rewarding (Carstensen, 1995; Carstensen, Gross, & Fung, 1998). Therefore, older mothers are likely to have fewer remaining social contacts than their daughters do, and to value each of those contacts highly. Furthermore, as was mentioned previously, differences in mothers' and daughters' familial contexts shape the mother/daughter tie.

FAMILY CONTEXT AND SALIENCE OF THE MOTHER/DAUGHTER TIE

Mother/daughter relationships are also part of a larger network of kinship ties. As is discussed in the next section, prior studies have focused on the important role the mother/daughter tie plays in maintaining the extended family (Rosenthal, 1987; Troll, 1988, 1996). Yet, few studies have considered the importance of the extended family to mothers and daughters themselves. As will be discussed in Part II of this book, mothers and daughters share an investment in the larger family that shapes the strong bond that they maintain. The remainder of this chapter considers how the presence or absence of other family members contributes to the importance each woman places on the mother/daughter tie.

The Mother's Family Context

Some studies have looked at mother/daughter ties as a function of the daughter's marital status or her status as a parent, but the mother's family context has rarely received attention. In this study, the mother's family context was associated with mothers' and daughters' ratings of their relationship. In other words, mothers and daughters rated one another differently depending upon whether or not the mother was widowed or divorced, and depending upon the number of siblings the daughter had.

Mothers who had more children rated their daughters as relatively less important ($r = -.27$, $p < .05$). In other words, a mother with two children rated the target daughter as among the three most important people in her life, a mother with four children rated her as among the top six, and a mother with more offspring rated the daughter as less important than that. Eleven mothers indicated that the target daughters had central billing by rating these daughters as the most important person in their lives; these mothers tended to be widowed and to have few offspring.

The number of children a mother had also determined the likelihood that she depended on this specific daughter for emotional support. Even mothers who were married rarely named their husbands as their preferred confidant, instead they tended to name one of their children. Mothers with many children sometimes named an offspring other than the target daughter when asked whom they confide in most. In other words, the target daughter's salience depended on competition from siblings available to fill a given slot.

The mother's family context also seemed to shape the daughter's ratings of the relationship. Daughters whose mothers were widowed or divorced were more likely to nominate these mothers as the person they get along with best than were daughters whose mothers were still married. Daughters of mothers who lived alone were more likely to name them as the person to whom they might speak when upset than were daughters of mothers who were married (McNemar's exact $p = .0347$).[2] The mother's marital status was not related to whether the daughter named the mother as the person who was most annoying. It seems that mothers who are alone serve as a greater emotional resource to their daughters, without the accompanying negative emotional costs of being annoying.

The presence of other family members did not relate to the primacy daughters gave their mothers. In general, daughters considered their husbands or lovers to be the most important person in their lives. They named their husbands as the person with whom they get along best and in whom they confide most. Daughters' husbands were not the dominant source of irritation in their lives, however. Daughters named their mothers, lovers, and children as annoying in nearly equal proportions.

Some researchers have argued that the relationships between mothers and daughters change for the better as daughters marry and have children. Presumably, mothers and daughters come to share greater empathy when their roles converge (Fischer, 1981, 1986). Daughters in the present study were fairly homogeneous with regard to family structure, however. It is possible that a sample in which daughters had a wider range of family structures would reveal greater variation in mothers' and daughters' sense of their relationship as a function of the daughters' family. Yet, as will be discussed in the third section of this book, other research suggests that it is the daughter's maturation into full adulthood, rather than her family roles, that sets the tone for her relationship with her mother in midlife (Blenkner, 1963; Fingerman, 2000; Walker, Thompson, & Morgan, 1987).

Cohort and Family Structure

The relative salience of the mother or daughter in the other party's life may reflect cohort as well as age differences. The mothers and the daughters were born at different periods of history. Although daughters varied in age, nearly all of them were born during the baby boom after World War II, when fertility rates in the United States were high. Indeed, the mothers in this study had one more child on average than did their daughters.

In addition, the baby boom brought child rearing to the center of American life. Although they were well-educated women with careers, the older mothers may have found their children to be particularly salient and important throughout their lives. Their daughters, on the other hand, were the product of this baby boom, and may have found their peer group, their careers, and a wider constellation of relationships important throughout life. In other words, the patterns here may not be those of midlife and later life, but rather may reflect period differences in the size of family and the importance of children within those families.

CONCLUSIONS

In summary, although mothers and daughters alike possessed rich social resources, they valued their relationships highly. At the same time, family roles and size of family appeared to effect the ways in which they experience one another. Regardless of whether their husbands were still living, mothers perceived their offspring as a source of pleasure, emotional support, and enjoyment. The daughters who participated in this study appeared to fit into a general category of *family* in these mothers' minds. Mothers did not consistently name the target daughters as most favored nor as most irritating person in their lives. In fact, the daughters' relative importance and salience depended upon how many siblings she had. The value mothers placed on the daughter in this study appeared to reflect a greater sense of the value of their grown children, as a collective. In the third section of this book, we will see that this phenomenon was also evident in mothers' descriptions of problems with their daughters.

After they discussed the context of their relationships and provided some general background information about themselves, mothers and daughters turned to the task of describing what goes on when they get together. Specifically, mothers and daughters provided information about a time when they had a particularly enjoyable visit together. The next section examines the types of events that contribute to mothers' and daughters' investment in one another.

NOTES

[1]Initially, 51 sets of mothers and daughters participated in the study. Three of these dyads of mothers and daughters were excluded subsequently because they did not meet study criteria. One dyad was excluded because the mother resided in a nursing home, a second because the mother refused to answer many of the questions, and the third because the mother and daughter resided in the same household and patterns of aid, conflict, and affective have been found to be distinct in multigenerational households (Speare & Avery, 1993; Suitor & Pillimer, 1991).

[2]Throughout this study, several types of statistics were used to examine differences and similarities within mother/daughter pairs. McNemar's Test of symmetry is a nonparametric measure used to assess the same variable at different times or to compare matched pairs in a 2 × 2 contingency table (Fleiss, 1981). It was used in this study wherever comparisons between paired dichotomous variables were estimated. The McNemar's test examines differences in the off-diagonal cells, upper right cell and lower left cell, in the 2 × 2 table, ignoring the main diagonal. A significant finding indicates lack of symmetry or greater imbalance in one direction than the other. When fewer than 30 cases change values or have different values in the matched pair, an exact p value can be calculated using the binomial distribution rather than calculating the approximate chi-square statistic. Exact p values are reported for this study. In cases where ordinal variables were involved, the nonparametric sign test was used. It is also possible to estimate the exact p value or probability for the sign test. Where continuous variables were involved, paired t-tests or an appropriate correlation was calculated.

■ two

POSITIVE FEATURES OF THE MOTHER/ DAUGHTER TIE

■ 3
Theories About Mother/Daughter Ties

> *We usually try to have lunch together at least once a week without my husband interrupting us, which is very important to us. . . . Sometimes I feel a little left out when she is talking with her father. I don't seem to be brought in to the conversation they are having. It's usually about some activity that they are geared into. I'm geared into it, too, but not to the same competence level. They are both at the same level you know, education wise. I really want her to talk to her father, but I love to have her to myself. Isn't that how it is with most mothers and daughters?*
>
> —*Grace, 79-year-old mother*

I am often asked why I chose to study healthy older mothers and their middle-aged daughters. Why not sons, fathers, husbands, or wives? Why not younger women or older women with sickly mothers? Relationships between older mothers and daughters are distinct from other social ties across a number of dimensions. The bonds tend to be tighter, the intimacy greater, the interactions more frequent and of a more emotional quality. Although marital couples may divorce, it is rare for a mother and daughter to sever their tie. Their relationship lasts a lifetime. When mothers are still healthy, the relationship serves as a social resource to both parties; mothers and daughters alike benefit from the other party's aid and assistance, from her emotional support and advice. Indeed, both women derive a sense of definition and identity from the mother/daughter tie.

I am fascinated by the question of why mothers and daughters maintain such strong ties throughout their lives. By looking at mothers and daughters in old age, we gain insights into the complexities of a relationship that has endured for nearly half a century. The mother/daughter relationship is shaped by the fact that both partners are women, that the mother has always been the mother in this relationship, and both parties are aware that their current relationship will end soon, due to either the mother's declining health or her death. Researchers and theorists have given particular attention to the first two aspects of the mother/daughter tie, but have rarely considered specific experiences in the relationship in late life. Moreover, there has been little attention to the ways in which mothers and daughters themselves view their relationship in late life.

This section of the book deals with the positive features of mothers' and daughters' ties. Specifically, it looks at why women maintain more intimate intergenerational bonds than do men. This chapter reviews existing theories that help explain the strong relationships that mothers and daughters experience. The next chapter presents the mothers' and daughters' descriptions of enjoyable visits from this study. Throughout this book, theory is presented in each section followed by findings from the study.

Three types of theories help explain the strength of the mother/daughter bond: sociopolitical, familial, and psychological explanations. Women's disadvantaged status in society fosters close ties to kin, and particularly close ties between mothers and daughters. Women's special position in the family further enhances the bond between mother and daughter at midlife; both women are deeply invested in kinship ties. Finally, a number of psychological factors contribute to this relationship. Women initially define themselves in relationship to their mothers, and later, take on the role of mother themselves. Daughters are socialized from an early age to retain ties to their family of origin, and particularly to their mother. The mother's sense of herself perpetuated in her daughter enhances the special qualities of this relationship in late life. In the next chapter, I describe the ways in which mothers and daughters themselves think about the strengths of their relationships in late life.

SOCIAL AND POLITICAL CONTRIBUTIONS TO THE MOTHER/DAUGHTER BOND

Factors such as longevity and economic vulnerability render relationships between mothers and daughters distinct from relationships involving fathers or sons. It is important to bear in mind, however, that although societal factors contribute to the strength of the mother/daughter tie in late life, societal factors do not fully explain emotional qualities of these bonds. Mothers and daughters subjectively experience their tie as a unique relationship, not as the outcome of a set of social forces. The psychological aspects of the mother/daughter relationship will be explored later. First, we consider the social context of the mother/daughter bond.

Longevity and Mother/Daughter Ties

The general increase in life expectancy over the past 100 years is particularly important for women. Recent projections for life expectancy indicate that women born in 1996 have an average life expectancy of 79.0 years, whereas men born that year are expected to live 73.1 years on average (NCHS, 2000; Singh, Kochanek, & MacDorman, 1994). Because women often marry men who are older than they are, the likelihood that they will be widowed in old age is high. In the early 1990s, only 35% of women over the age of 65 had a living spouse. Women are likely to live 12 to 15 years of their lives as widows. Widowed women find themselves in the precarious position of turning to their daughters for assistance and emotional support.

Gender differences in longevity present the following scenario in family ties. A husband turns to his wife for contact, support, and his emotional needs (Troll, 1988; Troll & Stapley, 1985). As he grows older, his health declines. Physical impairments lead to functional disability. This man may find himself in need of assistance to get about the house, wash himself, and eventually even to use the toilet or eat. His wife takes on the caregiving role, turning to her daughter for her own emotional needs. Through this process, the mother/daughter bond is intensified in a way that the father/daughter or mother/son bond is not.

For example, Kim, a 45-year-old daughter in this study, described changes in her relationship with her mother, Edna. Edna is 74 years old, and her husband is still alive, but his health has deteriorated. Kim described her aggravation during a recent situation when her mother had broken her foot:

> She loves to play helpless. She loves attention. She won't obey the doctor and it is really hard to recover if you are not going to do what you are supposed to do. My dad used to do all of this, he used to really take care of her and listen to her and help her. Now, it's all falling on me.

Kim loved her mother and found their relationship rewarding; she also described the pleasure she derived from long conversations with her mother and how relaxed she feels with her mother. There was a new tension in their relationship, however, since Kim's father was no longer able to provide the spousal care roles he had previously performed in Edna's life.

On the other hand, Paula, a 34-year-old daughter, found reassurance when her mother Gwen called to tell her about her father's health problems. Paula liked to be a part of this situation and to be informed:

> My father has fainting episodes and she called me to tell me that he had one last night, and called me for support—which made me feel extremely good, but at the same time a little helpless because I couldn't really do anything but give her verbal support. Unfortunately, since my daughter was sick, I couldn't run over there and just hug her, and I told her that. It was the first time she's really reached out like that to me.

Paula also noted that her mother had not informed her children of their father's health problems at first, and Paula and her siblings felt left out and hurt. Paula found her mother's call reassuring; it was a sign that Paula had achieved a new position in relationship to her mother as confidant and supporter. At the same time, Paula noted that she could not fulfill that role completely because her daughter had competing needs. Over time, as her father's health continues to decline, Paula and Gwen may grow closer, but the demands on Paula's time may increase as well.

Of course, gender differences in parent/offspring ties are apparent before the father's health begins to decline. Indeed, women rely on their spouses less than men do throughout adulthood. Rather, women have traditionally turned to their family of origin and to their children for a variety of support functions (Baruch & Barnett, 1983; Kranichfeld, 1987). Differences in longevity and health status in later life appear to accentuate existent patterns rather than generating new ones.

Social Vulnerability and Mother/Daughter Ties

In general, women's status in society is more volatile than men's status in society. In 1998, women employed full time earned approximately 75% of what men employed full time earned (White & Rogers, 1999). Women often hold jobs that do not provide health insurance or retirement accounts. Even when they have jobs with adequate salaries and benefits, women are more likely to experience discontinuities in their employment status; women take time off from work to care for children or sick parents.

Financial instability may contribute to women's strong ties to their families of origin. When unexpected crises arise, women suffer more than their male counterparts and are more likely to need help from kin. For example, when a marriage fails, the man's income tends to go up, whereas the woman's income tends to go down (Rossi & Rossi, 1990). Divorced daughters who are raising children depend on their parents for support, particularly while they are in the throws of divorce (Aldous, 1987; Johnson, 1988; Robertson, 1994).

Indeed, the daughters' children play a role in the daughters' ties to their own mothers. Daughters often rely on their mothers for help with their children, even when they are not in a crisis. Although the majority of women in the United States today are employed outside the home, women still shoulder the burden for childcare (Booth & Crouter, 1998). Childcare remains scarce, expensive, and unreliable in American society, and mothers often assist their daughters with child care.

Problems with a Social Contextual Understanding of Mother/Daughter Ties

Although women's relationships are shaped by the larger social context, there are several reasons why social contextual explanations for mother/daughter bonds are dissatisfying. Although social constraints encourage women to be more dependent upon kin than men, it is not clear that such dependency generates closer relationships. In fact, parents are less satisfied with offspring who need them most. They may feel that they have failed as parents when their grown children cannot function independently (Pillimer & Suitor, 1991; Ryff, Lee, Essex, & Schmutte, 1994). Furthermore, if economic incentives were the motivation underlying intergenerational ties, we might expect daughters to maintain closer ties to fathers because they usually have greater financial resources than do mothers.

A model of mother/daughter relationships premised on their need for support presents a portrait of women who are constantly planning for their next crisis, and who invest in their relationships as a result. Women's subjective experiences of their relationships do not match this portrait. Moreover, this model excludes women who are able to weather storms without assistance. Well-educated mothers and daughters with high incomes would be expected to maintain little intimacy if social vulnerability were the driving force behind strong relationships.

Indeed, it seems that the pattern of association goes in the opposite direction. Women rely on their mothers and daughters in times of crises because their relationships are so strong already. Troll (1994b) pointed out the importance of looking at mother/daughter connectedness in positive terms, as a sophisticated relationship, rather than framing their bond in terms of dependency. This is not say that we should discount gender differences in opportunity and social position. Rather, social context does not fully explain mothers' and daughters' strong investment in one another, other factors also play an equal or more important role.

WOMEN'S ROLES IN THE FAMILY

The cohesive bonds that characterize mother/daughter relationships also stem from the central role that women play in families across the life span. Women are socialized to value ties to the family, whereas men are socialized to succeed in the extra-familial world. When men demonstrate independence from their families of origin, they feel grown up, accomplished, and secure. When women demonstrate such independence from their families of origin, they feel guilty.

One of the most salient functions women serve in the family involves maintaining ties between relatives. A woman, and usually an older one, serves the role of "kinkeeper" in the family (Nydegger, 1983; Rosenthal, 1987). It is this matriarch who keeps each family member appraised of other family members' status. The kinkeeper knows when cousin Louis is ill and conveys this news to other relatives during weekly phone calls. The kinkeeper organizes family gatherings and holiday rituals. The kinkeeper decides which family members should bake pies and which ones bring salads (the kinkeeper herself makes the turkey). The kinkeeper is a general who musters the family army for family celebrations and crises. Indeed, kinkeeping is an extension of the maternal role.

Even when women do not serve in the role as kinkeeper, they tend to exhibit greater activity and consistency in their ties to relatives (Hagestad, 1984; Sussman, 1985; Walker & Thompson, 1983). Indeed, women are participants as well as activists in the family. Someone has to serve as the "kinkeepees," who responds to the kinkeeper's organizational efforts by mustering support for family gatherings. Daughters tend to fill the ranks of "kinkeepers." Moreover, women of different generations engage in what has been labeled "family work." They get in touch with family members and offer help, advice, and emotional support. They remember to send birthday, anniversary, and holiday greetings (Di Leonardo, 1992; Fingerman & Griffiths, 1999). They care for the sick. Mothers and daughters share this aspect of family life, and their relationships are stronger as a result.

Mothers and daughters also tend to have insular relationships. They interact within a dyad, mother to daughter. Relationships involving men tend to include triadic interactions, usually with a spouse (Troll & Smith, 1976). For example, older fathers read the paper as their wives speak to their daughters on the phone occasionally offering instructions to ask about the grandchildren or gather other information about the daughter's life. Daughters-in-law are usually present when sons visit with their parents, whereas daughters often visit their mothers alone.

Of course, some of the family patterns we find in middle-aged and older adults today reflect prior societal gender values. As today's young cohorts grow older, current gender differences in men and women's affiliation with their families of origin may begin to dissipate. In the future, parents may place less emphasis on daughters' maintenance of family ties or more emphasis on seeing their sons. Mobility and changes in women's roles in the past 3 decades have been accompanied by shifts in the definition of men's and women's roles.

Yet, the nature of family relationships is slow to evolve. The daughters who participated in this study grew up after World War II, a time when mothers dominated middle-class family life, regardless of whether or not they also had outside employment. Although the society in which these daughters currently live is different in many ways from the one in which they grew up, their early experiences continue to color their relationships with their mothers. Moreover, these women developed psychologically in a manner that encouraged them to enhance, rather than to sever their ties to their mothers.

PSYCHOLOGICAL ASPECTS OF MOTHER/DAUGHTER BONDS

In addition to societal and familial pressures on women to maintain a strong tie, individual psychological factors contribute to their investment in this relationship. In this section, I review psychoanalytic and feminist theories of the mother/daughter bond. Although it was the first theoretical camp to deal with motherhood in a developmental context, psychoanalytic theory does not provide insights into the strengths of mother/daughter ties in old age. Early psychoanalytic theories are reviewed here because these theories played a role in the development of subsequent conceptualizations of mother/daughter ties rather than for the insights these theories provide. Feminist theories of mother/daughter ties appear to better incorporate a current understanding of this relationship. Yet, both classes of theories fail to consider the mother as a developing individual in her own right, an issue that will be discussed at the end of this section.

Psychoanalytic Theory

Psychoanalytic perspectives initially portrayed the mother/child relationship as central in early psychological growth. Autonomy and independence were deemed the end-state of development. Indeed, early psychoanalytic theories conceived of the relationship between mother and child as one that is supposed to move from symbiosis to separation. Accordingly, women's interdependence and connection were deemed inferior to men's more detached relationship style in adulthood. As will be discussed, feminist scholars have argued that early psychoanalytic conceptions of the mother/child relationship reflect men's experiences rather than women's (Gilligan & Rogers, 1993).

Psychoanalytic theories initially focused on the parent/child tie during the early years of life. Freudian theory describes a process through which children pull away from the opposite sex parent to identify with the same sex parent. In particular, Freud was interested in the male child's love of his mother and competition with his father during what Freud called the Oedipal phase (Freud, 1910). There is no explicit attention to women in later life in Freudian theory, and young women are portrayed as victims of their own stunted psychological growth.

Other psychoanalytic theorists gave greater attention to changes in adulthood. Erikson (1950) proposed a lifespan theory of development. Although Erikson's theory is one of individual development, it includes relational themes. Three of the eight stages of development in Erikson's theory explicitly involve the ability to maintain appropriate ties to other people: basic trust versus basic mistrust, intimacy versus isolation, and generativity versus stagnation. Erikson argued that the individual must achieve an appropriate connection to other people in each of these stages to advance successfully to the next stage of development.

This is not to say that Erikson's perspective adequately describes women's experiences with their mothers and daughters. Erikson, like Freud, tended to view the mother as an agent who responds to the infant's needs. According to Erikson's theory, a mother's lack of sensitivity to the infant leads to future psychological problems the child encounters as each stage of development builds upon the previous one. Although development arises from relationships, there is no sense of the developing individual as an active agent in these relationships; the child's contribution to a relationship is not considered. Furthermore, as will be discussed, feminist theorists have criticized Erikson's theory for its emphasis on the formation of identity prior to the establishment of intimacy, as though well-adjusted adults do not define themselves in relationship to other people. This premise may apply to many European American males, particularly at the time that Erikson developed his theory, but is not applicable to most women or to many men in non-European ethnic groups (Gilligan, 1982; Sampson, 1988, 1989).

Moreover, Erikson did not adequately describe the experiences of older women. Although Erikson's theory addresses development throughout the life span, his last stage of development, ego integrity versus despair, does not articulate the salience of relationships in later life. In his subsequent work, Erikson addressed this issue to some extent by emphasizing older adults' investment in younger family members (Erikson, Erikson, & Kivnick, 1986). Yet, the unique features of being a mother, of having been a mother over a lifetime are not considered in Erikson's descriptions of the life span. From an Eriksonian perspective, mothers are relational objects for the developing child; the mother herself as a developing being is sorely neglected.

Jungian psychology dealt with motherhood in a different manner. Jung considered the mother an archetype or shared universal symbol. He referred to "the collective image of the mother," arguing, "The mother–child relationship is certainly the deepest and most poignant one we know; in fact, for some time the child is, so to speak, a part of the mother's body" (Jung, 1931/1981, p. 373). Jung, like other psychoanalytic theorists of his era believed that well-adjusted individuals pulled away from their mothers as they developed. Nonetheless, he viewed the mother image as a symbolic and universal force in adult life.

Jung, unlike other psychoanalytic theorists of his time, dealt with issues surrounding aging and with older women more specifically. Indeed, Jung described an analysis of a woman in her late 60's who had dreamt about her weaknesses as a mother. He explained:

> She was still hearty, and moderately intelligent. It was not for want of brains that she was unable to understand her dreams. It was unfortu-

> nately only too clear that she did not *want* (sic) to understand them. Her dreams were very plain, but also very disagreeable. She had got it fixed in her head that she was a faultless mother to her children, but the children did not share this view at all, and the dreams too displayed a conviction very much to the contrary. (Jung, 1934/1981, p. 411)

Jung goes on to describe this woman's epiphany in the final months before her death when she realized that she was, in fact, a poor mother. At this stage of her life, Jung pointed out that she was in a "sort of delirious or somnambulistic state" (p. 411). Yet, Jung purports that the reality of this woman's existence was her weakness as a mother, rather than the strengths she had considered herself to possess prior to her delirium. As will be discussed throughout this book, it is normal, and perhaps beneficial, for parents to view their relationships with offspring in more favorable terms than do those offspring (Fingerman, 1995). Jung's preference of a description of the mother as viewed by her children is indicative of the general failure of psychoanalytic theory to look at the mother as an individual in her own right.

In summary, psychoanalytic theories began as theories about the developmental trajectories of well-to-do European males. In these initial theories, mothers received considerable attention. They were portrayed as powerful beings who determined their children's developmental trajectory early in life and then faded into the background. To the extent that psychoanalytic theories dealt with old age, they did not consider maternal identity or the mother as an individual who held a perspective of equal importance to that of their children. Moreover, the important role that "daughterhood" plays in a woman's identity was all but ignored. Being a mother or daughter in late life is a central aspect of women's lives. Today, we know that mothers and daughters continue to grow in their relationships and to derive benefits from these ties into late life.

Feminist Perspectives

As opposed to the pathological conceptions of the mother/daughter tie evident in psychoanalytic writing, the mother/daughter tie has been portrayed as the epicenter of women's development in feminist scholarship. Feminist scholars have focused considerable attention on women's development of a relational self, or a sense of identity in connection to others. Feminist theory called into question the premise that autonomy is the final virtue to be equated with maturity. The emphasis in feminist writing has been on the bond that mothers and daughters share, rather than on the role the mother plays in launching her child (e.g., male child) into autonomy. The mother/daughter tie is both the context in which women establish identity and an aspect of their identities.

Feminist scholars have given particular attention to how the mother/daughter tie shapes a woman's sense of identity. As opposed to psychoanalytic theorists who concentrated on the maternal role in early life, feminist scholars concentrated on the importance of mother/daughter ties in adolescence. Gilligan and her colleagues describe political pressures that subvert girls' voices in early adolescence (Brown & Gilligan, 1993; Gilligan & Rogers, 1993; Taylor, Gilligan, & Sullivan, 1995). Grown women confront new challenges when they watch their daughters pass through this stage of life. The mother is a witness and a participant in relationship with her daughter. The relationship is a catalyst for the growth of both parties, yet feminist scholars have not considered how this tie contributes to women's growth later in life.

In addition to emphasizing the role that mothers play in their daughters' development, feminist writing also places the maternal role as a more central aspect of women's identity. Motherhood is an accomplished skill with personal and societal meaning. Indeed, Ruddick (1989) suggested that forming a maternal identity is a political act, one through which women are empowered.

Furthermore, feminist theories describe unique skills that women possess in connecting to other people. The close tie between mothers and daughters is viewed as a strength rather than as a deficit. In their analysis of women's cognitive development, Belenky and colleagues wrote:

> With an increasing awareness of how much the sense of connectedness to others deepens with maturity, we believe that important causal factors that occur later in the life cycle must be considered. For many women, being a mother as well as having a woman as a mother

> provides a profound experience of human connection. That adult experiences as well as childhood experiences contribute to the evolution of a sense of connection is consistent with our observations that connectedness with others is one of the most complicated human achievements, requiring a high level of development. (Belenky, Clinchy, Goldberger, & Tarule, 1986, p. 178)

Feminist writing points out the importance of the tie between mother and daughter and the key functions that it serves. Given their skills in maintaining social ties, it is not surprising that mothers and daughters share stronger relationships than fathers and sons in adulthood.

Although feminist theory has provided considerable insights into the mother/daughter tie, there are also gaps in this literature. Feminist scholars, like their psychoanalytic nemeses, tend to focus more on the daughter's development than on the mother's development. Troll (1988) argued that feminist women tend to conceive of themselves as daughters breaking free from their mothers rather than as aging mothers who struggle with the investment they feel for their daughters. A number of researchers have taken a feminist perspective to understand the mother/daughter in late life since Troll first issued this complaint (e.g., Allen & Walker, 1992a, 1992b; Blieszner et al., 1996; Henwood, 1993; Walker, 1994), but the mother's voice remains weak in descriptions of this tie in late life. Moreover, there has been little attention to the tensions that women incur in these ties. The negative emotions that women experience for their mothers and daughters are not necessarily antithetical to the positive feelings that pass between them. Rather, as will be discussed, women are also skilled at identifying and managing interpersonal tensions that might disrupt their intergenerational relationships.

Recent Psychological Perspectives

Following the onset of feminist work on relationships and women's identity, many researchers have looked at mother/daughter ties in late life. Recent work on mothers and daughters suggests that they may not be as interconnected in late life as was once thought. There is a strong degree of affiliation, companionship, and interdependence in the tie, but there is also a degree of independence and autonomy (Boyd, 1989; Walker, 1994). In one study comparing young adult daughters and their mothers to middle-aged daughters and their mothers, I found age differences in their sense of connection. The younger daughters and their mothers reveled in the daughters' newfound adult status and described their bond as tight and insular. They seemed to idealize their relationship and the other party. By contrast, middle-aged daughters and their mothers seemed to view their relationships in more complex terms that suggested that they viewed the other party as another adult. These middle-aged daughters and their mothers valued their relationships, but also demonstrated some distance from the other person (Fingerman, 2000a).

Indeed, the strongest mother/daughter ties in late life seem to involve a careful balance of positive and negative feelings, of connection and autonomy. When older mothers feel demanded upon by offspring, they become resentful and less invested in the tie (Cohler, 1983; Talbott, 1990). Likewise, when older widows feel that their daughters overlook their weaknesses and vulnerabilities, they may wish their daughters understood them better (Morgan, 1989). At the same time, older women do not like their daughters to proffer help they do not require (Smith & Goodnow, 1999). The balancing act in this tie involves a careful mix of closeness and distance in old age.

CONCLUSIONS

In summary, mothers and daughters maintain strong ties for a variety of reasons that stem from their shared experiences as women. Their relationship is central in both parties' lives. The primacy of this bond appears to fade somewhat from early adulthood to later life (Fingerman, 2000a). The bond between mother and daughter shifts from an idealized interconnectedness in young adulthood to a sophisticated interdependence between two individuals in later life. Yet, mothers and daughters continue to value their shared investment in family and one another throughout adulthood. Few theorists have considered the mother's experiences in the mother/daughter tie or her personal growth in this relationship. A more inclusive approach to understanding the mother/daughter tie involves examination of both parties' perspectives.

Many questions remain about the emotional experiences, positive and negative, that serve as filaments underlying this connection. Although theorists have attempted to describe the strength of their bond, the mother/daughter tie also involves a subjective experience. Women have their own explanations for their motivation to maintain such strong bonds with their mothers or daughters. The remainder of this section considers the benefits that mothers and daughters report that they receive from their relationship.

4
The Pleasure of Her Company

She's an ideal daughter. She's never given me one minute of trouble. I am never annoyed with Amy. To me, she just does everything perfectly. She has a good husband. She loves to paint, and he helps with the housework so she's free to do that. She loves her job. She's a very loving person. I don't know if she feels the same way about me.

—Gloria, 73-year-old mother

I'd like to think of something spectacularly enjoyable, but nothing outstanding comes to mind. In our family tradition, we used to go out every Friday night—fish fry sort of thing. Because we were big time Catholics and in the old days we used to not be able to eat meat on Fridays . . . We sort of tried to carry that tradition through and still do it occasionally. And that's always fun. Afterwards, we play games. In our family, we're big game players, always have been. So she and I play Scrabble and we play word games. We end up laughing a lot.

—Margaret, 39-year-old daughter

Researchers have rarely asked women what they perceive to be the benefits of their relationship with their mother or daughter. These ties are voluntary to a large extent, and women could presumably sever their ties or at least engage in less frequent contact if they were dissatisfied. Although mothers and daughters in this study described difficulties fitting this relationship into their schedules, they made it a priority to do so. A central goal of this study was to understand what mothers and daughters enjoy about their contact.

After the interviewer had obtained some basic information about the participant's background and social context, she asked each woman to, "Tell me about the last time you had a particularly enjoyable visit with your mother (daughter)." The question focused on a specific situation rather than pleasant situations in general in order to obtain rich descriptions of their relationships. Women might recall a recent situation in detail, whereas as descriptions of pleasant feelings in general might produce global generalizations. Follow-up questions allowed a greater understanding of the typicality and meaning of the incident. As is described in Part III, participants responded to a similar series of questions pertaining to situations when they felt irritated, hurt, or annoyed with the other party.

Nearly all mothers and daughters readily recalled a recent visit that had been notably pleasant. By contrast, as will be discussed, many mothers and a few daughters hesitated to describe problems in their relationships. One mother and one daughter, from different families, were also unable to describe an enjoyable visit. Penny, a 55-year-old daughter, claimed that as her mother Ruth grew older, she did not provide such pleasure:

> In a way, it (our relationship) doesn't make me happy anymore. I think she could make me happy when I was younger, but I think I have to make my own happiness now. I think it's past a point, there with her illness, I don't have the sense that she makes me happy. I mean, I'm pleased when she's doing physically well. She's doing well after having a very bad summer. I don't mean to seem like an ungrateful daughter, it's just that now I have to be happy on my own.

It was unclear why this daughter felt none of her recent visits with her mother were enjoyable. Penny valued her mother, but now that her mother had begun to grow old, she was less able to derive pleasure from their visits. The mother who couldn't remember a specific enjoyable visit repeated several times, "We just don't have that kind of relationship." Yet, these women did not consider their relationships with their respective daughter or mother to be poor. Neither the mother nor the daughter reported an excessive degree of tension when they answered questions about the downside of their relationships. The inability to think of a particularly enjoyable visit was linked to having more neutral, rather than more negative feelings about the other party.

SOURCES OF PLEASURE

Conceptually, mothers' and daughters' pleasant visits might be considered under three general areas. The first area involves pleasure derived from the other party. A mother's or daughter's presence, her traits, or a shared activity made that particular visit enjoyable. These situations illustrate the importance of the mother/daughter relationship itself as a source of reward. Second, mothers and daughters described situations involving other people. These events appeared to reflect the shared investment in family described in the previous chapter. Third, mothers and daughters discussed being nurtured and nurturing the other. Finally, mothers and daughters mentioned difficulties in the relationship. The first three areas are considered sources of pleasure in the relationship, while the latter may provide insight into the ambivalence older mothers and daughters experience in their ties.

The proportions of mothers and daughters whose descriptions of enjoyable visits fell under each area are found in Table 4.1. In general, mothers and daughters described the same types of agreeable events. Their descriptions of pleasant events were multifaceted. Mothers and daughters derived pleasure from a sense of identification with the other party, from interacting with her, from sharing their extended family, and from being nurtured—all in the same situation. Although typologies of mother and daughter relationships have been developed with regard to different categories of caregivers (Walker & Allen, 1991) and with regard to different relationships across ethnic backgrounds (Blieszner et al., 1996), the complexity of participants' descriptions of enjoyable visits made this task impossible. A given participant's discussion of a pleasant situation did not clearly differentiate her from other mothers or daughters in the study. Nor did the types of events that bring happiness distinguish

TABLE 4.1 Proportions of Mothers and Daughters Whose Responses Fit Each Code

Response	Daughter (n = 47)	Mother (n = 47)
Activities		
Shared events	0.30	0.60
Traditional activities	0.26	0.19
Conversations	0.40	0.50
The other's presence		
Just being with her	0.38	0.50
Identification with her	0.21	0.11
Family and kinkeeping		
Family mentioned	0.40	0.60
Daughter's children	0.21	0.40
Nurturance		
She did something for me	0.22	0.39
I did something for her	0.21	0.09
Negative comments		
Absence of something bad	0.25	0.10
Gratuitous negative comments	0.33	0.23

the quality of mothers' and daughters' relationships. As will be seen in the next chapter, when participants described *difficulties* in the relationship, mother/daughter typologies emerged. Different sources of problems were related to poorer quality relationships and to better quality relationships. Yet, a few shared classes of events seemed to render mothers and daughters happy in each other's presence, with little impact on the quality of their relationships overall.

Positive visits were frequent occurrences in these women's lives. Two thirds of the mothers and daughters reported having visits as enjoyable as the one they described at least once a week. They tended to select everyday events such as a lunch together, or helping the other fold laundry as a source of enjoyment. When they did select exceptional events, such as a birthday celebration or holiday, the aspect of the event that they found enjoyable still stemmed from something more mundane. A conversation with the other, her presence, the ability to please her, her happiness were considered pleasurable. The frequency with which mothers and daughters have pleasant visits seems to reflect the minimal criteria for making one another happy.

Pleasure Derived from Activities

The mere act of visiting with the other party was a primary source of pleasure for most mothers and daughters. Nearly all the older mothers, and over two thirds of the daughters described such situations. These responses might reflect the nature of the question—women were asked to discuss a recent enjoyable visit. Despite instructions to the contrary, some participants may have understood this question as a request for a description of a specific activity. Yet, a range of situations fell under this category. Mothers and daughters found it gratifying to go out together, to talk with the other party, or simply to be in her presence. It seems that these mothers and daughters maintain such frequent contact because they enjoy the contact itself.

Shared Events

The types of activities women enjoyed varied, but many women focused on an outing they had taken with the other party. Several mothers and daughters described going to lunch as their most recent pleasant visit. Ruth, Penny's mother, was almost apologetic that she took pleasure in simple events with her daughter. "Oh, you can just put down that we had lunch at a local department store." When asked more specifically what she had enjoyed, Ruth continued, "Oh, I don't know what I enjoyed—just a quiet little talk together and a club sandwich. So, that's a wonderful day for me . . . " she concluded by laughing. Louise, an 85-year-old mother with a college education, pointed out that she and her daughter shared the same sorority. "We're both Theta's, my daughter was in the same sorority that I had joined. And we went to the Founder's Day Dinner last week and that was just a really happy occasion for me."

Likewise, daughters took pleasure in activities they shared with their mothers. Sue, Louise's 55-year-old daughter, was grateful that her mother had been willing to fill in for her husband when he had been unable to go out with her:

> "Well, it was last night, going to a concert. My husband let me know practically at the last minute that he wasn't going. So, she hurried up and got ready and—which isn't easy—and came with me. And, it was just a lot of fun to experience that. I felt very grateful because music is a very big part of her life and a big part of my life."

Sue clearly enjoyed the sense that she and her mother shared an interest in the same activity. Whereas younger women might assume that their mothers should spend time with them, Sue was able to recognize that her mother was sacrificing something by making arrangements to respond to a last-minute invitation. This shift in the mother/daughter tie provides a distinct characteristic to the relationship in late life; daughters increasingly recognize their mother's vulnerabilities and appreciate their strengths.

Traditional Activities

In addition, daughters seemed to enjoy the sense that their mothers served as a tie to their extended family history. My colleague Lillian Troll and I have proposed that the emotion underlying offspring's connections to their parents in old age may include feelings of nostalgia, belongingness, or coming home (Troll & Fingerman, 1996). To offspring, a parent may represent their roots and where they came from (Bahr & Bahr, 1996). Although the mother/daughter relationship has been described as a repository for the traditions of the larger kin network, little was known about whether mothers and daughters themselves enjoyed this aspect of the relationship.

For some women in this study, pleasurable visits included a purposeful effort to build a sense of continuity into the relationship. Such mothers and daughters described events that had become a part of the tapestry of their relationships over time. Sunday dinners, an afternoon baking holiday cookies, an evening out together once a month constituted the special traditions that mothers and daughters had built into their relationships. Other women described the joy they derived from reminiscing about the past with their mothers.

Over a quarter of the daughters and nearly a fifth of the mothers described activities of this nature. Personal traditions appear to be a unique aspect of mothers' and daughters' ties as they grow older; such events rarely show up in younger mothers' and daughters' descriptions of enjoyable visits (Fingerman, 2000a).

For example, Valerie a 40-year-old daughter, described an activity she had shared with her son and her mother:

> Tommy and I went over to her place to go through her basement where she stores things. And we were helping her go through some stuff. She was just deciding that if she hadn't used it in 4 years, she probably wasn't going to use it. And so we ran across some of the photograph albums. And we looked at some old pictures of me when I was little. And my brother Allen when he was little, and Grandma when she was little, and it was a nice time.

Likewise, Rebecca, a 47-year-old daughter, was pleased that her mother was teaching her daughter new activities:

> Well, we went over there for dinner, Tuesday night. We had a meal and I guess there's one special thing that I remember. Molly and I went over and Mom was showing Molly how to knit and pearl. And so we had dinner; Molly, and Mom and I, and then Mom was showing Molly how to do that. And we were just talking about how much fun it was to be together.

In some cases, older mothers helped their daughters' sons acquire new skills, but more frequently, teaching situations involved activities across three generations of women.

Other traditional activities centered around holidays. For example, several mothers and daughters mentioned Thanksgiving, Christmas, or Easter dinners or activities. Kelly, a 43-year-old daughter, described the pleasure she took in a recent party:

> A particularly enjoyable time was our Christmas party. No one was totally responsible to take care of everyone else. We all chipped in. So, it was kind of nice to just relax and not have to take care of things. Most of the times when I see her, she comes to visit at my house. We feed her and she loves my husband's cooking. It's nice to see her get fed. She's fed everybody so much and she really appreciates how much we put in. She's so appreciative. We played charades. It was a really nice party.

Nancy, Rebecca's 81-year-old mother, also referred to a situation involving the holidays.

> She and Molly are always coming over. They came over and saw Grandma hadn't put up anything for Christmas. And I said it was too much work. I have to get it upstairs and then later get it downstairs. I mean, when you're in your eighties, you don't feel like climbing the stairs doing all this kind of stuff. So nothing to do, they came over on a Saturday afternoon, when Rebecca wasn't working, and they got all the Christmas stuff down and put up the tree. And I said, "Well you're going to put it up, you're going to have to take it down." So they carried the boxes all upstairs. It was nice to have it up, I will admit. Rebecca said to me, "Mom, isn't it nice to have it up?" I said, "Yeah, but it's a lot of work." And you don't realize when you get older how . . . you like it but, still on the other hand, it's just so much work. Your mind stays, but your body is different. So I really appreciate them putting it up.

Of course, whether or not mothers and daughters mentioned holidays might vary depending upon when they were interviewed. These interviews took place from September through April. Mothers and daughters discussed a range of holidays including Thanksgiving, Christmas, New Year's, Valentine's Day, St. Patrick's Day, and Easter. In addition, several mothers and daughters referred to their own family celebrations such as anniversaries, birthdays, new jobs, and graduations. In other words, the season itself did not seem to matter, mothers and daughters recognize and generate reasons for family traditions and celebrations.

Conversations

In addition to specific activities, many mothers and daughters claimed to enjoy a good discussion. Several women mentioned that simply talking with the other party had been a source of pleasure in their visits. Marianne, an 80-year-old mother, explained:

> Amanda and I serve Motor Meals together to seniors. My husband George has his Lion's club meeting at that time. We have lunch together and we always enjoy that because we're together, the two of us, for quite

> some time. We can talk that way. Of course, we've also gone to concerts and we go shopping, but this is a more personal thing.

From Marianne's perspective, their conversations and discussions forge the personal bond that exists between them.

Mothers also explicitly expressed pleasure from confiding in their daughters. When asked to describe the last time she had had an enjoyable visit with her daughter, Martha, a 71-year-old mother, explained, "I enjoy talking with her, being with her . . . and her family. I think it's the mother and daughter relationship, and little things that she'll ask me. I like to be with her, to talk with her." Mothers at this stage of life appear to recognize their daughters' maturation as a gift. When daughters are younger, mothers have to spend more time listening to them and assisting them with their own problems (Fingerman, 2000a). When their daughters are middle-aged, mothers feel free to treat them like mature women in whom they can confide.

Mothers enjoyed learning about their daughters' activities. They seemed to feel that they remained a part of their daughters' lives through these conversations. For example, Pauline, a 76-year-old widow, explained:

> She knows I like to hear about her job in the English department and the people there. And she makes it a point to come in and tell me what all is going on. She tells me, you know, how she handles some problems. She discusses her daughter with me and her husband's kids and it's just as though they were her own. And that, to me, is very enjoyable. . . .

Doris also described conversations she has with her 46-year-old daughter Jennifer:

> She tells me about her work, and sometimes her problems, which includes me in her world. It makes me happy. I don't think she is aware of it. She doesn't realize how much I enjoy being a part of her life.

Of course, some daughters reported that they enjoyed discussions with their mothers as well. Jennifer, Doris's daughter, was in fact aware of the importance of conversation in their relationship:

> I mean, she knows so much. She knows everything about my life. I probably talk to her almost every single or every other day. It's not like

> we have a phenomenal visit each time because she just kind of knows what my life is like. I fill her in on the last 2 days and then I fill her in on, you know what's happened. So, there are not individual visits per se. You know its like if you see somebody or talk to them that often, it's not like a visit stands out because it's just part of the regular routine.

Daughters also often derived pleasure from listening to their mothers rather than from talking to them. For example, Danielle, a 39-year-old daughter, indicated that she loves to listen to the stories her mother tells:

> I always get a kick out of when she starts to talk about things that she remembers from when she was little—reminiscing about her life with her sisters or stories she'll share. I think we talked about that when I was at her house last.

Some daughters also claimed to enjoy hearing about their mothers' present concerns. These middle-aged daughters took pleasure in being able to serve as a confidant to their mothers. In continuing to describe their last pleasant visit, Danielle explained:

> Then, we always talk about my other siblings. She sort of airs her worries about them, her concerns, that sort of thing . . . I felt good. Oftentimes when we're with the whole family, you don't get a chance for that one-on-one. So, that's real nice.

As will be seen in the next chapter, daughters also appear to experience ambivalence over listening to their mothers' concerns. Like Roberta in the first chapter, many daughters found it difficult to deal with their mothers' problems, or felt drained by their mothers' desire to unburden their anxieties. There was a distinction between having a mother who tells stories about the past and having a mother who calls to talk about a current problem in her life. A mother's stories about the past are a consistent part of the mother/daughter relationship beginning in childhood and continuing into old age. When mothers discuss their own problems with their daughters, these conversations may reflect a change in the nature of their relationships. As will be discussed, some middle-aged daughters feel conflicted over what they refer to as a "role reversal." Although mother and daughter roles do not actually reverse, middle-aged daughters feel both pride and distress over shifts in their responsibilities in the relationship (Fingerman, 1997b). Thus, some daughters find their mothers' confidences pleasurable, other daughters experience such disclosure as problematic, and still other daughters experience both states of emotion over the same phenomenon.

THE OTHER'S PRESENCE AS A SOURCE OF PLEASURE

Mothers and daughters did not need to engage in activities or even in conversations to find their visits enjoyable. The presence of the other party often sufficed to render a situation pleasant. Mothers and daughters may maintain frequent contact in part because they enjoy their relationship and view this contact as an inherent feature of this tie.

Just Being with Her

Alice, a 74-year-old widow, described her sense that whatever she and her daughter did together was enjoyable because they were together:

> We don't really see each other that often because of her working hours. She works, gets home so late, and then being married, I hate to interrupt her weekends because they spend so little time together. But when I do see her we have an enjoyable time. And we went shopping. She took me shopping last Saturday and it was very nice. {Pause} Oh, just being with her. Just the companionship and the care that she gives me. She always wants to do things for me and gets upset sometimes if I do them myself. I just love being with her.

A daughter's ability to spend time with her mother appeared to be a simple pleasure, as well. As was mentioned in Part I, some daughters expressed their regret that they were so busy, it was hard to fit their mothers into their lives. Although the mothers in this study tended to be active women, they lived alone or with a spouse. Their daughters experienced stress over the division of their scant leisure time among competing social contacts (e.g., husbands, children, parents, friends). Yet, daughters reported pleasure from the time they did spend with their mothers.

For example, Allison, a 35-year-old daughter, described a trip she had taken to Florida with her mother as their last pleasant visit, noting, " . . . part of what was nice was seeing her when I wasn't really busy. I feel like otherwise I try to carve time out of my busy schedule to sort of do obligatory things."

Daughters were also aware that their mothers were aging, and they often expressed the hidden message that they took pleasure in being able to spend time with them before they died. Kathy, a 46-year-old daughter, described a number of health problems that her 78-year-old mother, Phyllis, had incurred. Although Phyllis considered herself to be healthy and she did not require her daughter's daily care, she had heart problems and her physical state was precarious:

> She has 3 million things that are seriously wrong with her. She has a very simplistic view of medicine and not too much knowledge, so it works for her. To her, if she's taking a pill for her heart, it's curing her heart problem. But, actually, she has a major blockage and so we've been told. Her doctor calls it a walking time bomb, which I love that expression, but it's made us aware. She also is arthritic and she has high blood pressure and several other things. I mean, I felt very happy to be with her. But I kind of came away feeling also kind of sad. The last couple of years, my sisters and I have talked about that we all sort of feel this way when we're with her. It's bittersweet because she's not well, and she's almost 80. So, you know you're not going to have a whole lot of those.

Identification with the Other Party

Experiencing pleasure in another party's company may be inherent to many types of intimate relationships in adulthood. Parent/child relationships may be distinct, however, because both parties derive a sense of their own identity from the relationship. Descriptions of a sense of identification or connection to the other party were not dominant in this study, but did appear meaningful to the women who brought up such issues. A few mothers and daughters felt gratified by a sense of connection with someone like oneself in so many ways.

After describing her bittersweet feelings about her mother's health, Kathy went on to describe her sense of identification with mother:

> About 2 weeks ago, I was making a care package to bring my son at college. I was baking cookies and I was making a roast and I was doing all of these things. I was in the kitchen and real happy about doing all this stuff for him. I knew he was going to love all this and I thought, "Where is this coming from?" I mean, I work full-time and I've never been Sally home-maker. I just don't normally get into this kind of stuff, and here I was having a wonderful day doing all those things for him. And I thought, "Where is this coming from?" and then I realized where it comes from. It would've been just what my mother would've done for us when we were growing up. And she enjoyed it all the time, or so it appeared to us. I called her up and we talked about that.

The sense of being similar to someone else, of using her as a role model was important in the mother/daughter tie to the women who derived such pleasures.

Glenda, a 73-year-old mother, described her visit with her daughter Sandy in glowing terms, "I enjoy Sandy a great deal. I'm very fond of Sandy. I like Sandy's company. Sandy and I are much alike in many ways. We have lots of things to talk about . . . "

Other women pointed out the pleasure they take in the other person because of her personal attributes. Jacqueline described her pleasure from interacting with her daughter, Annette, slipping in her pride over her daughter's prowess at backgammon:

> Usually, when we travel, we play backgammon in the evening . . . and we fight like mad over it, in a kidding sort of way. And I cheat, and she tells me I cheat. And, you know, if I win it's because I'm lucky. And if she wins, it's because she's smart. So, you now, that's part of why I enjoy it.

This type of pride, which might be anticipated with regard to parents, was also evident in daughters' descriptions of enjoyable visits. Sara, a 42-year-old daughter, explained:

> She's a really good model for mothering because she is a very unselfish person. She's a very giving mother. Nothing, even if she's tired, nothing is too much for her children or her grandchildren. She's just fun to be with.

Again, as daughters mature, they may be more able to see their mothers as individual human beings with virtues and foibles. As they notice their mothers' aging, they may become more aware of the things they enjoy about her.

Young adult daughters and their mothers commonly describe enjoying a sense of identification and connection in their visits (Fingerman, 2000a). For older mothers and daughters, the bond may be taken for granted, or the need for that type of identification may have been outgrown. Indeed, more mothers and daughters described activities, conversation, or time spent with the other party than a sense of identification or relating to her. The relationship itself is a source pleasure, but that pleasure is derived from relating to the other person as an individual, rather than identifying with her or the relationship.

FAMILY AND KINKEEPING IN MOTHERS' AND DAUGHTERS' RELATIONSHIPS

Although mothers and daughters were asked to talk specifically about their relationship with one another, their descriptions of pleasant visits often included fathers, sons-in-law, grandchildren, and siblings. Indeed, family appeared to be a more salient theme than a sense of identification in this relationship for most women. Nearly two thirds of the mothers and nearly half of the daughters described enjoyable visits involving other people. These individuals were central to the mothers' and daughters' sense that the visit was so positive. For example, Glenda included other family members when she expanded on the details of her enjoyable visit with Sandy:

> I guess the last time we got together was yesterday and she came over. She called to ask me if she could bring the baby over and leave him here for awhile so she could get out. She did and she came back. And then, just then, also just yesterday, her sisters and their families were by my house and she had a chance to see them. And we all chatted a bit 'cause we always do that. Whether the baby kept everyone up all night, how her son Zachary is doing in preschool, things like that.

Much of the time when mothers discussed other family members, they specifically mentioned grandchildren in their pleasurable visits. Sometimes the grandchildren were present and other times, they were the focus of discussion. Several such examples have already been mentioned, such as Rebecca and her daughter Molly who helped her mother Nancy put up the Christmas tree and Valerie and her son Tommy who spent the afternoon looking at old photographs with her mother. Grace described a visit with her 38-year-old daughter Denise:

> She came to the house to pick up her daughter, Samantha, my granddaughter that is. And, we had a very short visit, but it was a very pleasant visit. Sort of, in summary, it was about how happy she and Mike had been to get away together and then she took off to go take Samantha home and to pick up Andy to go swimming. So, it is that type of contact that I have with her frequently, very often, related to the two children but still very much related to my interest in her and in the children.

In another example, Lucille described a situation when she simply talked on the phone with her daughter Carol. Their phone conversation focused on Carol's children. "We talked about shopping for my granddaughters and what I could get them for Christmas." Thus, the pleasure Lucille experienced was not only that of talking with Carol, but of sharing a connection to Carol's children, Lucille's granddaughters.

Daughters also enjoyed the collective sense of connection across generations. Denise, described the pleasure she derived in passing on a family recipe to her own daughter with her mother:

> Last Sunday, Ashley and I went over to my mom's house and we made applesauce together. It was really fun because it was all three of us and I used to do that with my mom when I was a kid. Ashley can be a really sweet kid, and she worked really hard with us. And we just, we were just working together doing all the different parts of the applesauce and conversing. And it was just a real regular time. We were all acting like friends, but at the same time there was that bond there—that grandmom, mom, daughter thing. It was neat. That wasn't the last time we got together. The last time we got together was for supper (with the rest of my family), and that was great, too. But this was real special with the three of us together. Passing down crafts is sort of a generational thing.

Of note in Denise's description is the joy she feels from her own embeddedness in a family chain. As was mentioned in the previous chapter, mother/daughter bonds across the life span often serve to link together families. Denise's description conveys the emotional importance of these bonds to mothers and daughters. Her pleasure is not only a function of being in her mother's and her daughter's presence (both were also present at the supper she chose not to describe as a notably special visit), but from her own sense of linking together a family chain, " . . . that grandmom, mom, daughter thing."

The inclusion of connection to others distinguishes descriptions of pleasant visits from descriptions of unpleasant ones. As will be noted in the next section, mothers were more likely to describe other people as part of problematic situations than were their daughters. Mothers referred to a larger group when asked to describe a time when they were irritated or annoyed with their daughters. By contrast, in these instances, daughters focused solely on their mothers. Moreover, mothers' aggravations included a wider range of people than had their descriptions of enjoyable situations. Whereas mothers' pleasure tended to stem from connection to their daughter's children, mothers' displeasure was derived from a variety of others, including the daughter's fathers (the mothers' husbands), the daughter's siblings, her lovers, and even her friends, as well as the daughters' children. Again, the pleasure mothers and daughters derive from their relationship appears to be more similar across participants than the displeasure they experience.

PLEASURE DERIVED FROM BEING NURTURED

In addition to the kinkeeping functions mothers and daughters serve in later life, caregiving is often seen as a central function of this relationship. Researchers have suggested that daughters derive benefits from their ability to care for their mothers when needed (Fingerman, 1997b; Walker & Allen, 1991). Yet, little is known about whether or not mothers and daughters enjoy caring for, and being cared for by the other when both parties are healthy. In this study, many mothers and daughters described situations involving nurturance, whether they provided care for or received care from the other party. Nearly a third of mothers' responses fell under this category and just over a third of daughters' responses fell under this category. Provision of care appeared to be a means of communicating affection for the other person, rather than an inherent responsibility. Descriptions of nurturance involved sharing food and presents, assisting with special tasks, and providing emotional support.

In some dyads, mother and daughter alike derived a sense of pleasure in being nurtured by the other. For example, Barbara described a situation in which her 49-year-old daughter Ellen had made her lunch. She expounded on the soup and salad her daughter fixed in detail, savoring it again in memory, "We had gone shopping, and stopped at Ellen's. She made a lovely lunch of cream of tomato soup, homemade. She's very talented like that. She also made a salad with some hard-boiled eggs that was very nice. I always enjoy it. This is the last time we had done that." In her own account of their last enjoyable visit Ellen also described a meal they had shared. However, the meal Ellen remembered as constituting their most recent enjoyable visit involved a family dinner that her mother had made for Ellen, Ellen's children, and Ellen's siblings the previous Sunday. While Barbara and Ellen share a sense of enjoyment from food, they also derived a sense of enjoyment from having the other party prepare that food.

Although the proportions of mothers and daughters who described nurturance as a source of pleasure were comparable, there were generational differences in who received that nurturance. Daughters were as likely to report incidences involving caring for their mothers as they were to describe situations in which their mothers cared for them. Eight daughters described events in which their mothers did something kind for them and nine daughters described events in which they did something kind for their mothers. For example, Claire, a 46-year-old daughter, described the many things she had done to help her mother prepare for Christmas:

> I went to help her specifically to do some Christmas things. We had lunch together. Then, I helped her turn an old-fashioned bread maker. She can't turn it. I did that for her. We do that for her every year. Then I helped her decorate her house where she couldn't reach. That was fun because it brought back memories. Then we both went outside and wrapped her light post in green garlands. That was really cold, but we did it! Then we went in and had a little coffee and a chat. It was fun because it was Christmas kinds of things. I felt good because I really thought I had helped her do things that needed doing that weren't hard for me to do. I didn't think it was laborious—they were fun tasks.

Claire's enjoyment was related to helping her mother, but also to nostalgia and memories pertaining to the tasks at hand. Claire's pleasure is "daughterly" in the sense that she derives pleasure from pleasing her mother. At the same time, the ways in which she is helping her mother reflect changes inherent to relationships between middle-aged daughters and older mothers. Her mother requires help with tasks that, in the past, would not have fallen under her daughter's province. Part of Claire's pleasure was related to her ability to deal with these changes and to experience them as positive.

By contrast, when mothers described enjoyable events involving nurturance, they themselves tended to be the target of that care. Twelve mothers supplied scenarios in which they derived pleasure from their daughters' ministries. Only three mothers described situations in which they had provided care for their daughters. Some of these situations were simple tasks that made the mother's life easier, but did not demand a great deal of time from the daughter. For example, Phyllis mentioned that her daughter Kathy had helped them with a television:

> Well, we didn't have a television. Our television broke. Then, my husband bought one that didn't work either. We had to take that back. So, she gave us this one and just told us to keep it. She does things like that. Gosh, she gave us that telephone, too.

Other mothers mentioned assistance with shelves they could not reach, heavy cleaning, or decorating for a party or holiday.

Although these mothers were relatively healthy, they did incur short-term health problems. Their daughters had already begun to provide assistance in these situations. Nancy mentioned that she had received care from her daughter in addition to the assistance with her tree:

> Rebecca also helped me when I had my knee operation. She was here—she takes care of me for short times. She came over almost every day to see that I had groceries, that the meals, that I had my meals very definitely. She's always very worried that mother's eating right. And the other girls are far away and they can't come. So I go to visit them. And so Rebecca is here for me all the time.

The generational differences in the target of care may reflect mothers' and daughters' conceptions of their roles. As was mentioned, mothers and daughters reported that they were only required to provide care for the other party on an infrequent basis, less often than once a year. Given that the mothers were relatively healthy, the care they provide their daughters may be part of the continuity of their role as mother. It is the mother's role to care for their daughters beginning in infancy. Mothers may be less likely to describe provision of care for daughters as characterizing a particularly enjoyable visit because they see such care as integral to their relationships with their daughters throughout life. To mothers, care for daughters does not define a specific visit, it defines the relationship itself (Ruddick, 1989). On the other hand, as they age, mothers may provide less care, or take less pleasure from doing so. When daughters provide care for their mothers, there is something special about the act of giving for the daughters and the state of receiving for the mothers.

The differences in care as a source of pleasure are paralleled by comments about care as a source of irritation. As will be seen in the next section, some mothers felt their daughters were being intrusive by offering unsolicited or unneeded care. In addition, daughters sometimes resented having to help their mothers in situations where they felt demanded upon. Thus, even when mothers are healthy, caregiving appears to be fraught with ambivalence.

THE NEGATIVE IN POSITIVE EVENTS

Although participants were generally loquacious and animate in their responses to questions about enjoyable visits, some mothers and daughters spontaneously mentioned something unpleasant as well. Daughters were more likely to mention the downside of their relationships than were mothers. More than half of daughters referred to something negative when discussing the positive aspects of the relationship, as did one third of mothers. In some instances, daughters appeared to be trying to present a balanced portrait of the relationship.

For example, Sue, the 43-year-old daughter, who had described the concert her mother attended at the last minute also acknowledged that their relationship is not perfect. At the end of her scenario, she commented, "Of course, my mother and I can disagree with one another as well as having nice evenings out." As will be mentioned again in subsequent chapters, daughters appear to experience more ambivalence in their relationships with their mothers than do mothers. Thus, when they talk about their relationship, daughters seek to portray its strengths and weaknesses.

Mothers were less likely to introduce something unpleasant into their discourse on pleasant visits. When they did bring up negative situations, the situations tended to be ones that were unavoidable. The pleasant aspect of the event in these cases involved the removal of some unpleasantness. For example, Hazel, a 79-year-old widow, talked about her husband's death, and how sad she felt at Easter. However, she described that day as her last enjoyable visit because, "Allison had a brunch for the family. She really helped me get through the day."

Some daughters also included instances where the pleasantness of the event involved the aversion of something negative. Hazel's daughter, Allison, focused on the absence of negative feelings as what made their last visit so enjoyable. As was mentioned previously, Allison had commented that she and her mother had spent time in Florida together, and Allison's pleasure stemmed from having time free to spend with her mother. The pleasure was described as the absence of an overly hectic schedule. Allison was relieved that she didn't feel overwhelmed by the combined demands of work, family, and her mother, and that she could spend time solely with her mother.

Brenda, a 43-year-old daughter, cited an instance in which she and her 16-year-old daughter had been at her mothers' house. First, she described how much she appreciated her mother's love for her and her daughter and described how her mother had made a special evening for them. However, she also noted, "I like it when I feel some control of the time and the structure. . . . I like to be real clear on the beginning and the ending time. This time I didn't feel like she had all the control."

Here again, subtle generational differences appeared in the perspectives that mothers and daughters took, even with regard to the same types of issues. Whereas mothers tended to focus on ways in which their daughters helped them avoid difficult personal problems, daughters tended to focus on avoiding interpersonal tension with their mothers as defining the pleasant situation. In the next section, we look at daughters' ambivalence in their ties to their mothers more closely.

COMMUNICATION OF FEELINGS DURING THE ENJOYABLE VISITS

In addition to understanding how mothers and daughters perceived the pleasant aspects of their relationships, this study focused on how emotions are communicated. After the women had described a recent enjoyable visit, interviewers asked mothers and daughters whether the other party was aware of her feelings during that visit. Nearly 90% of mothers and daughters said that the other knew how they felt during the pleasant incident. Yet, few mothers and daughters reported directly telling the other party how she felt.

Knowing How the Other Party Felt

When asked *how* the other person knew what they were feeling, fewer than 40% of mothers and daughters indicated that they had actually told the other person how much they were enjoying the visit. This failure to explicitly communicate feelings is important for understanding negative emotions in the relationship, as well. As will be discussed in the last section of the book, mothers and daughters seem to assume that the other person knows and understands how they feel, regardless of whether or not they have actively expressed those feelings.

Indeed, mothers and daughters appeared surprised when the interviewer asked them if the other person knew how they felt. For example, Claire paused and then explained:

> I don't know. I remember saying 'Well, thanks for the lunch.' But I'm not sure that I used the word 'fun' or 'that was really great' or 'I enjoyed it today' or made those kinds of statements. I mean, she looked happy and she said, 'Thanks,' for all the help I'd given her, and I said 'You're welcome.' . . . I think she felt positive.

Claire's sense that she had communicated her feelings was derived not from anything she said, but from her observation that her mother was also happy.

Likewise, other mothers and daughters seemed to be aware of the other person's pleasure or displeasure. In fact, many mothers included their daughters' positive affect as a source of their own enjoyment. When asked how she had felt during the visit when her daughter Ellen had made her such a memorable lunch, Barbara explained, "I felt great because I could see that she felt great." Bernice, an 85-year-old retired teacher, also expressed this sentiment. Bernice's immediate response to the question about the last enjoyable visit was, " . . . she seemed happy. I'm happy when she's happy."

Correspondence Between Responses

Finally, we might expect mothers and daughters with more open communication patterns to describe the same events as their most recent pleasant and unpleasant visits. Mothers and daughters sometimes had a different perspective on why a particular event was pleasant. For example, a daughter might claim she enjoyed the event because her mother fixed her supper the previous Sunday, whereas the mother might describe pleasure derived from being with her entire family at supper the previous Sunday. Mothers' and daughters' responses were considered to correspond if they both clearly described the same situation, regardless of why it was considered pleasurable. Nearly a third of mothers and daughters described the same situation as their last enjoyable visit. The correspondence between their responses does not associate with explicitly telling the other party one's feelings, however.

It is not clear why some mothers and daughters named the same incident when asked about their last pleasant visit while others did not. It is possible that some events were particularly salient. It is also possible that mothers and daughters who named the same incident merely selected the last time they were together, and, thus described the same incident. Again, the issue of mothers' and daughters' viewing the same visit as a recent emotional encounter was more important with regard to problematic situations than it was with regard to pleasant situations.

CONCLUSIONS

In summary, the older mothers and daughters who participated in this study enjoyed the time they spent together. Mothers and daughters alike claimed that their relationships were distinguished by the positive regard they experience for one another. In general, mothers and daughters described activities as central features of their enjoyable visits. The research literature has emphasized a number of themes that appeared in mothers' and daughters' descriptions of enjoyable visits such as family life and nurturance, but there has been little research attention to the notion of companionship in this tie. It is clear that mothers and daughters simply enjoy the other party's company.

Although they generally characterized their relationships as good, several mothers and daughters commented on negative aspects of the relationship when asked to discuss its positive features, revealing a wide range of emotions for the other party. It is also notable that mother/daughter ties were characterized by a lack of overt communication about pleasurable emotions that they experience. The next two sections focus on sources of tension and communication of difficulties. As shall be discussed in detail in the remaining chapters, mothers and daughters experience a wide range of feelings for the other party, and their negative experiences provide greater insights into variation in their ties than their positive experiences.

■ three

PROBLEMS IN THE MOTHER/DAUGHTER TIE

■ 5 The Developmental Schism

My mother has expressed the fact that she respects me as an adult. That was said to me so many years ago that a lot of that tension that is sometimes present in mother/daughter relationships even in later life, just isn't in ours. You want a time when I was annoyed? Well, I wasn't personally annoyed. I just feel bad that she won't do something that I think would be good for her—which is to get a flu shot. She was with me when I got mine last year, and at that time we had the discussion that it would be a good idea. After all, she is elderly. And she said she just doesn't believe in putting that kind of stuff in her body. So I said, "All right," and I went ahead and got mine and then we went home. And this year, she was with me when I got mine. And I didn't even bring it up, because I knew how she felt. I wish she would do it, but obviously, I'm not going to harp at her. She is an adult, and she has the right to make her own decisions. I felt a little irritated, but you get irritated when people aren't doing what you think is the right thing for them to do.

—Amanda, 58-year-old daughter

Although mothers and daughters love one another a great deal, they may still get annoyed with the other party from time to time. Researchers have noted that it is the nature of conflict, rather than the degree of intimacy and love, that best differentiates relationships (Canary, Cupach, & Messman, 1995; Cohan & Bradbury, 1997; Gottman, 1979, 1993a, 1998). The strengths of relationships are often similar in nature. Positive affection, frequent contact, and exchanges of support build strong relationships. To get a better sense of variation in mother/daughter ties, we must examine problems they experience and how they handle those problems.

Indeed, as a general rule, problematic features of relationships outweigh positive features of relationships (Rook, 1984, 1992). Rook (1992) pointed out that one nasty argument in the middle of an otherwise pleasant dinner taints the entire evening. By contrast, one pleasant encounter in the midst of a stormy fight does not redeem the evening. Therefore, we might expect mothers and daughters who are frequently irritated with the other party to have weaker relationships. Yet, it is not clear that the mother/daughter tie follows this general pattern for negative encounters. In such a long-lasting relationship, parties may become accustomed to issues that rancor. By late life, mothers and daughters may be aware that the other party has unpleasant habits, but they may come to accept this unpleasantness rather than resenting it.

It is clear, however, that mothers and daughters do not always feel positively about the other party. Indeed, Luescher and Pillemer (1998) introduced the term "intergenerational ambivalence" to describe ties between parents and offspring in adulthood. These authors argued that intergenerational relationships are inherently emotionally complicated. Moreover, such complications are particularly evident in ties between mothers and daughters (Troll & Fingerman, 1996).

This section considers mothers' and daughters' reports of problems in their relationships. Although the implications of mother/daughter tensions are not well understood, existent data suggests that difficulties in mother/daughter ties may harm both parties. Daughters with weak ties to mothers score lower on indicators of mental health than do daughters with strong ties (Barnett, Kibria, Baruch, & Pleck, 1991; Welsh & Stewart, 1995). Elderly mothers who have poor relationships with offspring have higher rates of morbidity and mortality. Aging mothers who are dissatisfied with their grown children show more symptoms of psychological distress and are less happy with their lives (Davey & Eggebeen, 1998; Kobrin & Hendershot, 1977; Pruchno, Peters, & Burant, 1996; Umberson & Gove, 1989). Given the potential implications of mother/daughter tensions, we know surprisingly little about the types of problems that they encounter.

DEVELOPMENTAL SCHISMS

The field of gerontology has shown that individuals do not reach adulthood and then stop developing. Rather, development continues throughout adulthood. Accordingly, in many aspects of functioning, older adults are at a different point in their development than are middle-aged adults, and middle-aged adults are at a different point in their development than are young adults. Disparities in life stage may contribute to problems between parents and offspring throughout life. Elsewhere, I introduced the "developmental schism framework" to explain why parents and offspring experience tensions (Fingerman, 1996).

The developmental schism is premised on the idea that problems arise because parents and offspring have discrepant developmental needs. The developmental schism reflects more general principles about interpersonal ties. When individuals come together in an intimate relationship, they each bring their own goals and beliefs to that relationship. When these goals are not in synchrony, conflicts erupt. In many types of relationships, it is possible to understand interpersonal conflicts by looking at systematic differences in relationship partners' needs. Indeed, the developmental schism might be understood by looking at the parallel case of gender differences in marriage.

Researchers who study marriage have suggested that problems arise because men and women come to the marital relationship with differing perspectives, needs, and communication styles based in gender differences (e.g., Acitelli & Antonucci, 1994; Bradbury, Campbell, & Fincham, 1995; Gottman, 1998). Here, gender is a proxy for the ways in which men and women were socialized, how they are treated by the larger society, the resources available to them outside the marriage, and so forth. Men and women are not interchangeable in the marital tie because they come from inherently different backgrounds. Similarly, parents' and offspring's ages and roles present a polarity that is never reconciled. Parents are always parents, and offspring are always offspring.

Notably, when "age" is examined in parent/offspring relationships, it is generally the child's age that is assumed to drive the relationship. Indeed, much of the literature on the family lifecycle is premised on transitions involving a child (e.g., birth of a child, child's entry into school, empty next). Of course, some features of this proposition are undeniably true. At early stages of development, there are clear differences in parent/child ties as a function of the child's age: a baby who cannot talk or walk evokes different responses than a 9-year-old with budding interests in the outside world. Yet, it is also true that older family members incur changes over time. Parents have developmental needs.

Problems arise when the developmental needs of one individual conflict with the needs of the other. For example, the so-called "terrible twos" would not be a problem if the parent did not mind the child's explorations, stubbornness, or desire to do things for herself (at a maddeningly slow pace). Problems arise because the parent has competing needs, such as an ambition to advance in the work world that does not allow the 45 minutes necessary for the 2-year-old to put on her own coat. The adolescent years present difficulties not only due to the teenager's increasing desire for independence, but because parents must struggle with their role in this relationship as the teenager enters adulthood. The interplay between the two parties generates conflicts and tensions. When daughters enter midlife, they experience an increased awareness of their own mortality; they may shift these concerns onto their aging parents (Cicirelli, 1988; Fingerman, 1997a). Tensions erupt if mothers feel belittled by their daughters' concerns.

The developmental schism stems from the large age gaps between parents and offspring, rather than specific developmental tasks. Chronological age itself is not a clear marker of development in adulthood (Uttal & Perlmutter, 1989). A 20-year-old adult might be living in the mother's home, a 20-year-old might be enrolled in college, or a 20-year-old might be raising children of her own. Although these patterns vary, a more general issue in the mother/daughter relationship at this stage of life stems from the fact that 20-year-old women are establishing themselves in the grown-up world for the first time. Their anxieties and life concerns are distinct from the issues their mothers confront.

Not all developmental differences generate tensions, of course, just as not all gender differences generate marital discord. It is not differences in age, per se, but rather, conflicting needs that underlie problems. Moreover, differences in life stage do not always lead to tensions. Rather, they may explain patterns of tension that do arise. Again, to use marriage as a parallel example, when problems arise in a marriage, they may reflect gender differences in perspectives, needs, and communication styles. Gender, per se, does not lead to marital conflict. Rather, it serves as a proxy for these other issues.

In contrast to gender, however, developmental needs change across the life span. At one point in life, parents and offspring may deal with the offspring's identity formation, at another stage of life, the parent's health may be a key concern. Although developmental differences always exist between parents and offspring, these differences wax and wane. Luescher and Pillemer (1998) suggested that intergenerational ambivalence peaks when parents and offspring confront a transition; during transitions, norms for the relationship are weak. These authors provided the specific example of widowhood as a time when daughters and mothers experience ambivalence over their relationship. Transitions are not directly linked to tensions, however. Although transitions introduce new demands on the mother/daughter tie, such shifts in the relationship arise repeatedly. Childhood markers such as walking, talking, puberty, and moving from the parent's household shape the relationship between mothers and daughters in positive ways. The developmental schism approach looks more generally at disparities in individuals' goals, perspectives, and relationship attributions, rather than focusing on specific life contexts or transitions.

STATUS, COHORTS, AND ROLES DISPARITIES

In addition to being at different points in life, mothers and daughters also differ in other significant ways. Sociologists have noted that parents and offspring occupy different roles in their relationship and that disparities in their status may lead to relationship tensions. Bengtson and Kuypers (1971) argued that parents have a "developmental stake" in their offspring, leading them to be highly invested in the parent/offspring tie. Offspring wish to establish their own mark on the world, and wish to separate from their parents. Although it is important to consider such continuities in parents' and offspring's roles in the relationship, it is also important to consider changes in their relationships. Parental investment in the relationship is not constant throughout life. At different stages of life, differences in investment are likely to be more or less salient. Moreover, level of investment is not the only disparity that parents and offspring experience. The developmental schism framework subsumes the idea of role-related differences between parents and offspring.

Cohort Differences

Parents and offspring were born into different cohorts. The historical events they have experienced and the social climate in which each party was raised influences their relationship. For example the so-called "generation gap" of the 1960s and 1970s received considerable research attention (Bengtson, 1970; Bengtson, Olander, & Haddad, 1976; Troll, 1971). During this period, widespread social changes in sexual mores and gender roles allowed young women opportunities that had not been available to their mothers 20 years previously. Existent data suggest, however, that parents and offspring of this period did not differ in their *fundamental* values.

Indeed, tensions between parents and offspring have been noted since Grecian times (Reinhold, 1976). Although certain cohorts may be more aware of the tensions they experience or better able to define the reasons underlying those tensions, cohort differences alone do not seem to account for parent/offspring tensions. A more fruitful way of considering tensions between mothers and daughters may involve examination of disparities in their goals and beliefs about the relationship, the approach taken using a developmental schism framework. Of course, some of those differences may stem from the larger cohort experiences in which mothers and daughters are entrenched. Moreover, individuals born in different historical periods experience life tasks at different ages. Therefore, developmental tasks themselves are partly shaped by cohort.

Role Convergence

Sociologists have also pointed that mother/daughter relationships tend to improve as daughters acquire life roles that are similar to their mothers. As daughters marry and have children of their own, they presumably understand their mothers better, and thus, there are fewer difficulties in their relationship. The data pertaining to the idea of role convergence and mother/daughter tensions are equivocal, however. Some studies find that when daughters have partners and children, their ties to their own mothers improve (Fischer, 1981, 1986; Umberson, 1992), other studies find no effects (Suitor, Pillemer, Keeton, & Robison, 1996), and still other studies suggest these factors only matter at certain times of life (Fingerman, 2000a).

A problem with the role convergence approach to understanding mother/daughter ties stems from the focus on role acquisition patterns that were common for middle-class women in the 1950s and 1960s, but are no longer as common. Women who remain single, who divorce, who have no children, and who select a family form that differs from that of their mother also report decreased tensions with their mothers across adulthood. A more microanalytic approach to parent/offspring ties suggests that differences in *perspective* are more important than differences in social roles in explaining mother/daughter tensions. As women's roles converge, they are more likely to share perspectives, but it is not essential that roles converge for daughters to come to see their mother's point of view. Life experience may substitute for convergence of roles. As daughters achieve positions of authority and responsibility, they may sympathize with the challenges their mothers have faced. The developmental schism framework does not contradict role convergence theory, but it focuses more broadly on changes associated with life experience and current goals and needs.

DEVELOPMENT IN THE MOTHER/DAUGHTER TIE AT MIDLIFE

Although the developmental schism framework can be applied to parents and children across the life span, this study focused specifically on schisms at midlife. Longitudinal and cross-sectional studies of parent/offspring ties indicate that negative qualities of the tie decrease and positive qualities increase across adulthood. Middle-aged offspring report fewer tensions with parents than do young adult offspring (Carstensen, 1992; Hagestad, 1984, 1987; Suitor & Pillemer, 1987, 1988; Umberson, 1989; Weishaus, 1978).

A parallel, but separate literature suggests that decreases in tensions coincide with offspring's increasing sense of their parents as individuals. Offspring who are in their 20's perceive their parents as older and different from themselves. Although offspring in this age range can clearly interact as adults in the adult world, they continue to perceive their parents as parental figures. By contrast, offspring in their late 30's may achieve "filial maturity," an awareness that their parents are complex individuals with weaknesses (Blenkner, 1963; Fingerman, 1997b; Labouvie-Vief, Diehl, Chiodo, & Coyle, 1995). Not all individuals achieve "filial maturity," but those who do are able to relate to their parents on more equal terms. It is easier to accept a parent's faults if the parent is just another adult like oneself. Many middle-aged daughters have achieved this sense of their mothers.

Less is known about parents' conceptions of offspring than offspring's conceptions of parents in adulthood (Nydegger, 1991). There is some evidence that parents conceive of young adult offspring as an extension of themselves, rather than as adults in their own right (Aldous et al., 1985; Ryff, Lee, Essex, & Schmutte, 1994; Ryff & Seltzer, 1996). Parents, like offspring, may undergo a transformation in their conceptions of the relationship as offspring enter midlife. Nydegger (1991) suggested that parents might undergo "parental maturity," parallel to their offspring's filial maturity. Parental maturity involves the ability to view offspring as full-fledged, independent adults with inherent weaknesses. As will be discussed, mothers seem to struggle with this transition more than daughters do. Indeed, there is no empirical evidence that parents change their conceptions of their offspring when offspring are in their 30's. Throughout life, mothers may retain a parental investment in their daughters, including an ability to see their daughters' strengths more readily than their daughters' weaknesses.

In summary, mothers and daughters continue to develop after daughters reach adulthood and before mothers incur dramatic health problems. Although there has been less research attention to this period of life than to other periods, the mother/daughter relationship in midlife appears to be distinct from prior stages in this relationship.

Role Enhancement at Midlife

Daughters are particularly sensitive to changes in their relationships with their mothers at midlife. The popular press is filled with descriptions of a "role reversal" in later life. Middle-aged daughters presumably assume the position of "parent" to their mothers. Although there are undeniable changes in mothers' and daughters' roles in late life, the gerontological literature has discounted the premise of a role reversal (Brody, 1990; Bromberg, 1987; Fingerman, 1997b; Seltzer, 1990). In order for roles to reverse, each person would have to take over the functions and status of the other party. The phrase "role reversal" does not do justice to the myriad of changes that take place between mothers and daughters in later life. Moreover, it glosses over the continuities in this tie.

The first chapter began with a quote from Brenda, a 49-year-old daughter, who first expressed her concerns about her mother's frailty, "I feel like I have to watch over her a lot. I'm always kind of amazed at how vulnerable she seems. She's getting older," and then comments on her mother's vitality, "I'm always amazed at how independent she is." The quotation from Marion at the start of this chapter mimics the same sentiment. When daughters are concerned about their mothers' health, they may use the popular term "role reversal." Yet, these daughters also realize that their mothers are still healthy women with the right to make their own decisions. The roles have not truly reversed.

Elsewhere, I have suggested that the term "role expansion" provides a more accurate description of changes in the daughters' role at midlife (Fingerman, 1997b). Daughters are increasingly aware of their mothers' health and they may feel protective of their mothers, even when their mothers are in relatively good health (Cicirelli, 1988). Daughters' roles are enhanced in midlife, as they begin to assist their mother with day-to-day tasks such as heavy cleaning or holiday decorations, described in the previous chapter.

Developmental Schisms at Midlife

There are two principal areas where mothers and daughters differ in the goals they bring to their relationships. Given the salience of the mother's aging to middle-aged daughters, we might expect this issue to come up in their relationships with their mothers. Daughters may feel irritated if their mothers take risks that they feel are inappropriate. Yet, as was discussed in the first section of this book, middle-aged daughters still crave their mother's approval and wish to please them. Mothers may continue to feel that they are mothers and that is it is they, and not their daughters, who should proffer advice in the relationship. Tensions may erupt over these differences in perceptions of the relationship.

The second area of difference revolves around available time for, and investment in, the mother/daughter tie. Older and middle-aged adults have different types of social networks. Older adults tend to have fewer social contacts than younger adults, but they tend to be more invested in those ties and to derive greater emotional rewards from those ties (Carstensen, 1995; Carstensen et al., 1998). Moreover, as was mentioned in the prior section, the social contexts in which older and younger women live look very different. Older women are more likely to be widowed and less likely to be working. As a result of these disparities, mothers and daughters may experience tensions over the value they place on their relationship.

Of course, the manifestation of developmental schisms is likely to vary as a function of women's cultural, educational, and past experiences. The issues examined here are most applicable to well-educated, European American samples. Unfortunately, research on parents and offspring in adulthood has rarely included multiple ethnic or cultural groups. Moreover, most developmental theories were derived based on European American samples (Erikson, 1950; Havighurst, 1972). In other ethnic or cultural groups, different issues might arise in the mother/daughter tie.

CONCLUSIONS

Developmental differences between mothers and daughters encompass a wide range of issues and may result in interpersonal tensions regardless of the quality of their relationship. The basis for these tensions may vary over a lifetime. Preschool children and their mothers may find themselves in conflict over the child's behavior, whereas middle-aged daughters and their mothers may be upset over plans for a family gathering. In each instance, however, these tensions stem from the fact that the parties involved have different goals.

The next chapter addresses mothers' and daughters' memories of early experiences in their relationship. Mothers and daughters in this study remembered past problems in their relationship either in stereotypical terms (e.g., "Everyone fights during the teenage years") or as the outcome of a specific crisis that occurred at that period. Few mothers or daughters explicitly linked problems in the past to the quality of their relationship at present. Chapter 7 presents mothers' and daughters' reports of tensions in their current relationship. In many instances, their problems appear to stem from the types of developmental schisms anticipated when daughters enter midlife. The final chapter in this section includes information from the joint interviews, when mothers and daughters discussed their problems together.

In summary, the developmental schism framework builds on prior work by considering how disparities in perspectives on the relationship contribute to interpersonal tensions. These disparities arise from differences in relationship status, prior life experience, and current needs and goals. Mothers and daughters spend their entire lives in different positions in their relationship and different points in their own development. These differences can foster tensions between them. The simplest way to look at a developmental schism is to ask, "Does it matter that mothers and daughters are at different stages of life?" When daughters are middle aged and mothers enter late life, the answer is, "Yes."

■ 6 The History of the Mother/Daughter Tie

When Paula was about 13 to 18, we had the same things that come up with other mothers and daughters. There was a time when she was very sharp with her friends. Paula felt she was right all the time. She never wanted to clean her room. It was clean, but it was a mess. We disagreed about that. I felt she was cold at that time. If I put my arms around her to hug her or kiss her, I didn't get the same response. Just small everyday things, like curfews. There were questions about schooling. Paula thought we should be able to send her anywhere she wanted to go to school, and we couldn't afford to. Now, looking back, it doesn't even seem important, but at the time, there was tension.

—*Gwen, 70-year-old mother*

Although this study focused on mothers and daughters in late life, mothers and daughters share a long history prior to this stage. The early years of the mother/daughter tie may have an impact on the relationship in midlife. Indeed, researchers have found that memories of childhood experiences with parents are associated with the quality of the relationship and willingness to care for the parent in late life (Field, 1989; Fingerman, 1997a; Webster & Herzog, 1995;

Whitbeck, Hoyt, & Huck, 1994; Whitbeck, Simons, & Conger, 1991). Of course, retrospective accounts of past relationship experiences may be subject to error because these memories are reconstructed in the present. A mother or daughter might remember the past as problem-ridden because the present is problem-ridden or she might remember the past as pleasant in comparison to a more difficult present. Yet, women's memories of their early experiences provide insights into their beliefs about how their present relationships evolved.

TENSIONS DURING DIFFERENT TIME PERIODS

Mothers and daughters provided information about five time periods in their relationship. They rated the degree of tension they experienced when the daughter was ages: 5 to 12, 13 to 17, 18 to 25, 25 to 35, and 35 to present. They did not provide information about their relationship in the earliest years. Although mothers might remember the first years of their daughters' lives vividly, daughters probably would not. Mothers' and daughters' average ratings of tensions at each time period are found in Figure 6.1.

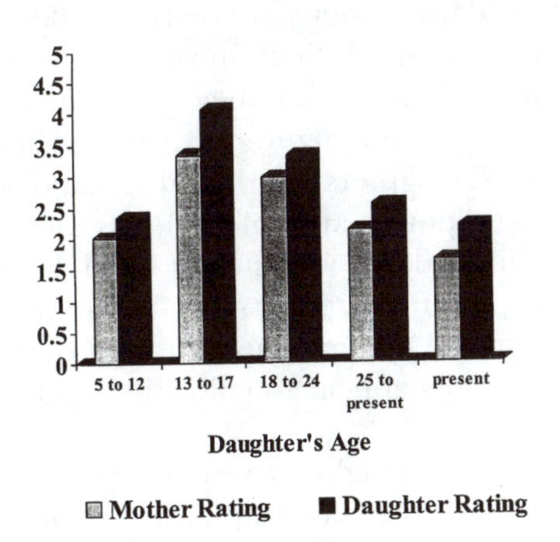

FIGURE 6.1 Mothers' and daughters' average ratings of conflict at each time period.

Mothers consistently reported fewer tensions than daughters did across time periods. Therefore, data were examined again by comparing mothers' and daughters' selection of the most difficult time period. Just over half of mothers and nearly half of daughters claimed that they experienced the most conflict during the teenage years. This finding is not surprising given that most Americans perceive parent/child conflict as characteristic of the teenage years (Arnett, 1999; Buchanan et al., 1990). It should be noted, however, that many mothers and daughters viewed other time periods as more strife-ridden than adolescence. Twenty-six percent of daughters and 28% of mothers viewed young adulthood, when the daughter was ages 18 to 24, as the most difficult period. Another 20% of daughters thought the years leading up to the present, when they were ages 25 or older, had been marked by the most difficulties. Therefore, nothing inherent to the teenage years induces problems, and nothing inherent to the adult years alleviates them.

Within dyads, just under half of mothers and daughters (48%) named the same period as most conflict ridden. For the remaining dyads, mothers tended to select earlier time periods, whereas daughters tended to select later time periods. Mothers were more likely to view the child and adolescent years as most problem ridden and daughters more likely to view the young adult years as most problem ridden. This intergenerational discrepancy may stem from the demands mothers faced when they were rearing children. Mothers may view their children as more difficult during earlier stages of life due to the time and investment that they require; mothers may feel liberated when their grown daughters are able to interact with them in an adult manner. Daughters, on the other hand, start life viewing their mothers as omnipotent and infallible. As they become increasingly aware of their mothers' weaknesses in adolescence and adulthood, they may experience greater stress in the relationship. Thus, the parties' status in the relationship and their developmental state at different time periods appear to color their perceptions of when problems arose.

Not all mothers and daughters remembered early relationship experiences in the same way. We might ask, do mothers and daughters who remember more problems during one time period also remember more problems during other time periods? Mothers rated adjacent time periods in a similar manner, but they were not consistent across the entire life span. For example, mothers' ratings of conflict in the childhood and adolescent years were associated, and mothers' ratings of conflict in the adolescent and young adult years were associated. Mothers' ratings of the childhood and adult years were not associated, however. It is possible that the age breaks used were not appropriate for mothers. Perhaps they rated the level of conflict similarly in the childhood years in this study (ages 5 to 12) and the adolescent years (ages 13 to 17) because the daughter was particularly difficult around puberty (ages 10 to 15).

For daughters, ratings of conflict prior to the age of 24 were associated. Daughters who remembered a lot of conflict in the childhood or adolescent years, also remembered a lot of conflict up to the age of 24. Daughters' ratings of tensions after the age of 25 were associated with their ratings of tension in their more recent relationship, but not their past relationship. These disjointed ratings are somewhat surprising given cultural beliefs that early relationships shape later ones. Mothers and daughters remembered certain periods as strife-ridden, but other periods as calm.

On the whole, memories for past tensions were not strongly associated across the life span. Several explanations are available for these findings. Few prior studies have asked women to rate past tensions across different time periods. It is possible that the nature of the mother/daughter tie changes considerably over time. Mothers and daughters who have close relationships during the childhood and teenage years may incur difficulties when the daughter tries to separate in the adult years. In other words, problems in the early years may stem from individuation issues (as suggested by other models of parent/child tensions) and dealing with these issues at an early age may inoculate against problems in later years. Alternately, mothers and daughters who experience conflicts in the early years of life may develop means of negotiating their difficulties such that by the adult years, their relationships are relatively problem-free. Finally, it is possible that these findings simply represent memory distortions. Mothers and daughters who experienced many difficulties while the daughter was growing up may see more recent years as better, whereas mothers and daughters who view the present as tension-laden may remember the early years fondly. Longitudinal data are needed to examine the actual pattern of tensions, but it is clear that women do not perceive the qualities of the mother/daughter tie as continuous over time.

TYPES OF PROBLEMS IN THE PAST

Mothers and daughters also provided descriptions of the types of problems that they encountered in the past. Their responses provide an initial test for the developmental schism framework. It is possible to ask whether the types of tensions mothers and daughters described reflect developmental issues associated with each stage of life. They were asked to elaborate on the period they had rated as most tension laden. If they rated a recent period as most difficult, they were asked to describe problems during an earlier stage of life.

The Childhood Years

Few mothers and daughters considered the childhood years to be the most conflict-ridden. Those mothers and daughters who did rate this period as the most contentious tended to focus on daily matters such as schoolwork, grooming, and eating. For example, Linda remembered these years as particularly problematic with her mother:

> She used to make me eat and do all kinds of things. So, probably there was more tension until I was about 7 or 8. By the time I was 7 or 8, she got the lay of the land. And she said, "She will do it or she won't do it

TABLE 6.1 Proportions of Mothers and Daughters Whose Reports of Past Tension Fell Under Each Content Code

Code	Mother ($n = 48$)	Daughter ($n = 48$)
Daily matters	0.52	0.45
Independence	0.23	0.42
Arguments	0.44	0.49
Sexuality	0.35	0.28
Mother did not meet daughter's needs	0.25	0.25

> and I can't push her beyond what she's going to do." So, that reduced the tension. Until I was 8, she did make me do all kinds of things, like go to sleep early. When she got the lay of the land and I could do those things, she relaxed. Maybe until 12 it lasted. I think maybe it took a while for me to realize that I was going to be able to tell her how things would be. When I began to speak up, she began to understand.

A developmental schism is evident in this subjective description of early tensions. Even when discussing the childhood years, Linda framed the situation in terms of her mother's development as well as her own. Likewise, Glenda remembered the problems she had with her daughter, Sandy, in terms of her own frustrations as a mother of small children:

> Well, grade school was better than the preschool years, but the years after that were better. I got a job after she was 12. I did not like homemaking, I hated every aspect of it. I was just overjoyed when I could get a job. So, I became more happy with myself and with my situation once she hit junior high. In every way, things just got better as they got older.

Martha, a 70-year-old mother, remembered problems with her daughter, Emily, over her eating patterns, but also mentioned that part of the problem was that she had her own needs at the time:

> Food. That's about it. That's the only thing that stands out. She's very strong-willed. If she made up her mind about wanting to do something, she wouldn't let go. She didn't like to eat anything. . . . What is there to eat? You go down the list and she'd go, "I don't like that, I don't like that, I don't like that." It was throughout childhood . . . I was upset because I had other things to do.

Julie, a 42-year-old daughter, commented on problems she had with her mother during the later childhood years. She framed her problems in terms of her transition to puberty:

> I'm thinking primarily of when I was 10, 11, 12. I was at the point where I was most conscious about what the other kids were wearing and who can do this and who can do that. I certainly went through a period when what my mother thought was best for me was not what I thought everyone else was doing. By the time I was in high school, I had sort of come to

> grips with some of those things. We were conflicting most when I was maybe 10 or 11.

Julie's response also sounds stereotypical. Her problem could be framed in terms of the childhood refrain, "Everybody else's mom let's them do it." Yet, she also captures a pervasive theme in memories of the mother/daughter relationship, mainly, tensions around the daughter's desire to set her own agenda.

In some cases, the problems that mothers and daughters encountered in the childhood years appeared to stem from external factors that shaped the relationship. Claire, a 46-year-old daughter, described problems during the childhood period:

> I was born with congenital heart disease. I was very restricted in my physical activity. I was a "blue baby," that's the cardiac term. I was very much restrained in my activities, the games I played. They always wanted to carry me everywhere. I don't know if they thought I would die if I overexerted myself. I wasn't allowed to try it out. At age 9, on my ninth birthday, they took me and admitted to children's hospital for surgery. In those days, a parent couldn't stay with a child at the hospital. Or at least, they did not stay with me. I was in the hospital for 27 days, alone. My sister couldn't visit me. I went to the window and waved to her. . . . They treated me very differently. I had to repeat a grade. I certainly didn't have a normal 6- to 12-year-old life. My father wasn't home a great deal. My mother was in charge of the home. She imposed her will, had a Germanic background. She ran a very Germanic home. I don't remember being spanked or locked in my room, so there's nothing like that. Lots of things were imposed on me, what she thought I could do or couldn't do. I was never given the opportunity to make many choices.

Although Claire attributed difficulties to her health problems at an early age, she also saw the situation as one involving her mother, who had a Germanic background. Her mother's attributes added to tensions in this context.

Likewise, Nancy, an 81-year-old widow, felt that the tensions she experienced with her daughter, Rebecca, stemmed from the way other children treated Rebecca:

> This was the time she was going through problems at school. The kids at school, she was always put down. I think it was because of her low self-esteem. She just never felt that she was equal to the other kids. I

> think that's what caused her to seek attention. She would come home and tell me the kids would go and write on the bathroom walls. They'd write something about her, everything putting her down. She never really had a chance to feel she was equal to the others. That used to bother me. I'd think, we brought the girls up the same way, why is Rebecca always condemned? . . . I didn't realize then the things that I realize now. She started telling me lies. She was lying to me about a lot of things.

Nancy's concerns were those of a parent whose child was experiencing problems she felt she could not control. She did not view the problem as embedded in the mother/daughter tie, but rather as imposed by circumstances. Nancy was concerned that the other children were treating her daughter badly and attributed the difficulties in their tie to this situation.

In summary, mothers and daughters who discussed the childhood years as most problematic often focused on the day-to-day tasks that are part of children's socialization. At the same time, several mothers and daughters who thought this period was most problematic viewed these problems as an artifact of external factors that had arisen in the daughter's life as she negotiated some specific difficulty of childhood. It is possible that these responses are partially an artifact of autobiographical memory. Memories of experiences in the childhood period are far removed from recent experiences in late life. Therefore, some mothers and daughters described these experiences in terms that were vague and diffuse. Those mothers and daughters who remembered this period with precision did so because their conflicts were linked to specific and salient crises that had taken place at the time.

Adolescence

The majority of mothers and daughters felt the teenage years, when the daughter was ages 13 to 18, were the most difficult years in their relationship. Their tensions revolved around issues of separation and autonomy. Mothers' and daughters' descriptions of past tensions in the adolescent years revealed the presence of a developmental schism. It was not only that the daughter was establishing herself in adulthood, but that the mother was struggling with this transition.

During the adolescent years, mothers and daughters remembered frequent arguments over curfews and rules. Frieda, a 71-year-old widow, joked about the problems she had with her daughter Pam at this time:

> That was the period when I ruined her social life. I told her she had to be home at a certain time . . . (We disagreed about) everything. Teenage kids, you were a teenager yourself, did you think your parents were as smart as they thought they were? . . . She didn't think I was as smart. She wanted to stay out later than I wanted her to. She thought that I was more restrictive than a lot of her friends' parents, which she probably was right about. Her taste and mine in clothes are still miles apart, but when she was a kid, how can I say this? If I thought she wanted to do something totally off the wall, because I was the parent and she was the kid, I could make it stick, and that didn't sit too well with her. It wasn't that there was daily conflict, but there was conflict between us as she was in her teenage years. There might have been after that, but she married young.

Rose, a 73-year-old mother, also described problems in the teenage years that were closely linked to efforts to parent her daughter:

> She didn't want to listen to my rules. We disagreed about who she was dating and the hours she was supposed to be home. I can't say there was anything in particular. Those years, there were just more discussions.

Danielle, Rose's daughter, also remembered the teenage years as most conflict-ridden in their relationship, but the conflicts she described were relatively mild:

> Oh, I wished that I could have had more clothes or different clothes or whatever. Since they had had two sons before me and one after, those sorts of things were more important to me than they realized. Plus, money was an issue, we didn't have a lot of money. There may have been a couple of occasions when I wanted to do something and she didn't let me do it. Maybe going to a ball game or something. The activity was fine, but for some reason, she didn't want me to go. I don't know if they just wanted me to be able to take "No" for an answer once in a while or what it was.

Sandy also remembered the teenage years as particularly difficult in her tie with her mother, Glenda. She explicitly stated that these memories were tainted by the present:

> It was just related to how hard it was to separate and how badly I wanted to. I look back and I can see some conflict I wasn't even aware of. I was very interested in theater my whole life. It wasn't until after I graduated from college that I found out that some people went to college and majored in theater so they could do it as a profession. She had so ingrained it in me that that was a hobby and not an intellectual pursuit. So, I look back on that and I resent it, and some of those tensions are evident now. There were certain kinds of pressures to pursue certain kinds of professions. I never managed to separate. And, plus, you're an adolescent like that, there's always trouble, independent of anything she did.

Wendy, a 39-year-old daughter, also talked about problems she had with her mother, Bea, during the teenage years. As will be discussed in the next chapter, Wendy's and Bea's relationship included a great deal of strife at present. Wendy's memories of their tie included the types of issues other women raised, but she also suggested that their relationship had included extreme difficulties in the past:

> The tension was about me growing up and my mother worrying about decisions that I was making then, regarding how I did in school and who my friends were. And, our growing apart. Oh, and I ran home away from home then, too, a great source of tension.

Although Wendy mentioned that she ran away from home, she did not elaborate on the details of the situation. Indeed, although most mothers and daughters remembered past difficulties, they described these events with a sense of distance that made them seem trivial and unimportant for their present relationship.

In many cases, mothers and daughters remembered past tensions in terms of the mother's inability to meet the daughter's needs, or her inability to parent effectively. Barbara, a 75-year-old mother, described tensions when her daughter was a teenager in terms of her own worries, rather than her daughter's behavior:

> Well, I was working, but I had a neighbor that they stayed with after school until my husband came home at 5:00 p.m. She had an older brother at home, too. But she always had a lot of friends, girlfriends and boyfriends. Not that she did anything wrong, I was just worried about leaving her and not being there.

Ellen, Barbara's 49-year-old daughter, also described her mother's inability to connect to her during the teenage years:

> I needed her to help me deal with problems, some physical problems, some more psychological problems. She wasn't able to help me. She didn't know what to do. She couldn't help me with what I needed. I was frustrated, angry, lonely.

In some cases, daughters mentioned instances where their mothers wanted more from them than could give, but these situations did not seem to come up until after daughters entered adulthood. During the childhood and adolescent years, daughters expected their mothers to assist and nurture them. Mothers and daughters alike experienced tension when they were not able to do so.

Young Adulthood

Several mothers and daughters viewed the young adult years as more problematic than the adolescent years. The problems they described tended to involve adult decisions the daughter was making. Some mothers and daughters felt that the daughter's "adolescence" had been delayed until these years. Emma, a 75-year-old widow, who was upset about her daughter Priscilla's behavior when she was aged 18 to 24, described the situation in these terms:

> I think she had a delayed effort to be her own person. So, she began to throw herself away, more like an adolescent kind of thing. She began to see herself as not as conservative or as traditional as we may have thought she was. She was seeing people that she wasn't really happy to bring home—not that I required that I approve of who she saw. She went through a long period of separation, and some experimentation in behavior, and, I thought, a penchant for choosing the wrong man to date. We didn't argue about it except once or twice. We argued about how she was thinking about the future and whether she was being serious enough about her lifestyle. Now, it seems it was a very moderate lifestyle, but I worried then. I wished that she were doing otherwise.

Emma's response is specific to both her daughter's stage of life and her cohort. Priscilla came of age during the late 1960s and early

1970s, when social turmoil was pervasive. Thirty years later, mothers are also dissatisfied with their young adult daughters' choice of partners and their future plans. Mothers today may be less likely to frame the problem in terms of breaking away from being conservative or traditional, however. Thus, the type of issue Emma described may be a consistent developmental schism as young women make choices about their lives in early adulthood. The manner in which Emma framed the problem, however, may reflect values of the period in which her daughter came of age.

Theresa, a 39-year-old daughter, also described problems she and her mother, Clara encountered pertaining to a boyfriend Theresa had:

> We literally didn't speak to each other for 3 years, so I suppose you can count it as a lot of conflict, but you can't really disagree if you don't talk. I was living with my boyfriend and she didn't like it. . . . She hadn't met him, so she didn't dislike him. It was mostly that I was living with him, that I was growing up. I resemble my father a great deal, and he was pretty wild when he was young. And I was pretty wild when I was young, and she just couldn't deal with it. Her thing was, "You're just like you're father." I had a mind of my own.

Disputes over the daughter's romantic liaisons were pervasive in young adulthood, more so than in adolescence. In young adulthood, daughters select long-lasting and serious partners, and mothers are likely to react to these relationships. Yet, the extremity of Clara's reaction, not speaking to her daughter for 3 years, also may be specific to their cohort. Although some parents today may react to their children's residing with a partner by not speaking to their offspring as Clara did, her reaction seems linked to the historical period as well as her daughter's development in young adulthood. Theresa came of age during a period when young adults were more likely to live with their partners prior to marriage than their parents had been. At the same time, Theresa framed their problem as her mother struggling with Theresa's entry into adulthood, an issue that transcends a specific time in history.

Marianne, an 80-year-old mother, also described problems involving her daughter's partner. This situation was time limited and unique; their tensions were resolved when her daughter got divorced:

> In her first marriage, when she was 22, she married a man who was schizophrenic. He tried to cause trouble. He got violent. Eventually, she got divorced. . . . Well, if you said something that displeased him, he might not say anything. Later on, he'd write me a letter that I better shape up or he wouldn't let me see my daughter. I worried about my daughter. I thought a horsewhip would be a good thing to have for him, but I never had one. Then, she had a little daughter. That's when she left when she was afraid he would do something to her.

It is notable that mothers' and daughters' problems in the young adult years often involved other family members. As will be seen, this is a pervasive theme in the mother/daughter tie in late life. Although mothers and daughters maintain a cohesive and tight bond, that bond is set in the context of the larger family. Other family members are a source of both joy and aggravation in the adult years.

Brenda, a 38-year-old daughter, also described problems with her mother during the young adult years. She framed her problems in terms of the mismatch between her own needs and her mother's needs at the time:

> Really, there was probably only one time span of a couple years within that time when there was a lot of disagreeable things. I was probably about 21 and I had gotten married and she was, I think, going through her change of life. It had been about 4 or 5 years after my dad had died. I left home. It just seemed like a real difficult period of time for her. She was very depressed and seemed very argumentative and unreasonable. She expected a lot of attention. I was trying to begin a life of my own and dealing with all of the problems that go with that. There was a lot of tension at the particular time.

Laura, a 51-year-old daughter, also described a situation during her young adult years, but in this case, she herself had suffered from depression:

> I was going through a period of depression. My doctor recommended a psychiatrist. The worst thing I ever did in my life. In retrospect, he had that Freudian philosophy. If you broke a toenail or fingernail, it's because your mother did something terrible to you. I know that's a slight exaggeration, but it's not too far from Freudian philosophy. Anyway, he suggested I confront my mother on an issue or just stand up to her a

> lot. He felt that I was a really good kid, and that it was not normal not to rebel, and part of my problem was that I had not rebelled. She has a way of making people feel guilty and she was doing that to my kids. I brought that up to her and tried to explain to her when she did these things, it didn't bring the kids closer to her. It pushed them away. And, she got very defensive. And we had an argument. It went on for a while.

Several mothers and daughters framed their past tensions in terms of a mental health problem, whether their own, the other party's, or another family member's. Yet, these women reported few symptoms of depression or mental health problems at present. Rather, when women do encounter mental health problems, the mother/daughter tie seems to be strongly affected. Indeed, mothers' and daughters' memories of past tensions were strongly linked to past crises in general. As will be seen, their reports of present day tensions were not as strongly linked to exceptional circumstances.

CONCLUSIONS

The popular press suggests that adult behavior patterns are established in early life. Kagan (1996) refers to this premise as one of "three pleasing ideas" espoused by American culture. The mothers and daughters in this study, however, did not seem to view their current relationship as an artifact of their past experience. Rather, they remembered changes in their relationships, with some periods more conflict ridden than other periods.

Some mothers and daughters described past conflict in vague terms that covered the typical developmental issues of the period. For example, mothers and daughters described daily matters in the childhood years and arguments during the teenage years. Other mothers and daughters remembered specific events that tainted a particular period. In both these types of situations, mothers and daughters seemed to view their tensions as isolated to that particular time period. Moreover, mothers' and daughters' ratings of tensions at past time periods were not strongly associated across the life span.

Of course, these memories may obscure the actual continuity that exists in mother/daughter ties. Nonetheless, mothers and daughters do not seem to link the problems they experience in late life to the early history of their relationship. The next chapter provides information about the types of problems mothers and daughters reported in their present relationship.

7
A Problematic Encounter

Now, I'd like to know a little about the things your mother/daughter does that bother you. People we love and value can also make us irritated or annoyed at times. Can you tell me about the last time that you were bothered during a visit with your mother/daughter? By visit, I mean a time when you got together, went to the other's house, or talked on the phone. I'd like you to tell me a little about what happened and why you were upset.

—The interviewer

Although the women who participated in this study viewed their relationships with their mothers and daughters as strong and close, they also described frustrations, irritations, and annoyances in these relationships. Daughters, in particular, reported that their mothers bothered them in different ways. This chapter looks at mothers' and daughters' descriptions of a recent problematic visit. First, however, we consider how often such problems arise in this relationship.

The frequency with which mothers and daughters get upset with the other party sets the tempo for the relationship. Do mothers and daughters get angry with one another often? Is some degree of irritation with one's mother or daughter part and parcel of everyday interactions? Are negative feelings isolated events? If problems come up frequently in mothers' and daughters' encounters, they may eat away at positive features of the relationship.

FREQUENCY OF PROBLEMATIC ENCOUNTERS

Previously, I noted that mothers and daughters might experience tensions in their relationship, without experiencing overt confrontation. The women in this study provided separate ratings of how often they engage in conflicts with the other party and how often they get upset with the other party. Early in the individual interviews, they indicated how often they have open disagreements or overt confrontations with their mother or daughter. Later in the interview, mothers and daughters described the last time they had experienced an unpleasant visit. They then indicated how often such unpleasant situations come up in their relationships. Table 7.1 shows mothers' and daughters' reports of how often they have disagreements or experience unpleasant visits.

Overt conflicts are not everyday occurrences between mothers and daughters. In fact, 81% of mothers and 60% of daughters said

TABLE 7.1 Reported Frequencies of Conflicts and Unpleasant Visits

Conflict frequency	Mother (n = 48)	Daughter (n =48)
How often have overt disagreements		
Once a week or more often	.04	.08
2 to 3 times a month	.08	.17
Monthly	.06	.15
1 × every few months	.42	.32
1 × year or less	.39	.28
How often experience unpleasant visits		
Once a week or more often	.05	.11
2 to 3 times a month	.10	.22
Monthly	.17	.09
1 × every few months	.44	.38
1 × year or less	.25	.20

they engage in an open conflict once every few months or less frequently. Of course, there was variation in mothers' and daughters' reports of conflict—12% of mothers and 25% of daughters reported conflicts at least every other week. Moreover, if we consider negative feelings rather than overt conflict, nearly a third of mothers and 40% of daughters reported feeling upset with the other party at least once a month. Although tensions might not come up everyday, they are a regular part of the relationship.

Indeed, for daughters, visits with their mothers seemed to generate some sort of affective response, whether positive or negative. Daughters who saw their mothers more often also reported more frequent positive visits ($r = .32$) and more frequent problematic visits ($r = .30$). In fact, daughters who had more frequent positive visits also reported more frequent negative visits ($r = .32$). Thus, in midlife, it is not a question of whether women's relationships with their mothers are "good" or "bad." Daughters' contact with their mothers seems to evoke some sort of reaction, both good and bad.

For mothers, the pattern was different. Mothers generally enjoyed time they spent with their daughters. The more often they saw their daughters, the more often they claimed to have enjoyable visits ($r = .64$). By contrast, older mothers who had more frequent visits did not report having more conflict or tension with their daughters.

As will be discussed, daughters' perspectives on their relationships with their mothers include more ambivalence than mothers' perspectives on their relationships with their daughters. Daughters experience pleasure from their ties to their mothers, but also experience difficulties in these ties. Older mothers tend to find interactions with their daughters almost exclusively positive and rewarding. When mothers are upset, their irritations do not stem from contact with their daughters.

MOTHERS' AND DAUGHTERS' DESCRIPTIONS OF PROBLEMS

Although irritations are not everyday occurrences between mothers and daughters in late life, tensions do arise with regularity. The specific problems that mothers and daughters encounter may distinguish their relationships from intergenerational ties involving men.

Prior research suggests that women report more problems in their intergenerational ties beginning in adolescence and continuing into late life (Collins, 1990; Hagestad, 1984; Lehr, 1984; Troll & Fingerman, 1996). Indeed, these gender differences appear to stem from the nature of their disparities. In late life, women's intergenerational tensions have been associated with more personal issues, such as criticism of themselves or their children, whereas men's tensions pertain to occupation, political beliefs, or leisure events (Hagestad, 1984, 1987; Lehr, 1984). Although fathers and sons share a long history and also have disparate goals and needs, they do not usually share the intimacy that mothers and daughters do. The closeness that shrouds ties between mothers and daughters forces them to deal with personal issues in this relationship, and their tensions stem from this intimacy.

After they had described their most recent pleasant visits during the individual interviews, women described a recent time when they had been irritated, hurt, or annoyed with their mother or daughter. Although most mothers and daughters peppered their responses about positive visits with descriptions of gentle lunches, chit-chats, and shared celebrations with the family, their descriptions of problematic visits involved greater variation.

Moreover, whereas all but one mother and one daughter were able to think of a time when they had an enjoyable visit, eight mothers were unable to come up with a time when they were upset with their daughters when asked to do so alone. As will be discussed, all of these mothers readily participated in the discussion of problems with their daughters during the joint interviews. It is not clear if these mothers failed to come up with a response because they do not experience problems with their daughters, because they were concerned about presenting themselves and their daughters in a positive light, because they experienced memory problems, or due to other unknown factors. Of note, however, is that every daughter came up with a time when she was irked with her mother.

The remainder of this chapter focuses on the problems mothers and daughters described. The developmental schism framework is used to consider the ways in which disparities in investment and awareness of the mother's aging contribute to tensions in this relationship. Table 7.2 provides the distribution of mothers' and daugh-

TABLE 7.2 Proportion of Mothers and Daughters Mentioning Each Type of Problem

Type of problem	Mother response	Daughter response	McNemar's exact *p* value
Refused to answer	.17	.00	$p = .0039$
Parameters of relationship			
Intruded on	.23	.46	$p = .0500$
Excluded	.15	.10	NS
Discussed other people	.56	.35	$p = .0301$
Worries or concerns			
Self care	.13	.23	NS
Mother's aging	.15	.48	$p = .0009$
Habits or traits	.30	.27	NS

Note: McNemar's test was conducted in a conservative manner using only those mother/daughter dyads in which mothers responded.

ters' perceptions of problems by category. More specific descriptions of problems are provided as follows.

THE PARAMETERS OF THE RELATIONSHIP

A central problem in the mother/daughter tie involves setting the parameters of the relationship. In the first section of this book, it became clear that mothers are more invested in their daughters than their daughters are in them. Moreover, mothers have more available time to devote to their daughters and fewer competing demands in their lives than their daughters have. Tensions may arise from these disparities.

In fact, nearly half of daughters felt intruded upon by their mothers in some way. Some daughters felt intruded upon by their mother's advice, other daughters felt criticized by their mothers, and still other daughters were unable to provide their mothers with the time and attention they felt their mothers wanted. All of these daughters expressed a desire for more distance from their mothers than their mothers seemed to want. Yet, it is also clear that mothers are not purposely intruding upon their daughters.

Daughters Who Felt Intruded Upon

A mother's solicitude may fuel a daughter's feelings of irritation. Some daughters described a sense of betrayal when their mothers asked questions about their personal lives or offered suggestions. Ellen, a 49-year-old daughter who was recently divorced, complained that her 76-year-old mother expressed concern about her marital status:

> The last time she came over, I felt upset and angry with her because she was pressuring me to get married again. I've been married for 27 years and I don't want to get married again. She wants to know if the man I'm seeing is serious. That bothered me because I'm enjoying having fun right now, and I'm feeling free. Then, she wondered if I could get Jack (my husband) back, and I sort of snapped at her, 'Why would I want to? I don't need to have him back.' I felt hurt because she doesn't think I'm OK just being me. She wants me to be an extension of a man. She doesn't have confidence that I can make it on my own. It hurts my feelings.

Ellen's mother may have been merely trying to make conversation by relying on a topic she knew was important and salient in her daughter's life. Ellen, however, viewed the comments as critical, unwelcome, and hurtful. This pattern arose repeatedly.

In particular, a mother's comments about her daughter's children served as a source of rancor. Leslie, a pediatric nurse, described a time when her mother told her that she should make her own daughter wear a hat when she plays outside on a chilly day. Like Ellen, Leslie felt that her mother did not respect her abilities or knowledge. "She gives me unsolicited advice about the kids, especially medical advice. I find that particularly annoying because I'm a registered nurse." Leslie threw up her hands and remarked, "I should know those things already. For goodness sake, I'm the one who gives other people advice about how to keep their children healthy." Comments about childrearing were rife with tension due to the daughter's investment in her own role as mother. Claire, a 46-year-old daughter with children of her own, was upset with her mother's suggestions for childrearing:

> This year my daughter is taking violin lessons and she also loves to take dancing lessons. She hasn't been practicing the violin as much as she

> should. My mother said to me, 'I don't understand why you can't tell Alicia that she can't take dance lessons if she doesn't practice the violin. Why don't you use the dance lessons as leverage to get her to practice the violin? I don't know why you let her get away with it. Why don't you make her practice?' I didn't say anything. I was going to make a comment and then I decided not to. It sort of irritates me when she gives me that kind of advice about what I should do with my children.

On the other hand, by midlife, some daughters come to view these issues with a sense of perspective. "She gets motherly sometimes and asks me if I've written to so-and-so lately," one daughter commented, "but that's how it is—once a mother, always a mother."

Not all intrusion involved overt criticism. In some cases, daughters felt their mothers were demanding more time than they could give, and daughters experienced these situations with trepidation. "She came over and stayed for 2 hours, unannounced. She wanted me to just sit and visit with her," Laura explained, "I had loads of things to do. I hate it when she does that and stays for more than half an hour." Likewise, Roberta, who was described in the first chapter, was upset with her mother for telephoning up to five times a day to ask her advice. Roberta understood the importance of the issues her mother wished to discuss, but her schedule did not allow her the time to interact with her mother on a moment-by-moment basis. Sally, a 47-year-old daughter, commented:

> I was annoyed that when I saw her on Thursday, she asked if I would see her again on Sunday. And it's kind of this ongoing theme in our relationship, her insatiable desire to be with me. I'm her number one choice; she chooses me all the time. She sucks me dry. It's annoying because I feel so much guilt. It wasn't good enough that I had seen her Thursday. I had seen her the day before as well. But, we had to make arrangements for an additional day. It pisses me off.

The complexities of Sally's negative feelings also suggest her positive feelings for her mother. If she did not care about her mother, she would not feel guilty. Although Sally expressed her negative feelings more strongly than many daughters did, she also maintained more frequent contact with her mother than many daughters did. Sally, like Roberta, felt trapped in her desire to please her mother.

Tensions stemming from discrepancies in mothers' and daughters' investment in the tie were also evident with regard to the emotional support processes in the tie. In this case, the discrepancy reflects differences in the mother role and the daughter role. Daughters resented it when their mothers relied on them for emotional support. Mothers who listed their daughters as their preferred confidant were more likely to have daughters who described their mothers as intrusive. These daughters may not reciprocate their mothers' investment in them, and thus, their mother's trust may feel intrusive rather than valuable. Denise, a 38-year-old daughter, commented that her mother, Grace, told her things that did not interest her:

> Sometimes during the course of any visit with Mom, there will be a brief period that may seem to go on forever where she'll tell me about friends of hers, people that I don't know, and tell me all about what they're doing. If I'm on the phone, I sort of stop listening. That happens frequently. I sort of shut down, and she rambles on, and then we sort of pick up again.

When daughters relied on their mothers for emotional support, their mothers did not report feelings of intrusion, however. Indeed, as was described in the previous section, many mothers claimed that they felt like they were a part of their daughters' lives when their daughters confided in them. Mothers enjoyed such conversations.

Mothers' Descriptions of Intrusion

When mothers felt intruded upon by their daughters, their complaints usually centered on their sense that their daughters were treating them as less capable than they felt themselves to be. On the whole, older adults resent unsolicited advice or help (Smith & Goodnow, 1999). Such help seems to be particularly difficult to accept when offered by one's offspring. Louise, an 85-year-old mother, complained that her daughter had been overly protective when they went to a concert together recently:

> She's very thoughtful, but sometimes, she makes me feel my age—which irritates me. I don't think I'm old until I get around her sometimes. The other night we came home from a concert, and there was a terrible storm. She didn't take me home. She made me stay with her. I wasn't frightened, but she was terribly frightened. She refused to take me home

> because she was afraid for me to walk from the car to the door. She thought I'd get hit by lightning. She finally took me home at 11:30, but she had me stay at her house until then.

Likewise, Clara, a 76-year-old mother, felt her daughter was overly solicitous:

> She wants me to have people help in the kitchen. And I cannot take it. Often, I have people for lunch, and she sends me this help. It drives me crazy. I've cooked all my life. And, I'm used to doing things my own way. When she sends people in to help me, I can't very well say, 'Do it this way, don't do it that way.' She would like me to have lots of help, but I don't want lots of help. I just want to be left alone, to get things done my way.

On the whole, however, fewer mothers than daughters felt demeaned, criticized, or intruded upon.

Inclusion of Other People

It is clear the mothers and daughters have different ideas about the parameters and boundaries of their relationships. In general, mothers desired more time and attention from their daughters than their daughters wished to provide. Indeed, mothers seemed to have a more diffuse sense of how their daughters fit into their lives. Mothers were likely to talk about tensions with their daughters involving other people, such as sons-in-law, their other offspring, their grandchildren, or their own husbands. They held an idea about their "family" that included their daughters.

June, an 82-year-old widow, complained that her daughter's husband kept turning the volume on the stereo up when she turned it down. The interviewer then prompted such women by reminding them of the target daughter, "We're interested in a time when you were irritated, hurt, or annoyed with your daughter Amy—can you tell me about a specific situation with *her*?" These mothers appeared to view problems with other people as problems with their daughters. "Well, that is the last time that I was upset with Amy. Her husband kept turning the stereo up," June explained. It is possible that mothers expect their daughters to show loyalty to them by asking the people associated with them (e.g., their husbands and children) to honor their mothers' wishes. On the other hand, mothers also expressed concerns over situations involving the daughters' siblings or their fathers (e.g., their own husbands), suggesting that the discrepancy is one involving a sense of family demarcation. For example, Doris, a 76-year-old mother, complained about her daughter Jennifer's children:

> That was last week. It has to do with my grandchildren. My granddaughter is very busy. She's involved in many other things besides just her studies. She gets over involved in things. Sometimes she just seems too tired. I think Jennifer should do something about that.

Glenda also claimed to have problems with her daughter Sandy's childrearing:

> I can't say when was the last time, but I do have questions about Sandy as a mother. I think her intent is excellent. Her love for her children is great. Zachary is a terrific kid in most ways, but from the get go, she didn't discipline him. She doesn't structure things for him. Consequently, he is given to being stubborn when he doesn't get his way. I read something the other day that said that if your child is repeatedly saying, "No" or asking for something he cannot have, you are doing something wrong raising him.

To older mothers, daughters seem to be part of a larger family, and problems in the family are problems with the daughter. By contrast, daughters view their relationships with their mothers in terms of a dyad, constrained to themselves and their mothers. When mothers try to become involved in their daughters' family relationships, tensions may arise if daughters feel intruded upon.

Daughters also sometimes included other people in their descriptions of tensions. Occasionally, they mentioned concerns involving their own children. For example, Sandy was upset that her mother, Glenda, planned a family dinner that ran past the children's bedtime. The children were irritable and unpleasant, and the event was rushed. Sandy felt her mother should have given more thought to their needs. Claire was upset with the advice her mother provided concerning dance lessons and violin practice for her daughter. She resented her mother's intrusion, but also felt her mother did not understand her granddaughter's need to make her own choices about outside activities. Daughters felt their mothers could be insensitive to their grandchildren.

When daughters included other family members, they also often discussed their siblings. For example, Paula was upset with her mother, Gwen, over a party she was planning for a sister who has breast cancer.

> Seems to me that there are a lot of those. When was the last time she really pissed me off? A couple of weeks ago, my sister was coming into town. And when she comes to town, it's always, how do we handle Mom when she gets here? Mom likes to schedule my sister's life. She scheduled this party for my sister, and she wasn't going to tell her. It was a birthday party for my sister's fortieth birthday. My sister is not going to be 40 until *next* year. My sister was diagnosed with breast cancer 2 months ago. She's handling it exceptionally well. I'm close to my sister. Being in the middle, I see both sides. My mother is devastated. It's eating her up alive. Having kids, I know no parent wants to see a child suffer. But my mother's not dealing with this very well. I explained to my mother that making a surprise birthday party for my sister a year before she turns 40 is going to make her think, "What's the matter, Mom? You don't think I'm going to live that long?" So, that's the gist of what happened. I was pissed off. Pissed off is the word.

Mothers also complained about their daughters' siblings and husbands. The distinction lay in the sense of a larger unit. Mothers seemed to attribute other people's behaviors to their daughters. Mothers' problems stemmed from the way the daughter's sibling, husband, or children behaved. By contrast, when daughters included other people in their responses, they were upset about the way their mother interacted with those people.

Mothers and Daughters Who Feel Unloved

At the opposite end of the spectrum from feeling intruded upon lies feeling excluded by the other party. These situations were rare. Only seven mothers and five daughters brought up situations in which the other party left them out of an event they wanted to attend or made them feel unwanted. These mothers and daughters showed more signs of distress and pain, however, than did mothers or daughters who described situations involving intrusiveness or other types of problems. Indeed, women seemed to equate being left out with being unloved.

Mothers, in particular, were upset when their daughters excluded them. Bea, an 85-year-old widow, was the only mother who cried during her interview. Her anguish stemmed from religious differences that made her feel like an outsider to her daughter's life. Bea was a devout Catholic who desperately wanted to take her grandchildren with her to Christmas Mass. Her daughter Wendy married a man who was Presbyterian, and Wendy's children attended church in his faith. Wendy would not take her children to Mass with Bea. Bea was heartbroken as a result. "She won't celebrate Christmas with me," she lamented. Several daughters in the study practiced different religions than their mothers did, and this discrepancy did not always result in tensions. Indeed, one mother who was Jewish discovered that her daughter's marriage to a non-Jew was a blessing; she did not have to fight for her daughter's attention during the Jewish holidays. In Bea's case, the situation went deeper than religious differences.

Bea continued her discussion of tensions with a scenario in which Wendy did not notify her of a family dinner until after she had already made other plans. Bea then went on to describe a time when she was unaware of her grandchildren's dance recital. Bea felt slighted by her daughter's failure to include her more generously in these family events. Bea was the most memorable woman in the study given the level of distress she incurred in her relationship with her daughter. Many daughters reported stressful relationships with their mothers, but Bea stood out as a mother who reported a stressful relationship with her daughter. Several mothers and daughters listed different religious affiliations; Wendy and Bea were the only mother and daughter to experience problems over this issue.

It is also interesting to note dyadic patterns in reports of tension. We will look at whether or not mothers and daughters reported the same situation as problematic when we consider communication of tensions in Part IV, but we consider similarities between general categories of problems (e.g., intrusion, care of self) here. The seven mothers who felt excluded were more likely to have daughters who found these mothers intrusive. For example, Bea's daughter, Wendy, reported that her principal complaint with her mother was that she would not accept the way Wendy was raising her children. Wendy calmly explained that her children were still young, and they found it confusing to try to understand that their grandmother worshipped in a different manner than they did. Wendy felt that her mother was trying to force her own religious beliefs onto her children. Moreover, Wendy seemed to resort to exclusion as a means of protecting herself from what she perceived as her mother's manipulative efforts. This pattern has also emerged in other studies of middle-aged women's relationships with their mothers. Approximately 10% to 20% of middle-aged daughters report deeply conflicted relationships with their mothers, and withdrawal is a common response to these feelings (Fingerman, 1997b).

In addition, mothers who valued their daughters highly were more likely to feel excluded. Mothers who rated their daughters among the top 3 most important people in their lives were more likely to feel left out by those daughters than were mothers who considered their daughters to be amongst the top 6 or 12 (McNemar's exact $p = .0001$). On the one hand, it is possible that these mothers perceive more exclusion because they place such a heavy value on their daughters and wish they could spend even more time with them than they do. On the other hand, they may be more excluded in actuality because their daughters feel a need to protect themselves against their mothers' investment in them. It does appear that mothers who feel excluded are, indeed, less valued by their daughters. When mothers felt excluded, their daughters rated them as less important in their lives than the mothers felt they were (McNemar's $p = .0005$).

A few daughters also felt excluded. Although their sagas did not demonstrate the emotion-laden anguish of the excluded mothers, these daughters showed a wistful sadness regarding their inability to capture their mothers' attention. Allison, a 35-year-old daughter, claimed that she had little time to devote to her mother, but that when she did try to see her mother, her mother was not always available:

> Thursday, we had a very brief visit. I stopped over there and she wasn't there. Then, I stopped over later and she was there, but she just wanted

to watch the news. So, I left. I felt like, 'Why did you tell me to come over if you weren't going to be around?'

Another daughter, Melissa, expressed her disappointment that her 74-year-old mother would not allow her to plan a party for her parents' fiftieth anniversary. She insisted that her mother's reasons for not wanting the party were trivial. She was hurt that her mother refused the party.

When daughters reported that their mothers had left them out or had refused their requests to assist them, these reports did not seem to reflect differences in their mothers' investment in them or their mothers' feeling intruded upon. Rather, these reports seemed to stem from the mother's inability to meet their daughters' needs.

Despite its rare occurrence within the sample, exclusion appears to play a powerful role in mother/daughter relationships in cases where it does occur. Daughters put up with feeling intruded upon, and mothers swallow their aggravations with daughters' husbands and children, but being left out seems to create sorrow that is difficult to reconcile.

CARE FOR SELF OR OTHERS

Mothers and daughters also experience developmental schisms over concerns for how the other party cares for herself and for people under her charge. Middle-aged daughters begin to confront their own mortality. Midlife is characterized by a shift in time perspective, where individuals go from thinking about how many years they have grown since birth to how many years they have left until death (Fingerman & Perlmutter, 1995; Kastenbaum & Aisenberg, 1972; Neugarten, 1968). Although midlife is not generally a sickly period, rates of disease increase and physical declines become evident. As a friend has a heart attack, a cousin requires knee surgery, and one's own energy levels feel depleted, the salience of aging begins to shade day-to-day thoughts. A preoccupation with mortality may spread to middle-aged daughters' thoughts about their mothers; they may be particularly aware of their mothers' aging process and limited life expectancy. Older mothers, on the other hand, have passed through this stage, and may not view death with such great trepidation. As a result, aging mothers may resent their daughters' concerns for their well-being, particularly when they are healthy. Indeed, as was mentioned previously, when daughters showed unwanted solicitude or provided unneeded assistance, their mothers felt intruded upon.

The Mother's Aging

Daughters in this study did seem aware of their mother's mortality, and they raised issues pertaining to her health and her age in their responses. Half of daughters said something about their mothers' aging process during their discussions of tensions. Only seven mothers mentioned their own aging and, as was the case for Louise, mothers generally complained that their daughters made them feel old, rather than that their age actually contributed to tensions in the relationship. For example, Kathy described a situation involving her mother's problems with medication:

> They were here for brunch on Sunday. This would be a typical irritation. My mother's in a fog a lot of the time. She's on so much medication that she doesn't remember things. She's almost 80 and she's got a lot of health problems. Sometimes she says inappropriate things. She'll say something that appears to be thoughtless. She isn't the same mother I might have had 10 or 20 years ago. I get irritated with her and I'll correct her, or I'll snap at her. Then, I feel really guilty because she can't control it at this point. It seems that the older she gets, the more judgmental and critical she gets. That really irritates me.

Yet, Kathy's mother was able to participate in the interviews and did not seem cognitively impaired. Kathy is particularly sensitive to changes in her mother. She feels her mother is not the same person she used to be, and the contrast is particularly salient.

Daughters' keen awareness of their mothers' senescence appears to reflect another aspect of midlife maturation. As was discussed, Blenkner (1963) suggested that offspring reach a state of filial maturity in their mid-30's, when they come to see their parents as human and fallible, like themselves. In their 40's, offspring may go one step further, to see their parents as vulnerable. Indeed, a different study of women in their 40's and 50's revealed that they experienced continuity with regard to the strength of their emotional bonds with their mothers, but discontinuity with regard to an increasing awareness of their mothers' physical limitations (Fingerman, 1997b).

Daughters' Concerns About Mothers

Eleven daughters expressed concerns about their mothers' self-care. Moreover, these concerns were about the present, when the mother was relatively healthy, rather than reflecting worries about future caregiving the mother might need. For example, Monica complained that her 76-year-old mother has terrible eating habits:

> My sister was visiting here for Thanksgiving. She's on kind of a health kick—she eats a lot of fruits and vegetables and my mother does, too when she's here. . . . As soon as she leaves, my mom goes back to the same old eating habits of mashed potatoes and gravy and roast beef and roast pork and a lot of bacon and eggs. That's the way she eats. That's the way she's always eaten. And yet, she's so tired, she has no energy. She's exhausted. Since Thanksgiving, I say to her, "Don't go back to those eating habits. Eat fruits and vegetables—the kinds of things Judy told you to eat." It's on deaf ears. The next time she calls, she's eating roast beef again.

As the quote at the start of chapter 5 revealed, Amanda was concerned that her 80-year-old mother, Marianne, had not gotten a flu shot as is recommended for older adults. Another daughter was upset that her mother refused to get assistance changing flights in the airport, despite the fact she could not easily make the long walk involved.

Daughters' concerns tended to be selfless. They were not worried about having to care for their mothers. They were worried about their mothers. Yet, there was also a unidimensionality in daughters' maturity with regard to their mothers. Daughters were keenly aware of their mothers' physical vulnerabilities, but some daughters appeared obtuse to the emotional issues, the embarrassment and sense of giving up independence, involved for their mothers.

Indeed, Stephanie complained that her 74-year-old mother, Alice, was being ridiculous by refusing to use an oxygen tank in public:

> I get mad because she worries too much and that annoys me. I shouldn't be annoyed, but I do. She'll worry about taking her oxygen tank with

> her in public. She thinks that other people will look at her. Then, she also thinks that then she'd admit that she is getting worse. It makes her feel inadequate. And, I get mad sometimes, if she doesn't get better. I think, "Why bother suffering if you could feel better?" I think, "Why not get a wheel chair, put your oxygen tank on the back and I'll just whip you around." She doesn't do a lot to annoy us. She doesn't call us a lot. Sometimes, I wish she would call us, tell us how she's doing. When I hear about other mothers, I think we are so lucky. She's not bothersome.

Stephanie seemed unaware that her mother's discomfort was also a form of vulnerability; fear of drawing attention to oneself in public might be every bit as important to Alice as her physical limitations. Yet, Stephanie also clearly appreciated and loved her mother.

As was mentioned previously, daughters showed continuity in their filial roles. Despite their increasing abilities to see their mothers as human, as physically frail, and as mortal, some daughters continued to view their mothers as emotionally stronger than the mothers actually were. This change in perspective on one dimension (e.g., my mother has physical limitations) with continuity in perspective on another dimension (e.g., my mother should be able to change her own behavior and not worry about what other people think) generates tensions for daughters who worry about their mothers.

Mothers' Concerns About Daughters

For mothers, concerns about their daughters' well-being appeared to reflect continuity in their roles as mothers. Fewer mothers described problems of this sort than did daughters. It is possible that as mothers, they were accustomed to being concerned about their daughters' well-being from the earliest years, and these concerns do not generate tensions. Alternately, as they grow older, mothers may stop worrying about their daughters' well-being and, therefore, they may not complain about their daughters in this regard.

Of the six mothers whose problems involved daughters' care, three expressed worries about the daughters' self care, and three expressed worries about individuals the daughters cared for, their grandchildren. As mentioned previously, Doris felt that her grandchildren were involved in too many outside activities and worried about their ability to do well in school and their general fatigue. Leslie's mother, Sarah, couldn't understand why her daughter, a pediatric nurse, did not do more to protect the children from catching cold. Finally, Lucille worried terribly because her daughter, Carol, allowed her own teenage daughters to do dangerous things like drive into the city by themselves:

> I'm trying to think of a time like that. I think there are times when she lets girls do things that I didn't let her do that are a little more dangerous. They have a car available for their oldest daughter, Emma. They let her drive into the city with some friends. I was anxious for her to do that because I wouldn't do it. I think it's dangerous. I said to Carol, "Why don't you tell her this is dangerous?" And she said, "She knows, she's been there. I did tell her she needs to be careful." I become annoyed when they do things that I would not feel safe doing. Emma has done a great many things that are dangerous, like going off to New York by herself, and she's just a young woman. I just don't think that's safe.

When mothers worried about their daughters themselves, their concerns showed complexity and recognition of their daughters' positive traits. Hedda first described her daughter's compassion and love for animals, then indicated that this love for animals was excessive, "She gets carried away." Hedda was worried that a wild dog her daughter brought home would harm her daughter:

> If something does come up, we don't get upset. I don't remember things that aren't lasting. I cannot honestly say. You know there are things that bother me. She can run out in the street to rescue an animal. It really upsets me. She just adopted a dog. She adores it. The dog has to have a muzzle on it because it fights with other dogs. I think to myself, "Why do you do it?" I'm sure she gave it a great deal of thought, but she probably felt so sorry for the dog. She gets carried away a little bit. She knows how I feel about it, but she makes her own choices. She loves animals.

In general, concerns about whether the other party was taking care of herself showed up more often in daughters' responses than in mothers' responses. Daughters are aware that their mothers are beginning to age. That half of the daughters spontaneously mentioned their mothers' aging, whereas fewer than one fifth of mothers did, indicates that midlife is a period when old age is salient and tension-laden. Moreover, to daughters, old age is represented by their mother who is already aging, despite the fact that she may be as healthy as many middle-aged adults.

THE OTHER'S HABITS OR TRAITS

In addition to differences related to developmental schisms, mothers and daughters may experience tensions that any two adults in an intimate relationship experience. Spouses, lovers, and friends get on one another's nerves, despite similarity in their life stages, cohort, and developmental positions. Mothers and daughters may view the other party's habits, traits, or behaviors as problematic, just as individuals get annoyed with partners in other types of relationships.

Expectations About Mothers and Daughters Who Perceive Flaws

It is likely that mothers and daughters who perceive problems in their relationships in terms of the other party's flaw differ from other mothers and daughters. According to attribution theory, the sense the other party is flawed in some way that she cannot change would be expected to damage the relationship. When individuals attribute another person's behaviors to internal flaws, they also tend to evaluate that person more negatively (Heider, 1958). Yet, this may not be the case for mothers and daughters. Mothers and daughters who view the other party as flawed may see the tensions that they experience as stemming from something outside the relationship.

For daughters, the ability to see a problem in their mothers without feeling personally attacked may represent an aspect of filial maturity; the daughter may be seeing her mother as more like a peer. When middle-aged and older adults find fault with a friend, the difficulty often pertains to the other party's personality (Blieszner & Adams, 1995). In midlife, daughters may be able to reframe tensions so that difficulties are no longer perceived as being based in the relationship but, rather, as being based in their mothers. The ability to perceive, and possibly accept, undesirable characteristics of a loved mother may indicate that difficulties of early life have been mitigated.

By contrast, mothers who see problems in the relationship in terms of their daughters' flaws are perceiving problems in a motherly fashion that is characteristic of prior stages of life. Beginning in early childhood, mothers correct their daughters' misbehaviors and seek to shape their daughters' behaviors in ways that they deem socially acceptable. When daughters reach adulthood, women may view their daughters' accomplishments, attributes, and behaviors as a reflection of their own abilities as mothers (Ryff et al., 1994). Mothers who are dissatisfied with their daughters' habits or attributes may feel that they themselves did not succeed in their job as a mother.

Daughters Who Described Their Mothers' Flaws

Just over a quarter of daughters described tensions that involved something about their mothers. For example, Danielle, a 45-year-old daughter, complained about her mother's bad taste:

> Her taste in clothes for the girls or for me is terrible. She finds something for me or the girls that she'll think we'll like, maybe second-hand. I find it sort of irritating. In my opinion, though, who cares? I just say, "Thanks. We'll try it on." Sometimes, it's actually something that somebody wants. But if not, we just are gracious and say, "Thank you." Then, we just bag it up ourselves and bring it to Good Will. So she's got bad taste, big deal.

As opposed to daughters who felt truly aggravated by their mothers' behaviors, Danielle felt the situation was trivial and unimportant. Valerie had a similar complaint about her mother:

> She worries about stuff that I think she's wasting her time worrying about. . . . The last time this happened, just a very tiny example, when the time change comes she can never reset her VCR. So, she always wants my husband to come over to do the resetting of it. She's kind of antsy about that until it's gotten done. That's probably the most recent one, and that's kind of a minor one. She just worries a lot.

Valerie was not upset with her mother nor did she seem to feel that her mother was doing anything to her in particular. Rather, Valerie's mother worries, and Valerie wishes that she did not.

Daughters' descriptions of their mothers' annoying habits or behaviors had a disengaged quality. It should be noted that situations were coded based on the way they were perceived and framed, rather than something inherent to the nature of the problem. For example, Valerie might have complained instead, "My mother is very demanding. She expects my husband to change her VCR every time there is a time change and pesters us until it gets done." That sort of response would reflect a sense of intrusion. Instead, Valerie was able to see the issue as her mother's problem, and a minor one at that.

Mothers Who Described Their Daughters' Flaws

Contrary to expectations, mothers who recognized their daughters' faults also seemed satisfied with their relationships. Nearly a quarter of mothers provided descriptions of these types of situations. These mothers tended to describe their daughters' positive features as well as their negative features. Thus, they did not frame tensions in terms of their daughters' flaws, but rather the ways in which their daughters' strengths also lead to limitations. Mary, a 75-year-old widow, expressed concerns that her daughter, Jean, does not save enough money:

> There's a number of things that bother me about Jean as a mother. Mothers always want to do the right thing for their children. I see things that she doesn't, and, of course, it's her life. I see some things that really irritate me. She spends money very unnecessarily. She's a very warm, compassionate person. She's a giving person, to an extent I think where it's an extreme. She's always giving, giving, giving, which is a wonderful attribute. She always thinks of the other person. But, I'd like to see her put the money away and have it for themselves in the future. She works hard, and so does he. I feel that they should do more for themselves, get themselves something nice. Money is to use in the future, not give away. But, that's how all mothers think.

Mary framed this concern in terms of Jean's strengths, however, remarking that Jean is such a generous person that she is always giving to other people rather than saving money to use for herself. If Mary had expressed her concerns in terms of how much Jean has put away in savings in case of emergency, the response might have been coded as pertaining to self-care.

Another older mother, Jacqueline, a 71-year-old widow, found it annoying that her daughter, Annette, always checked with someone else to make sure she is doing things correctly at work.

> I can't think of a time when I felt very irritated with her. I get annoyed with her because she seems to lack self-confidence. "Well," she'll say, "Well this happened at work. I didn't finish this or I didn't finish that." And I can't understand why she has to check with anybody, but she's always doing that. For some reason, she has to question herself. It's like getting the call from college, "I know I'm going to fail this exam, I'm going to fail," and then she gets an A. It's too bad she feels that way.

Jacqueline framed this issue in terms of Annette's lack of self-confidence, suggesting that her daughter's abilities warrant greater confidence.

Dyadic Patterns with Regard to the Other's Flaws

Daughters who perceived their mothers' flaws as the root of problems in the relationships appeared to be part of distinct dyads. Of the eight mothers who did not discuss a problem, six had daughters who described situations involving their mothers' annoying habits or traits. As will be discussed in the next section, how mothers and daughters communicate their feelings may be as important as their perceptions of problems. Daughters who think their mothers' flaws cannot be changed may be less likely to discuss these problems with their mothers. As a result, their mothers may assume that all is well in the relationship. Alternately, mothers who have no complaints may be less intrusive. It is also possible that personality plays a role in women's experiences of tensions; mothers who report no problems during the individual interviews may be more easygoing than mothers who do report problems. Their daughters, in turn, may also be more easygoing than other daughters.

PERCEPTIONS OF TENSION AND WELL-BEING

Finally, we must consider whether reports of different types of problems enhance or harm the relationship. It is possible that mothers and daughters who experience some types of problems view their relationship on the whole in a more positive light, whereas mothers and daughters who experience other types of problems view the relationship on the whole in a more negative light. Mothers and daughters tended to fall into distinct categories with regard to problematic relationships. They described one of the three categories of problems: the parameters of the relationship, the other party's care for self or dependents, or habits and traits as the source of problems. Mentioning the mother's aging and including other people overlapped with other categories of tensions, but mothers and daughters did not describe feeling intruded upon in the same situation that they mentioned the other party's unchangeable flaws. Therefore, it is possible to ask whether these different perceptions of problems are associated with the overall quality of the relationship.

Types of Problems and Relationship Quality

Given the premise that developmental schisms render more intense problems in mother/daughter relationships, we would expect mothers and daughters who considered the other party's annoying habits or traits to be the source of difficulty to rate their relationship more highly. Table 7.3 shows Spearman's correlations between mothers' and daughters' descriptions of tensions and each party's ratings of relationship quality.

For daughters, descriptions of problems were associated with their own ratings of the quality of the relationship. More specifically, daughters who considered their mothers intrusive rated the relationship more poorly. Daughters who saw problems in the relationship in terms of their mothers' habits or traits rated the relationship more favorably.

Mothers' ratings of the quality of their relationships was associated with both their own and their daughters' reports of tensions. Although only a few mothers felt excluded by their daughters, these mothers felt worse about their relationships on the whole. By contrast, mothers who considered their daughter's habits or traits to be the source of problems rated the relationship more positively. The ability to view faults in the daughter in an impersonal way seems to be protective for mothers' sense of their ties to their daughters. A mother's feeling that she is excluded is deeply personal, however,

TABLE 7.3 Correlations Between Relationship Quality and Perceptions of Tension

Type of problem	Daughter's ratings of relationship quality	
	Daughter's description of problems	**Mother's description of problems**
Parameters of the relationship		
Felt intruded on	$-.39^{***}$	–.06
Felt excluded	.08	–.20
Discussed other people	.11	–.07
Concerns about care		
Care of self or others	.07	–.06
Mothers' aging	–.20	.14
Habits or traits	$.41^{***}$	.05
No response	NA	.10

Type of problem	Mother's ratings of relationship quality	
	Mother's description of problems	**Daughter's description of problems**
Parameters of the relationship		
Felt intruded upon	–.07	$-.32^{*}$
Felt excluded	$-.38^{***}$	–.08
Discussed other people	$.25^{*}$	–.16
Concerns about care		
Mothers' aging	.10	.10
Care of self or others	–.07	–.08
Habits or traits	$.24^{*}$	$.27^{*}$
No response	$.33^{*}$	NA

$^{*}p < .05$
$^{**}p < .01$
$^{***}p < .005$

and includes a sense of being unloved or unwanted. Feeling excluded clearly colors the entire relationship.

Moreover, a dyadic pattern emerged with regard to mothers' ratings of the relationship. Daughters who saw their mothers as intrusive had mothers who rated the relationship less favorably. Of course, as was reported previously, daughters who felt intruded upon also had mothers who felt excluded, so these findings may reflect this specific pattern. Daughters who saw their mothers' habits and traits as the problem had mothers who rated the relationship more highly. In other words, daughters' perceptions of the mother as intrusive appeared to be worse for both parties' ratings of the relationship on the whole, but daughters' attributions that tensions in the relationship reflected their mothers' traits appeared to be better for both parties' ratings of the relationship.

The mothers who did not provide an example during the individual interviews also provided higher ratings of the relationship. Of course, a mother's failure to provide an example and a mother's tendency to rate the relationship highly might both reflect her efforts to appear socially desirable. Yet, the pattern of results indicates a more complex pattern. As was discussed, these mothers were more likely to have daughters who saw tensions in the relationship in terms of their mothers' habits or traits. Mothers and daughters who perceive problems as an aspect of the person rather than an aspect of the relationship may circumvent tensions in their relationships. They may be able to view the tensions they experience as distinct from the relationship, and thus, value the relationship itself more highly.

Parameters of the Relationship and Relationship Quality

That issues such as intrusion and exclusion play such an important role in relationship quality suggests that intergenerational differences in investment in the relationship and in perceptions of the boundaries of the relationship are central aspects of mother/daughter ties in later life. When mothers are perceived as too involved in the daughter's life, the relationship suffers. Moreover, when mothers feel excluded and they wish to be more involved in the daughter's life, the relationship also suffers. This pattern is associated with differences in investment in the relationship; daughters were more likely to feel intruded upon if their mothers preferred to confide in them. Other researchers have reported that the boundaries of the relationship and demands from the other party are problematic in mother/daughter relationships (Cohler, 1983; Talbott, 1990). Such findings suggest that developmental schisms with regard to investment in the relationship do generate tensions that have an impact on the quality of the relationship.

These differences, which most often resulted in daughters feeling intruded on, may become even more evident in the future, as mothers continue to age and their health declines. The mothers' demands may generate a larger developmental gap as daughters find their mothers' needs increasingly encroach upon their lives. It remains unclear whether the ability to view a mother's problems as just an inevitable part of who she is would strengthen mother/daughter ties in contexts when daughters must provide care. Clearly, future research might examine this question.

The importance of the parameters of the relationship in this study may reflect the values of middle-class European Americans. It is possible that mothers and daughters from cultural groups that place less emphasis on individuation and autonomy might be less affected by feelings of intrusion. Indeed, research suggests that mothers and daughters who do not feel that the other is placing unreasonable demands fare better. In ethnic groups where there is an expectation that parents will be involved in offspring's lives and offspring will be involved in parents' lives, demands from the other party are met with greater equanimity. For example, African American daughters who care for their ailing mothers show less distress than European American daughters who face comparable demands. These group differences stem from differences in values and beliefs (Dilworth-Anderson, Williams, & Cooper, 1999; Mui, 1995). Nonetheless, the sense that the other party has been insensitive to one's needs may present problems for parents and offspring from any background.

Complaints about habits or traits were considered to be problems outside the realm of a developmental schism, that is to say, such issues are less intrinsically related to adult developmental tasks. A daughter's complaints over her mother's habits or traits may reflect the daughter's ability to view the mother as an individual, rather than as a member of the mother/daughter relationship. Such daughters perceived the problem as "she is too generous" rather than "she gives my kids things I don't want them to have." In part, this approach to problems reflects a sense of the boundaries of the relationship as well. Mothers and daughters who view the problems of their relationship as involving the other's habits or traits see the other party as an individual, rather than merely as a partner in the relationship. A mother's or daughter's ability to take this perspective may provide a sense of distance that improves relationship quality.

It is unclear whether the ability to view the other person's habits as a source of tension is associated with higher quality relationships solely in later life, or whether it might enhance relationships at other points in time in the parent/child relationship. Do parents who perceive difficulties with toddlers as an aspect of the toddler's temperament and emerging personality feel more favorable about their relationship? Do adolescents who think their parents are "weird" rather than "mean to me" feel better about their relationships with these parents? The ability to look beyond the relationship itself might be more evident in late life, but may serve as a buffer against tensions at any stage of life.

CONCLUSIONS

Mothers and daughters described specific types of tensions when they answered questions about the problems in their relationships during the individual interviews. There were generational differences in perspectives on tensions in this relationship, however. Daughters tended to be more negative about problems in this tie, to see these situations as confined to themselves and their mothers, to be aware of their mother's aging, and to feel intruded upon. At the same time, dyadic patterns emerged suggesting that mothers and daughters who interact in certain ways are more likely to evoke specific reactions in their partners. A daughter who felt intruded upon was likely to have a mother who felt excluded. A mother who was more invested in the relationship was more likely to have a daughter who felt intruded upon. A mother who did not describe a problem during the individual interview was likely to have a daughter who viewed their difficulties in terms of her mother's unchangeable humanity, rather than in terms of the way her mother treats her.

Mothers' and daughters' perceptions of tensions in their relationships reveal insights into the complexities of their ties. Although the general quality of these ties is positive, issues also arise that cause irritations. Mothers and daughters had different ideas about problems in their relationship. Their perspectives reflect their stages of life and relative investment in the relationship, their roles in the relationship (mother vs. daughter), and individual factors that allow some women to view tensions from a more distant stance. What remains unclear is whether these differences in perceptions of tensions translate into differences in behavior. In the next section, we consider the ways in which mothers and daughters deal with the problems in their relationships.

■ 8
Shared Perceptions of Problems

I'd like to start this interview by asking you about the last time that one of you was bothered during a visit together. You may have had a disagreement or difference of opinion. Or one of you may have been upset, but the other person might not have known. I'd like you to agree on a recent situation when this happened. You don't have to tell me a lot about the situation, but you both have to agree on the same situation. I'd like to know a little about what happened.

—*The interviewer*

Mothers and daughters came together for a joint interview 1 to 2 weeks after their individual interviews. At the start of this interview, mothers and daughters described a time when one or both was upset, irritated, or annoyed with the other. This technique provided mothers and daughters with two separate opportunities to ponder their negative feelings. It also provided insights into their relationship based on variation in their responses in these settings. In contrast to the individual interviews where eight mothers had trouble coming up with a situation when they had been upset with their daughters, all mothers and daughters came up with something to discuss during the joint interviews. One mother and daughter insisted on using their discussion during the joint interview as their most recent example of a problematic situation, but the other women discussed situations that had happened prior to the interview. As we shall see in Part IV, most mothers and daughters participated equally in the discussions of a problematic situation, regardless of whether the mother had described a problem during the individual interview.

The types of issues that mothers and daughters talked about during the joint interviews were similar to those described in the individual interviews, but the tone of these discussions tended to be less forceful. Table 8.1 shows the proportions of mother/daughter dyads describing each type of problem. Negative emotions underlying tensions were attenuated. Mothers and daughters who had previously described intense aggravation described their feelings and the situation in more positive tones or they selected a different situation to discuss. The general themes remained constant, but the details of the situations were different.

TABLE 8.1 Proportion of Mothers and Daughters Discussing Each Type of Problem During the Joint Interview

Type of problems	Proportion of dyads ($n = 48$)
Parameters of the relationship	
Mother gave advice	.39
Daughter gave advice	.24
Included other people	.58
Inappropriate care	
Mother's care	.14
Daughter's care	.07
Disagreement or argument	.16
Whose jurisdiction situation falls under	
Mother only	.24
Daughter only	.47
Both/unclear	.29

OFFERING ADVICE TO THE OTHER PARTY

As was the case during the individual interviews, the majority of mothers and daughters discussed tensions involving the parameters of the relationship. Yet, their descriptions of these issues were different during the joint interviews. When mothers and daughters talked about the boundaries of the relationship in the other's presence, they often framed their discussion in terms of unsolicited advice, rather than intrusion or extrusion.

Danielle had originally described her mother's bad taste in clothes during the individual interviews. Her mother, Rose, had been unable to think of a time when she was irritated with Danielle. When the two were brought together, they discussed a time when Danielle convinced her mother to carry through with travel plans she wished to cancel:

Rose: Can you think of something?

Danielle: No, I can't really. I honestly don't know. (To the interviewer) How far back do you want us to go?

Interviewer: As recent as possible. Something you disagreed about or a time when one of you was upset.

Danielle: I guess we don't get into those kinds of conversations. We live parallel lives. We're both Christian families. We have the same views. The only thing I think about is maybe travel. Maybe you don't want to go someplace and I have to talk to you about it. And I say, "You should really go."

Rose: I think that's right.

Danielle: You were supposed to go up north and you didn't want to go up north.

Rose: Yes, and then you thought I should go and I did.

Although Danielle had readily described her mother's annoying habits the week before, in her mother's presence, she reminded her mother of a time when she had encouraged her mother to do something she wished to do. Danielle's description of the situation did not appear to involve much tension, and Rose readily agreed to Danielle's version of events.

Likewise, June and Amy outlined a discussion they'd had a few months previously when Amy's favorite aunt had died. June offered her daughter advice. During the individual interview, June had described how upset she was when her daughter's husband turned up the stereo. Amy had complained that her mother did not remember things accurately and told people she'd said things she had not said. Their joint interview revolved around a different discussion.

Amy: I'm not sure what it was about.
June: We need to figure out when we disagreed last.
Amy: I can't remember any disagreement.
June: This is hard.
Amy: I'm sure we've had a disagreement.
June: I'm pretty sure, too. . . . We've got to get on with it. . . . What did we do?
Amy: You tell me when I'm not wearing something warm enough.
June: I do? The only thing that comes to mind is the furniture in Aunt Trudie's apartment. It wasn't really a disagreement.
Amy: You thought that I should really take the furniture, and I was hesitating to take it.
June: Yes.
Amy: I didn't know what I was going to do with the furniture.
June: It was mostly the breakfront.
Amy: And the dresser, too, and the sofa was a great idea. It was overwhelming to see an apartment full of furniture when you already have a house full of furniture. You were right, though. I'm glad I have it all.

Like many mothers and daughters, Amy and June discussed the situation amicably. June had simply pointed out what Amy should do, and Amy had followed her advice. There is no hint of criticism, intrusion, or rejection in their discussion. Patricia and her daughter, Hillary, discussed a time when Patricia offered advice that Hillary did not appreciate.

Hillary: Can you think of some time we disagreed?
Pat: Does it have to be a disagreement? We don't have disagreements.

Hillary: Well, we disagree. I'm trying to think of a recent time.

Patricia: Well, the only thing that comes to my mind is when you were driving. Down at that intersection, you drove through where you were supposed to stop. And I said to you, "That's a stop sign. You're supposed to stop on this side." And . . .

Hillary: And I got really angry . . .

Pat: You got really angry and said, "You're always telling me how to drive."

Hillary: You're nervous when you're not driving and someone else is driving and . . .

Pat: That had nothing to do with the fact that you didn't stop at the stop sign.

Hillary: No.

Pat: And I was afraid that one day you were going to get clobbered there. And I said to you, "You always go through this stop sign, and you're supposed to stop back at the line."

Hillary: It was extremely unpleasant, but the thing that upset me most was being told while I was driving because at that point, I'd already done it. And, I had just done it. And I thought, I thought, when you got real upset, that I had done something much more severe. And I was scared because I'm not the greatest driver. And the hardest thing in the world for me to do was to learn to drive. I lost a girlfriend in an automobile accident.

Pat: Oh, yeah.

Hillary: And I take my heart every time, and it's on the steering wheel every time I get in the car. I guess what happened was I lost it completely.

Pat and Hillary's discussion was closer to the negative tone found during the individual interviews. The situation was one where both parties were upset, and both were still agitated to get their point across during the joint interview. Nonetheless, Pat and Hillary were able to talk about their problem cordially in the other's presence and to come to a consensus on why they were upset. In general, descriptions of intrusiveness were less extreme in the joint interviews. Instead, for most mothers and daughters, the situations involved gently resolved disagreements. One party offered advice. The other accepted it. There was little tension or negative emotion.

CONCERNS ABOUT SELF-CARE

A greater proportion of mothers and daughters talked about self-care when interviewed together than had when interviewed alone. Of the 48 dyads, seven focused on the mothers' failure to care for herself and three focused on the daughters' care for herself or others. Amanda, who had mentioned her mother's flu shot during the individual interview, brought this issue up again during the joint interview. Neither mother nor daughter seemed perturbed by the issue, but they were both aware that Amanda would have preferred that her mother receive the inoculation and that her mother had the right to refuse to do so.

Melissa (who discussed her mother's refusal of a fiftieth anniversary party during the individual interview) and her mother discussed concerns about whether or not her mother needed to use a wheel chair. Her mother, Bonnie, had been worried about the amount of money that Melissa was planning to spend on a present for her. In their joint interview, this mother and daughter discussed a recent time when Melissa was concerned for Bonnie's health:

Bonnie: What did you disagree with me about?
Melissa: I think the most recent thing we disagreed about was whether or not you should get the wheelchair.
Bonnie: Yes. Yesterday, tell her (the interviewer) why we disagreed.
Melissa: You were so adamant about not using it.
Bonnie: I can't walk, so I guess I should use it. I'm so crippled, I can't walk.
Melissa (To the interviewer): But she was adamant about not getting one.
Bonnie: We never got one. I didn't go there looking for no wheel chairs.

Conversations about self-care often involved this sort of joking back and forth. Marianne and Amanda brought up the situation involving Marianne's flu shot during the joint interview.

Marianne: What's a problem?
Amanda: I'm sure there's some, there must be.
Marianne: If you'd asked me yesterday, I'd know.
Amanda: Yes, I'd have been thinking about it.
Marianne: Tonight, in bed, we'll think of it when we should be sleeping. The only thing I can think about is when you told me to get a shot.
Amanda: Yes, the flu shot thing.
Marianne: We'll go with that. (Pause)
Interviewer: Can you say a little more about the general nature of what happened?
Marianne (To interviewer): She thinks I should have a flu shot, but I don't want to do it. So, I don't do it. She does it. I don't like putting things into my body.

Of note in this joint discussion is that Marianne could not think of a time when she was upset with Amanda during the individual interview. It was Amanda who raised the issue of the flu shot in her discussion of her mother. Yet, in the joint interview, Marianne recalls the incident.

PROBLEMS INVOLVING OTHER PEOPLE

During the joint interviews, more than half of the mothers and daughters brought up problems that centered on other people. As opposed to the individual interviews, however, these discussions did not consistently involve the parameters of the relationship. Rather, the mother/daughter tie seems to be embedded in the context of the larger family. Mothers' and daughters' descriptions of pleasant visits also often included other family members. When they are together, mothers and daughters appear to discuss and include their other relatives, whether the context is one of positive or negative feelings. During the individual interviews, daughters' complaints had centered primarily on their mothers, rather than other family members, but in the joint interviews they were as likely to discuss other family members as were their mothers. This pattern suggests that daughters' conceptions of the mother/daughter tie are not always consistent.

Some of these discussions involved disagreements pertaining to the treatment of these other people, particularly the daughters' children. For example, Lucille and Carol talked about the fact that Carol spent more money on her daughters than Lucille felt she should.

Carol: What have we disagreed about lately? I mentioned to the interviewer before that we were having trouble deciding what you were going to do with your money, but I guess we finally decided on that. What else have we disagreed about lately?

Lucille: How much you spend on your daughters.

Carol: I told her that's what we disagreed on. That's fine. It's more of an ongoing thing.

Lucille: It's something that has been all your life, that you wanted to spend more money than I thought you ought to.

Carol: It's more a general thing. She's looking for a recent time.

Lucille: Well, I guess when recently, on Sunday, you were anxious to get Lizzie that party dress. You said, 'Well, she has to have a party dress.' We don't disagree really. I may think that, but down underneath, I don't really think that. I mean, I know she has to have the party dress. And you have the money, so that's all right. Because I've had to be careful with money all my life, it's hard for me to realize that anyone who has money now can spend it. Even myself, but I'm not ready to spend it. You go to the store and buy whatever you want. Did you buy her that dress on Sunday?

Carol: Yes. But is she happy? No. Anyway, that's an ongoing saga.

Mothers and daughters did not limit themselves to situations involving the daughter's children. They talked about the daughter's siblings, father, and partner. Indeed, Roberta and Lois discussed the situation that each had raised during the individual interviews. Roberta had complained that her mother Lois called up to five times a day. During the joint interview, they discussed one of those phone calls. Lois was trying decide whether to hire a babysitter for Roberta's nephew (Lois's grandson) and Lois wanted Roberta's opinion. Roberta did not wish to give her opinion about her brother's children.

Likewise, Clarissa, a 71-year-old widow, and her 43-year-old daughter, Blythe, discussed a situation involving Blythe's husband:

Clarissa: This is where I couldn't think of something before.
Blythe: You couldn't think of a disagreement?
Clarissa: Can you?
Blythe: We're so dull. . . . The only problem is when you start riding on John (my husband) about getting the house finished.
Clarissa: Oh yes, there's that.
Blythe: That's it.
Clarissa: That's the only thing.
Blythe: We agree on that.
Clarissa: But, that's a long-standing problem. (Pause)
Interviewer: Can you say a little more about what happened?
Blythe (To interviewer): She tells me what my husband should do about fixing the house up. It pisses me off . . . because I told him the same thing.
Clarissa: That's right, but coming from someone else it's different.
Blythe: Well, you should tell him, not me.
Clarissa: I do every once in a while, but he doesn't say anything. That is sort of a sore spot. But, it's none of my business, if you're happy with it, why should I care about it?
Blythe: Well, I'm not happy about it, but I don't like to be reminded of it.

It is notable that during the joint interviews, mothers often explicitly stated that they did not wish to intrude in their daughters' lives. The paradox of the mother's desire to be involved, yet her recognition that she has no right to be involved is evident. As was clear in the individual interviews, however, daughters feel intruded upon by their mothers. A key issue may involve the mother's criticism or desire to change these situations. Although mothers may state that they do not mean to be intrusive, they are passing judgment on these situations. Their judgment comes across as intrusion to their daughters.

Not all cases involving other people involved overt conflicts. As will be discussed in the next section, mothers and daughters may have discussed problems involving someone else as a means of directing attention away from their relationship and diffusing tensions. For example, Pauline and her daughter, Monica, spoke about their different strategies for dealing with Monica's father (Pauline's husband) whom both agreed could be difficult at times. Although they disagreed on how to handle him, they framed the discussion in terms of *his* problems and demands, rather than their own. They were united in their sense that he generated tensions.

OVERT DISAGREEMENTS

A new category of problems emerged during the joint interviews that had not received consideration during the individual interviews, overt disagreements. During the individual interviews, mothers and daughters provided accounts of annoying things the other party did or annoying things about the other party. During the joint interviews, eight dyads described overt conflicts that they had had. The directions for the joint interview were slightly different from the directions offered during the individual interview. In the joint interview, the interviewer specifically encouraged descriptions of disagreements or differences of opinion, and mothers and daughters clearly gravitated toward these words. They did not seem as comfortable bringing up a situation when only one of them was irritated.

Mary had described her irritations with her daughter, Jean, for spending too much money on gifts during the individual interviews. During the joint interview, she and Jean talked about a time when they couldn't decide who should be included in the roster for Christmas gifts.

Jean: When was the last disagreement we had?
Mary: What happened? There's so little.
Jean: How about whether Matt and Jason's name should be included in the Christmas list.
Mary: Oh, yes. That's very good. That was a very touchy subject. I think it was hurtful for them, how it ended.
Jean: I tried supporting them.

Mary: I wasn't there to directly hear it, but I was in the other room. So, I could listen and add in my thoughts.

Jean (To interviewer): The basic argument was—we pick names for Christmas presents, and so we were deciding whose name should be on the list according to how old they are and that kind of thing. My mom, you (to mother) were supporting that Matt and Jason also *not* be on the list. I was saying, 'They're already out of college, so they should be on the list, but my other nephew who is still in college shouldn't be on the list.'

Mary: That was the discussion, and it ended favorably for us. We sort of agreed to disagree.

Although Mary initially described the situation as "a touchy subject," Mary and Jean were careful to point out that they had reached an agreement of sorts, even in their dispute. Their discussion had involved a difference of opinion.

Likewise, Phyllis and Kathy described a disagreement that they had about what time to have Thanksgiving dinner. They were each concerned about getting what they wanted from the situation, but also showed a clear desire to make the other party feel good about the situation.

Phyllis: I know what we were talking about right before.

Kathy: Yeah, what time to have Thanksgiving dinner.

Phyllis (To interviewer): She wanted to have Thanksgiving dinner at 2:00. We were invited to another relative's at 6:00. (To her daughter): Now, that's pretty close to eat a full Thanksgiving dinner at 2:00 and then eat another dinner at 6:00. It takes a whole hour to eat. And then go and eat hers. So I said, "Why don't you have it at 1:00?" (To the interviewer) My husband said, "Twelve," but he just turns his back when he says it. She says, "That's breakfast. Nobody eats that early." (To her daughter) I said, "How 'bout 1:00?" So you said, "How 'bout 2:00?" (Laugh).

Kathy: (Laugh) Yes.

Phyllis: So, I agreed. We'll manage it. We just won't eat that much at the other.

Kathy: And the other thing is, you won't be eating right at 6:00. You just have to be there at 6:00.

Phyllis: That's right.

Kathy: So, there will be more hours in between.

Phyllis: Yes, that's true. We won't eat right when we get there.

Angela, an 80-year-old widow, and her daughter, Stacey, described a more intense conflict. During the individual interview, Angela had complained that her daughter was trying to change her. Stacey had complained that her mother acted like Stacey did things to hurt her on purpose. They brought up a different problem in the joint interview:

Angela: I never disagreed with you.

Stacey: Yes, we argue. Have we had a *recent* disagreement?

Angela: A difference of opinion.

Stacey: It would have to be that you get a little bit angry that I don't ask Cindy (my sister) about her marriage. That would be it.

Angela: That would be the only thing. I'm dying to know, and I won't ask her.

Stacey: You get mad and say, 'You don't ask your sister. You're not concerned.'

Angela: I have to call her up to ask her what's happening.

Stacey (To the interviewer): My sister's marriage is very strange. She's always leaving her husband, every other week. So my mother will say to me, "Did you talk to your sister?" And, I'll say, "Yeah." And she'll ask, "Well, what's going on?" And I say, "I don't ask." And she'll say, "Don't you care?" And I say, "If she wants to tell me, she'll tell me." And she says, "Well, you should ask." And I say, "No, because if I bring it up, she'll have to deal with it." My sister doesn't like to deal with it. So, she won't talk about it. My mother always wants me to ask her.

Angela: Well, I don't want her to think I'm nosy. Better you, than me.

Stacey: She'll go, "Don't you care?" And I'll go, "Yeah, but Cindy doesn't like to talk about it." Then usually you

	see my side after awhile. That, or I don't call my sister.
Angela:	Or she doesn't call me!
Stacey:	That's ongoing.
Angela:	Yes, that's ongoing.

Many of the overt disagreements overlapped with other categories of problems in the joint interviews. Mothers and daughters argued about other family members, about the mother's self-care, and about the advice that one of them had proffered. Given the context of the interview, with both mother and daughter present and required to agree upon the same situation, it is not surprising that most of their situations appeared to involve an overt and explicit conflict.

JURISDICTION OF THE JOINT INTERVIEW PROBLEM

Finally, we might consider whose jurisdiction the problems fell under. Did mothers and daughters talk about a problem that had to do with the daughter's life or with the mother's life? Did they discuss a problem involving both of them? In some instances, it was not possible to determine whether problems arose from the mother or daughter. When it was possible to make such a determination, more problems stemmed from the daughter's life. Twenty-one dyads discussed issues involving the daughter's life compared to only 11 dyads that talked about problems strictly limited to the mother's life. The remaining 16 dyads either talked about an issue that involved both parties or an issue that was not clearly defined as involving the mother or the daughter.

The greater focus on daughters suggests that when mothers are still healthy, even in later life the mother/daughter relationship is one that deals with helping, assisting, and changing the daughter more than the mother. Socialization processes in early life focus the mother/daughter dyad on the daughter, and this pattern appears to carry through into old age.

COMPARISONS OF PROBLEMS DESCRIBED IN THE JOINT AND INDIVIDUAL INTERVIEWS

One of the most interesting aspects of the joint interview, of course, involves a comparison between information that mothers and daughters provided in the other's presence and information that they provided when sequestered in the comfort of the individual interviews.

Surprisingly, even the general categories of problems did not show much correspondence across interviews. Mothers and daughters who complained of the other's intrusiveness were no more likely to complain of unsolicited advice during the joint interviews than were other mothers or daughters. Daughters who brought up their mothers' aging during the individual interviews were not more likely to describe her self-care in the joint interviews.

The eight mothers who provided no response during the individual interviews might have been expected to be less likely to describe overt disagreements as a source of tension. Surely, if their problems with their daughters involved open confrontation they would be aware that there was a problem. This was not the case, however. Mothers who provided no response during the individual interviews were just as likely to concur that their problems revolved around an open disagreement as any other mother in the joint interviews.

As was mentioned previously, the tone of the joint interviews was not as negative as the tone of the individual interviews. Even when the same basic story came up, mothers and daughters painted the issue in more gentle hues. For example, during the individual interview, Claire portrayed the ways in which her mother Willa intruded upon her efforts to raise her children. Willa recommended that Claire withhold ballet lessons from her daughter until her daughter started to practice the violin as often as she should. Claire resented the advice, and felt that it showed insensitivity to her own daughter. During the joint interview, this issue arose again, but this time, mother and daughter presented the problem in terms of a disagreement over the age at which children should begin to make their own decisions. Willa felt Claire's daughter was not old enough to decide how much to practice the violin on her own and Claire felt that she was.

Willa: I haven't been upset with my daughter in the past month.
Claire: A disagreement?
Willa: You may have an idea, but I don't have any.
Claire: Well, it wasn't a disagreement, but there was a statement you made to me. I didn't respond, but I guess I could

have. Then, it would have become a disagreement.

Willa: I'm interested.

Claire: I guess it was when we went shopping. You said to me something about Alicia and the violin, and you asked why I don't use ballet lessons as leverage to make her practice the violin.

Willa: Oh, yes.

Claire: And, I just chose not to say anything, I listened to you.

Willa: Uh huh.

Claire: But, I was thinking, the thing is, there comes a time when she has to make some of her own decisions about how to run her life. So that she'll be able to do that better as a young adult and as an adult. If you always mandate, "You have to do this," she won't have the chance to do that. She's the one that has to practice, not me, not you.

Willa: I don't think she's at that age yet. I think she's still under her mother's tutoring and discipline. At the age of eleven, I don't think she's capable of making such decisions.

Claire: I'm not sure that's true. Like, this year, I told her she didn't have to take piano. It was hard battling with her everyday. It's not fun if you're battling. You don't do a good job if you're angry. So, I gave in to that with the piano. At least the tension is less, and that helps.

Willa: I think that's a little different than putting one thing against another.

Willa and Claire disagreed about Claire's approach to raising her daughter. Claire wanted her mother to understand the constraints she faces in dealing with her own daughter and the validity of her decisions concerning childrearing. In the individual interview, Claire described her mother as insensitive and intrusive. In the joint interview, Claire tried to explain her case and to convert her mother to her side of the matter. Daughters still seek their mother's approval and mother's still try to socialize and change their daughters, even in late life.

In other cases, both parties had been upset during the individual interviews, yet they discussed the problem amicably during the joint interview. For example, Bea and Wendy each spoke of their difficulties concerning their Christmas celebrations during the individual interviews. They brought this topic up again during the joint interview. Yet, neither party seemed upset during the joint interview. Rather, they agreed wholeheartedly about their problems.

At the opposite extreme, mothers and daughters who were reticent to describe any difficulties were equally forthcoming about problems when asked to do so together. Rose had had nothing to complain about during the individual interview and her daughter Danielle merely commented on her mother's bad taste in clothes. During the joint interview, they came up with the incident concerning Rose's travel plans. Although the problem was slight, they were able to think of a time when they had disagreed.

CONCLUSIONS

Patterns of discussion in the individual and joint interviews suggest that daughters are protective of their mothers in later life. They are willing to voice their dissatisfaction when asked to do so alone, but are reticent to do so in their mother's presence. When daughters and mothers do discuss problems together, they are generally calm and tone down their grievances. Mothers seemed more forthcoming in their daughters' presence than they were when interviewed alone. These behaviors seem almost "motherly." Mothers are unwilling to admit to their daughters' faults when asked to do so alone with a stranger. When interviewed in their daughters' presence, they take advantage of the opportunity to comment, "Well, you know, dear, you do . . . " and seek to socialize those daughters, even in midlife.

■ four

MOTHERS' AND DAUGHTERS' REACTIONS TO PROBLEMS

9 Interpersonal Conflict and Communication

There hasn't been any tension. Of course, I don't expect people to see things the way I do. We just don't talk about it. We don't have any trouble. Amanda has always been a peacemaker. . . . We do discuss things, but we don't get upset about things. I'm afraid I can't think of any time we've ever argued. We do have differences of opinion. I think that her politics are different than mine, but in that case we just don't talk about it, 'cause she pretty well knows how I feel, I pretty well know how she feels. Nothing to say about it.

—*Marianne, 82-year-old mother*

As was discussed in Part III, mothers' and daughters' perceptions of the problems they encounter clearly contribute to the nature of their relationship. Their reactions to those problems, however, may have an even greater impact on their relationship. There are many things people can do when they are upset with someone they care about, they can: yell, argue, explain their position, pout, hit, throw things, pray, ignore the other person, listen to the other person, understand, forgive, or simply pretend the problem does not exist.

Prior to this study, few researchers had considered mothers' and daughters' responses to tensions in their relationship. The marital literature is rife with studies examining the antecedents and consequences of behaviors wives and husbands use to deal with their negative feelings toward the other party (e.g., Cohan & Bradbury, 1997; Gottman, 1993b, 1998; Heavey, Layne, & Christensen, 1993; Pasch & Bradbury, 1998). Such research has included multiple assessments of spouse's reactions to irritations in their relationships. In fact, the dyadic approach used in this study of mothers and daughters was derived in large part from research and theory pertaining to romantic partners.

At the same time, there are limitations in using what we know about problems in romantic relationships to try to understand how aging mothers and their adult daughters might respond when upset with the other party. First, much of that research has focused on circumstances leading to the dissolution of a romantic partnership (e.g., Gottman, 1993a, 1998; Heavey et al., 1993; Kelly & Conley, 1987; Kurdek, 1993; Rusbult, Drigotas, & Verette, 1994; Veroff et al., 1997). The issue of dissolution is not relevant for most elderly women and their middle-aged daughters. It is improbable that a mother and a daughter who have maintained a relationship for over 35 years will go their separate ways in the face of new problems, regardless of their communication patterns or the scope of the problem.

Second, explanations for spouses' reactions to problems in the marital relationship often involve differences related to gender, power in the relationship, and the roles of husbands and wives (Acitelli, 1988; Acitelli & Antonucci, 1994; Levenson, Carstensen, & Gottman, 1993). The mother/daughter relationship involves two individuals of the same gender. Inequities of power in this relationship follow a different pattern than is the case in romantic relationships. In early life, mothers have more power than daughters. Although mothers and daughters come to share a more equitable relationship in adulthood, daughters still crave their mothers' approval. Moreover, mothers socialize their daughters, and, thus, in the early years of the relationship they are likely to share a common communication pattern, whereas romantic partners may not.

This chapter provides an overview of theory and research pertaining to responses to interpersonal problems. Despite the limitations of doings so, existent literature pertaining to conflict behaviors in romantic relationships is used to establish a framework for understanding how mothers and daughters might respond to tensions in their relationship. The next chapter provides information about the behaviors mothers and daughters used to deal with difficulties in their tie. This section addresses several questions. How do mothers and daughters respond to problems in their relationships? Do mothers and daughters do different things when they are annoyed? Do their self-reports of behavior match an outsider's observations of their behaviors? Do they have a sense of how the other party responds to difficulties? Most important, do their behaviors help explain the quality of their relationships? The literature pertaining to interpersonal conflict provides a theoretical basis for examining these issues.

CLASSIFICATIONS OF BEHAVIORS

The vast array of reactions to problems can be classified along two dimensions. First, behaviors fall along a constructive/destructive continuum. The constructive/destructive dimension involves the impact a specific behavior has on the other party or the relationship itself. Does the behavior improve or harm the relationship? Second, responses can be classified as active or passive. The passive/active dimension involves the directness with which an individual responds. Do individuals communicate their feelings openly to the other party? These categories provide a useful heuristic for understanding patterns in mother and daughter relationships.

Constructive/Destructive Dimension

Constructive approaches involve communication that is intended to facilitate mutual understanding of a problem or to strengthen the relationship in some way. Behaviors associated with constructive approaches include: listening to the other person, asking questions, accepting the other person's limitations, or talking about one's feelings. Destructive behaviors involve communication that is hurtful to the other person. Such responses may hinder resolution of difficulties, and ultimately harm the relationship. Behaviors associated with destructive approaches include: yelling, offending, sulking, and even hitting the other person. Parents and offspring appear to rarely engage in physical confrontations in late life (Pillimer & Finkelhor, 1988), and physical assaults are presumed to be almost nonexistent between mothers and daughters who describe their relationships as close. Therefore, mothers' and daughters' destructive behaviors in late life are more likely to be verbal or nonverbal actions that upset the other person, hurt her feelings, induce guilt, or otherwise disturb the relationship.

The constructive/destructive dimension has received considerable attention in the marital and family research literatures (Canary & Cupach, 1988; Canary et al., 1995; Gottman, 1979; Gottman & Krokoff, 1989; Straus, 1979). Classifying behaviors along this continuum with regard to strength of relationship is somewhat tautological, however. Constructive behaviors by definition foster better ties, whereas destructive behaviors lead to difficulties in the relationship. A more complex portrait emerges when behaviors are also considered along an active/passive dimension.

The Active/Passive Dimension

Active behaviors deal directly with the situation at hand. For example, speaking calmly to the other person, asking the other person why she is upset, storming out of the house, hanging up the phone, and screaming are active responses to an irritating situation. Passive responses include avoiding difficult situations, not talking about problems when they do arise, tolerating minor irritations, pouting, ignoring the other person, or expressing one's annoyance indirectly.

Passive approaches may also involve non-explicit communiqués that are idiomatic to that relationship. Individuals in long-term relationships may develop subtle cues to communicate their discomfort in the absence of actual discussion (Brown & Levinson, 1987; Cupach & Metts, 1994). For example, a daughter might refuse to answer when her mother mentions that she has not begun a search for a new job. This silence signals to the mother that it is time to switch topics. Such a pattern may grow out of years of shared interactions.

American popular psychology espouses the idea that open communication is the best way for women to resolve problems in their relationships (e.g., Lerner, 1985). The premise that "I" statements such as "I feel upset when you . . . " strengthen relationships gained credence throughout the 1970s and 1980s. It is unclear, however, whether women do fare better by discussing negative feelings across contexts. On the one hand, women's failure to express anger has been linked to increased risk of coronary and other diseases, and to decreased psychological well-being (Thomas, 1993). On the other hand, women who express negative feelings in an explosive manner may experience a variety of negative outcomes (Tavris, 1989; Thomas, 1993). Obviously, other factors—such as the partner's response—play a role in how effective active behaviors are in resolving a given problem.

Passive communication may also be positive or negative in nature. A daughter's willingness to ignore her mother's annoying flaws may strengthen their tie. A mother's acceptance of her daughter's autonomy can reduce friction. By contrast, passive communication may involve behaviors that harm the relationship obliquely (Brown & Levinson, 1987; Wodak & Schulz, 1986). A mother might be irritated that her daughter does not make her own children remain at the table during dinner. Rather than tell the daughter, the mother might point out how rude someone else's children are behaving when they run around at a restaurant. In this manner, the mother slyly insinuates disapproval of the daughter's parenting, but does not leave the daughter a means of responding.

The Efficacy of Different Behaviors

The efficacy of a specific behavior in resolving difficulties depends upon a number of factors, including: the mores of the larger society, the type of relationship, the relative status of the aggrieved and aggravating parties, and the individual attributes and backgrounds of the two individuals involved in the relationship. In addition, the effectiveness of behaviors varies as a function of the issue causing the problem. A mother might find her daughter's overt complaints about her personal characteristics (e.g., "You always talk too much") threatening or offensive (Cupach & Metts, 1994). By contrast, a mother might welcome a direct suggestion for a new outfit or a new hairstyle if she is looking for a quick-fix change in her appearance.

The effectiveness of behaviors may also vary as a function of personality. Some individuals may feel more comfortable with one type of behavior than another type of behavior. Individuals who are shy and quiet may prefer passive approaches when upset with another party. More aggressive individuals may tend toward confrontational approaches.

Throughout life, the types of behaviors individuals rely on to deal with problems influence the nature of their relationships and, in turn, their own well-being. In long-term relationships, patterns may evolve and change over time. Most research on conflict communication has dealt with the romantic relationship, a social tie that begins in adolescence or adulthood. We know little about patterns of conflict in relationships that have lasted a lifetime. By old age, mothers and daughters have had many years to accumulate patterns of interaction that sustain their tie.

BEHAVIORS IN THE MOTHER/DAUGHTER TIE IN LATE LIFE

Several researchers have examined the ways in which adult family members negotiate problematic issues as they age (Hagestad, 1982; Nydegger & Mitteness, 1988). Older generations skirt around issues that they know to be a source of rancor. For example, as the quote from Marianne at the start of this chapter indicates, a mother who is a registered Democrat and a daughter who is staunchly Republican may politely circumvent discussion of the upcoming election. Family harmony takes precedence over exerting one's own opinion. Moreover, individuals come to view other family members as intractable around certain issues, and thus, efforts to change them seem futile. Of course, mothers and daughters may not be able to skirt around all hot topics. As described in the prior section, mothers and daughters get annoyed with the other party from time to time, regardless of efforts to avoid problematic issues.

When daughters are young, mothers and daughters may engage in overt confrontations with some frequency. For example, although most parents and offspring rate their relationships favorably during adolescence, during this period, heated arguments are not uncommon (Arnett, 1999; Conger & Ge, 1999; Paikoff & Brooks-Gunn,

1991). Whereas destructive behaviors might lead to the decline of a marital relationship, there is some evidence that mother/daughter confrontations in the teen years strengthen the relationship in adulthood. Yet, the persistence of overt confrontations into the adult years does not appear to benefit the relationship. Indeed, mothers and daughters who engage in open hostilities toward the other party in late life appear to be the exception, rather than the rule.

There are a variety of reasons why older mothers and daughters would be expected to respond passively when they are irritated with the other party. Their goals in their relationship shape their responses. For example, spouses may voice their dissatisfactions based on their desire to change their partner's behaviors and to foster the growth of the marriage. It is not clear that mothers and daughters view relationship growth as a goal in their interactions. In fact, they may see their autonomy, and the ability to maintain a sense of separation as a superordinate goal (Walker, 1994). Alternately, their shared investment in the larger extended family may encourage them to suppress their desire to argue a point or to raise an issue that bothers them. In any case, mothers and daughters in this study were expected to deal with difficulties through constructive means rather than using destructive behaviors.

Intergenerational Differences in Behaviors

Although they might generally be expected to engage in passive and constructive approaches to difficulties, mothers and daughters might also behave differently from one another when irritated with the other party. Mothers' and daughters' reactions to tensions are influenced by their respective partners, friends, the media, self-help books, and even psychotherapy across adulthood. Some systematic differences in mothers' and daughters' responses to tensions were anticipated. In general, mothers were expected to respond more passively and with greater efforts at appeasement than were daughters.

As was mentioned previously, parents tend to perceive greater compatibility with their offspring than do those offspring (Bengtson & Kuypers, 1971; Fingerman, 1995). As a result, they may be less likely to get upset with their offspring or they may behave in a way that strengthens the relationship when they are upset. In early life, the parent is expected to be patient with the screaming toddler. In adulthood, this pattern may carry over to a parent who notices fewer irritations and who gets less upset when they do notice irritations with offspring. Moreover, if mothers are more invested in the relationship, they may have a stronger desire to see problems resolved quickly.

Cohort differences may also contribute to differences in mothers' and daughters' responses to tensions. The daughters in this study came of age in the late 1960s and 1970s, a period when self-expression was widely valued and espoused. As young women, these daughters may have developed overt and direct means of dealing with interpersonal problems. By contrast, their mothers were raised in an era when ladies did not raise their voices, and "letting it all hang out" was not the modus operandi. Clearly, there were individual differences in each generation, and clearly the older women have had access to television talk shows and other aspects of the popular culture that encourage greater discussion of personal problems. Yet, the fact that they lived through the Great Depression, and may have developed skills to deal with adversity without getting upset shapes their openness in bringing up problems with their grown daughters.

In addition, mothers are older and more mature than daughters, and this age difference may shape intergenerational differences in their behaviors. Older individuals respond with less active coping strategies than do younger individuals in situations that seem unchangeable (Folkman & Lazarus, 1980). Rather than trying to change the situation or the other person, they may focus on regulating their own emotional state (Fingerman, Gallagher-Thompson, Lovett, & Rose, 1996). In addition, older adults respond more passively to interpersonal problems involving greater emotional intensity. In one study, older and younger adults responded to vignettes about social problems that varied in emotional salience (e.g., a teenager wanting to borrow a car vs. placing a parent in a nursing home). There were age differences in the way adults approached the highly emotionally salient vignettes. Older adults suggested more passive means of dealing with these problems than did younger adults (Blanchard-Fields, Jahnke, & Camp, 1995).

Such findings suggest that older mothers might respond to difficulties with their daughters through greater acceptance and tolerance, whereas daughters might be more likely to voice their dissent. In addition to examining the ways in which mothers and daughters responded to problems in general, particular attention was given to intergenerational differences in their reactions.

MEASURING MOTHERS' AND DAUGHTERS' BEHAVIORS

If mothers and daughters do, in fact, react to minor irritations by ignoring them, it may be virtually impossible to assess their responses in this context. How do you measure a "non-reaction"? An analogy for this task draws on the field of astrophysics. Astronomers must piece together a sense of a distant planet, star, or a black hole by examining an accumulation of indirect evidence. An off-shoot of light a billion years old, a change in orbit in the patterns of celestial bodies, radio waves bounced back to a target are used in combination to garner information about a phenomenon of interest. In order to get a sense of mothers' and daughters' reactions to interpersonal tensions, multiple approaches must also be used. It is a bit like holding up mirrors, catching reflections, and describing an entity from a combination of tangential angles.

In this study, self-reports, behavioral observations, and hypothetical situations were used to try to piece together the ways in which mothers and daughters react when they are upset with each other. Unfortunately, due to time constraints, some of the methods were used in a more superficial manner than desirable. For example, the ratings of behaviors in general were limited to single items for each category of behavior. In addition, only two story completion tasks were used where it would have been preferable to include six story completions. Although each particular approach has several limitations, the combined battery provides insight into mothers' and daughters' reactions to problems in their relationship. More detailed descriptions of each measure are provided in Appendix B.

Mothers' and daughters' response patterns on these measures are reported in the next chapter. Ratings of behaviors in general are presented first, followed by observed behaviors, and then the story completion task. As will be seen, mothers and daughters respond in different ways when they are upset.

■ 10
Mothers' and Daughters' Responses to Tensions

We get along real well. We never argue. We discuss things. We never . . . I don't think we ever had an argument. It's just we talk about it. I feel free to say if I don't approve of something and we talk about it. Sounds like fairyland, don't it? But honestly, sometimes when I have to stop and think, I say she is a perfect daughter. She's never given me one minute's trouble.

—Pauline, 76-year-old mother

Although mothers and daughters do not describe their relationships as plagued with difficulties, they do recognize that tensions arise. Moreover, women had clear ideas about the strategies that are most useful for dealing with these problems. This study looked specifically at aging mothers' and adult daughters' responses to the difficulties that they confront in their relationships. This chapter describes findings from multiple assessments of mothers' and daughters' behaviors when upset with the other party.

SELF-REPORTED BEHAVIOR

The first type of assessment involved self-report data. Mothers and daughters provided information about what they claim to do in response to problems in their relationships. There are two ways to ask for self-reports of behaviors, in terms of what mothers and daughters think they do *most* of the time in their relationships, and in terms of what they remember doing the last time they were upset with the other party. The first approach lends insight into their general goals and beliefs about their own behaviors in the relationship. The latter approach provides mothers and daughters with a specific instance, and this approach should spark clearer and more accurate memories.

Responses to the Self-Report Items

Mothers' and daughters' ratings of their behaviors can be found in Table 10.1. The top part of the Table includes behaviors mothers

TABLE 10.1 Means and Standard Deviations for Self-Reports of of Behaviors

Self-Report	Mother	Daughter
Behaviors in general		
Constructive	2.58	3.50
	(1.38) *	(1.01)
Destructive	1.81	2.29
	(1.02)	(1.01)
Avoidant	2.98	3.02
	(1.30)	(1.28)
Behaviors in a specific situation		
Constructive	3.38	2.85
	(0.79)	(0.72)
Destructive	1.75	1.97
	(0.82)	(0.94)
Avoidant	1.72	1.71
	(0.63)	(0.77)

*Standard deviation shown in parenthesis

and daughters claimed to use in general when irritated with the other party. Some of the earliest questions in the individual interview asked what these women do when they are irritated, hurt, or annoyed with their mother or daughter. Mothers and daughters rated their likelihood of (a) telling the other party what is wrong and what she could do to improve matters, (b) expressing her feelings in a way that could hurt the other party, and (c) avoiding talking about what is wrong using 5-point Likert scales, ranging from almost never to almost always. These ratings might be thought of as (a) constructive and active, (b) destructive (passive or active), and (c) avoidant behaviors.

Mothers and daughters did not claim to use any particular type of behavior almost all of the time. Rather, they reported using constructive and avoidant behaviors some of the time, and destructive behaviors rarely or never. Mothers and daughters claimed that they use destructive behaviors less often than avoidant or constructive behaviors (t (47) = 3.52, $p < .001$ for mothers and t (47) = 2.83, $p < .01$ for daughters). They did not differentiate between their use of constructive and avoidant behaviors, however. In other words, in general, mothers and daughters reported that they avoid telling the other party what is wrong or tell her what is bothering them more often than they say or do things that could hurt her.

When mothers and daughters were asked to rate specific behaviors in a specific situation, they claimed to use constructive behaviors most often. Daughters rated constructive approaches as more true of their behavior than either destructive ($z = 3.35$, $p = .0008$)[1] or avoidant approaches ($z = 6.10$, $p = .0001$). Mothers also rated constructive approaches as more true of their behavior than destructive ($z = 5.76$, $p = .0001$), or avoidant approaches ($z = 6.33$, $p = .0001$) in the specific situation. For example, mothers and daughters reported listening to the other person and trying to find out how she was feeling more than ignoring the problem or yelling at her. They said that it was true or very true that they listened to the other's point of view or tried to find out what she was feeling. By contrast, they indicated that the avoidant and destructive behaviors were not true of their responses in that situation.

In summary, mothers and daughters claimed that they *generally* used destructive approaches less often than avoidant and constructive approaches, but they reported using constructive approaches more than other approaches in the last *specific* tense situation. Such subtle differences regarding self-reported use of constructive behavior in the global ratings and the specific incident may reflect differences in the nuances of the questions. The measure of constructive behaviors in the specific incident included listening to the other person and trying to find out what she was feeling. The global ratings were limited to expressing how one feels oneself. Mothers and daughters may not tell the other person how they feel more often than they ignore problems, but they may listen to the other party or ask questions more often than they brush things under the rug. In addition, the ratings of behaviors in general asked mothers and daughters to think back across many incidents and thus, their responses may reflect what they do on average across situations that are mildly frustrating. By contrast, when asked to think about their behaviors in specific instances, mothers and daughters may have selected situations that were particularly salient, where the conflict came to fruition, and where avoidant behaviors could not be used.

Intergenerational Differences in Self-Reported Behaviors

Mothers and daughters clearly had different ideas about the types of behaviors that they use. Mothers said that they used active behaviors less often than their daughters did in general. They reported that they told their daughters what was bothering them less often than their daughters claimed to do so (t (47) = 4.41, $p < .001$), and that they raised their voices or hurt their daughters' feelings less often than their daughters claimed to do so (t (47) = 2.48, $p < .01$). Mothers and daughters said that they used avoidant behaviors with similar frequency; both parties said they used avoidant behaviors some of the time.

With regard to the specific incident, intergenerational differences emerged only with regard to constructive behaviors. The findings flip-flopped in comparison to reports of general behavior, however. In the specific incident, mothers claimed that they listened to their daughters, asked questions, and told them what was wrong more than their daughters claimed to have done so ($z = 3.17$, $p = .0015$). Mothers and daughters indicated that they used destructive and avoidant behaviors to the same extent in the specific incident.

In summary, mothers and daughters reported that they try to avoid difficulties to a comparable degree in general and in a specific situation. When asked about their general behaviors, daughters saw themselves as more active in positive and negative ways than their mothers did, both using more constructive and more destructive behaviors. When asked about a specific situation, mothers remembered using more constructive behaviors than their daughters did, and there were no differences in use of harmful behaviors.

It is possible that daughters' ambivalence about the relationship colored their memories of their general behavior. They may remember instances where they have been particularly kind and particularly difficult with their mothers, and these memories may shape their reports of their behaviors overall. When asked to recall a specific recent incident, these extreme behaviors may not have been present. Mothers hold a different conception of the relationship than their daughters, and this paints their perceptions of their behaviors. Mothers appear to view their approach to difficulties in a detached way. If mothers have an overall sense of the relationship as strong and enduring, their general memories of tense situations may be sparse and unemotional. In a specific situation, they may view themselves as helpful, upbeat, and kind, again stemming from their more positive bias toward the relationship.

Of course, researchers ask people to report on their own behaviors all the time in studies of interpersonal conflicts and presume that these reports are adequate representations of what took place. Undoubtedly, mothers' and daughters' self-reports include an element of truth and do not solely reflect their beliefs about the relationship. Their behaviors themselves may be shaped by their sense of the relationship. Daughters may actually react with more extreme behaviors and mothers may be more solicitous overall. Indeed, other approaches to assessing behaviors revealed that mothers and daughters have elaborate means of handling the problems that arise in their relationships.

OBSERVED BEHAVIORS

In addition to looking at mothers' and daughters' ideas about their behaviors, the study included outsider's observations of mothers and daughters as they discussed a recent conflict in their relationship. Mothers' and daughters' behaviors during the joint interview were used to gain insights into their ways of dealing with tension-laden issues. Researchers have used discussions of recent conflicts to assess relationship patterns between parents and adolescents (Alexander, 1973; 1996; Prinz, Foster, Kent, & O'Leary, 1979) and marital partners (Bradbury et al., 1995; Gottman, 1979, 1993a, 1993b, 1998; Oggins, Veroff, & Leber, 1993; Pasch, Bradbury, & Davila, 1997; Weiss & Heyman, 1990). In this study, mothers' and daughters' behaviors during discussions about their last tense visit served as a window into their interaction styles pertaining to such difficulties.

There were several reasons for using a discussion about difficulties rather than trying to evoke an actual conflict between the parties. If a mother and daughter usually avoid telling the other party what is bothering them, forcing them into a confrontation would not be a valid context for assessing their behaviors. Moreover, it did not seem ethical to create a conflict between a mother over the age of 70 and her adult daughter without the certainty that that conflict could be resolved.

A mother's or daughter's openness talking about problems in the relationship with an interviewer was taken as a proxy for comfort discussing negative aspects of the relationship. Participants who were more hesitant to discuss relationship tensions during the interviews might feel less comfortable communicating such issues in general. Behaviors were coded from audiotapes of the individual and joint interviews. Videotaping was not used because theorists have suggested that older adults might be self-conscious when discussing problems with adult offspring (Mancini & Blieszner, 1989). Their embarrassment might be compounded if their responses were videotaped. In the present study, the observations of behaviors were intended to be unobtrusive as possible.

Mothers' and Daughters' Openness in Responding to Problems

Table 10.2 includes mothers' and daughters' behaviors from the individual and joint interviews.[2] As was mentioned previously, eight mothers were unable to come up with a time when they were irritated with their daughters when asked to do so alone. Yet, as was mentioned

TABLE 10.2 Proportions of Mothers and Daughters Whose Behaviors Fit Each Observation Code

Behaviors	Mothers	Daughters	Intergenerational differences*
Individual interview			
Direct response	.44	.92	$p = .0010$
Hesitated	.38	.08	
No response	.17	.00	
Joint interview behavior			
Direct response	.44	.68	$p = .0352$
Hesitated	.54	.32	
No response	.00	.00	
Initiated the discussion	.49	.51	Not significant
Asked questions of other	.44	.43	Not significant
Spoke to interviewer	.66	.62	Not significant
Disagreed with other	.25	.17	Not significant
Told what happened	.32	.58	$p = .0050$

*McNemar's test conducted on dichotomous variables. Sign test conducted on ordinal variables.

in chapter 8, all mothers participated in the discussions of problems during the joint interview.

In addition to the simple dichotomy of responding, or not responding women varied in their initial reactions to the questions about tensions. Several women hesitated when they first tried to remember a situation when they had been upset with the other party. These women prefaced their responses with verbal statements such as, "I don't think we ever have difficulties" or "I'm not sure I can remember such an event." Women who fell into this category did manage to remember a tense situation after a slight pause. Mothers hesitated to respond more often than their daughters did in both interviews. All daughters remembered at least one incident when they were been irritated, hurt, or annoyed with their mothers recently, and all but four daughters did so without hesitating during the individual interviews.

During the joint interviews, mothers and daughters behaved differently than they had in their individual interviews. In general, mothers were more open than they had been previously, but daughters were less open in their mothers' presence. In contrast to the individual interviews, all of the mothers joined in conversations during the joint interviews. Mothers were still more likely than their daughters to state explicit difficulties in remembering a situation involving tension; only 44% of mothers responded directly during the joint interview whereas 68% of daughters did so (McNemar's exact $p =$ .0352). It is notable, however, that daughters were more likely to disclaim in their mother's presence, "I can't think of anything can you, Mom?" than they had been when interviewed alone (McNemar's exact $p = .002$, calculated with 1 = responded directly, 2 = did not respond directly). In fact, the individual interviews preceded the joint interviews, so these daughters could have simply relied on their prior responses, but they did not do so. When daughters hesitated to respond, they did not seem to have actual difficulties remembering tensions. Rather, this behavior was associated with ways in which mothers and daughters think about and present their relationships.

For example, mothers did not readily describe problems with their daughters when asked to do so alone. Yet, something about their daughters' presence appeared to catalyze a willingness to join in discussions of difficulties with her. Such behavior seems almost stereotypically motherly. First, these women bragged to an outsider about their offspring. Then, after building greater rapport with the interviewer, the mothers took advantage of the opportunity to proffer advice in their daughters' presence, "Well, you know, Dear, there was the time that you let the children go outside without their hats on . . . "

As with the substance of their responses, mothers' behaviors appeared consistently more positive than their daughters' behaviors across interviews. Mothers disclaimed more in both interviews. Daughters were more open than their mothers in both interview contexts. Yet, in keeping with the more positive tone of the joint interviews in general, daughters appeared more hesitant to bring up negative material in their mothers' presence. Again, in midlife, daughters appear protective of their mothers' welfare and feelings.

Mother/Daughter Interactions

The joint interviews also provided an opportunity to examine mothers' and daughters' interactions during a discussion about their difficulties. On the whole, mothers and daughters were direct and cooperative when talking about their last tense situation. They were equally likely to start the conversation, and equally likely to ask questions of the other person. Once mothers and daughters had selected their last tense situation, however, more daughters than mothers narrated the story behind that situation ($\chi^2 = 12.84$, $df = 1$, $p < .005$). Neither mothers nor daughters engaged in many destructive behaviors. Fewer than a quarter of mothers or daughters disagreed with the other person in a contradictory manner at any point during the discussion.

Mothers' and daughters' indirect communication patterns or avoidant behaviors were more complicated. Many mothers and daughters used disclaimers or referred to positive aspects of the relationship when asked to describe tensions. Such behavior suggests a sense of loyalty to the relationship. In the joint interview, mothers and daughters seemed interested in protecting the other party. Nearly two thirds of mothers and daughters directed distracting questions or comments to the interviewer, rather than speaking with the other party. Such behavior may reflect a bias introduced by conducting research with an investigator present. The practicalities of research with older adults demanded that the interviewer travel to the women's homes, rather than asking them to travel to a study site. Decorum did not allow us to ask older women if a stranger could sit in an another room in their house while they talked with their daughters into a tape recorder and therefore, the interviewer remained in the room while the women held their discussion. Yet, the interviewer's presence does not completely explain these women's behaviors. Mothers and daughters did not add such distracters during the individual interviews. Some theorists have suggested that attempting to draw an outsider into family conflicts is indicative of a poor quality relationship (Bowen, 1978; Scheff, 1995). This did not appear to be the case in this relationship, however. Mothers' and daughters' efforts to include the interviewer appeared to diffuse tension through diversion. In other words, mothers and daughters seemed to want to keep the tone of the discussion low key, and used an available distraction (e.g., the interviewer), as a means of regulating the emotional tone of the situation.

Observed Versus Self-Reported Behaviors

Of particular note are similarities and differences between the observed and the self-reported behaviors. Mothers and daughters generally engaged in constructive behaviors during their discussions. Daughters were slightly more active than mothers were; daughters actually told the story of what had happened. Women rarely showed even mild destructive behavior such as contradictory disagreement. The women generally used constructive behaviors such as those that they had reported.

The most complicated patterns emerged with regard to observations of avoidant behavior. Mothers' behaviors during the interviews suggested that they are not consistently direct and open with regard to tensions in their relationships. Relatively few mothers responded in a forthright manner during the individual interviews, although more mothers joined the discussions in the joint interviews. By contrast, nearly all of the daughters responded directly to questions about problems during the individual interviews, but their behaviors became more avoidant in the joint interviews.

These findings suggest that similarities in mothers' and daughters' self-reports of avoidant behaviors may stem from different underlying causes. Mothers try to avoid difficult issues because they wish to maintain a positive relationship with their daughters, or alternately, because they simply do not perceive problems in the relationship. Their avoidance may reflect their motherly investment in keeping the relationship positive and strong. For daughters, the greater rates of disclaiming in the joint interview suggest they use avoidance to protect their mothers. Daughters recognize problems, they are upset by problems, but by midlife, they do not feel the need to confront their mothers with regard to these problems. On the whole, the observed behaviors were similar, but not identical to the self-reported behaviors.

CORRESPONDENCE BETWEEN INDIVIDUAL AND JOINT RESPONSES

Mothers and daughters who openly communicate their feelings when upset may be more aware of the other party's feelings. When both parties discuss their problems, they may be more likely to remember the same event as their most recent problematic situation. During the individual interviews, mothers and daughters independently described a recent time when they were irritated, hurt, or annoyed with the other party. During the joint interviews, mother/daughter pairs completed the same task. Thus, we can compare their responses across the interview formats to gather a sense of whether mothers and daughters agree that the same situation generated tension.

One third of mothers and daughters described the same situation during the individual interviews. Of course, it is possible that the mothers and daughters who described the same situation in these individual interviews did not communicate directly about the situation, but rather, that the situation was very salient and memorable. Nonetheless, in some way, mothers and daughters who are both upset over the same situation share their emotions in a different way than do mothers and daughters who are upset over different situations.

Correspondence between the individual and the joint interviews constitutes a more persuasive indicator of openness. Mothers and daughters who feel comfortable discussing negative feelings with the other might be more likely to bring up the same issues they had raised during the individual interviews in front of the other person. Mothers and daughters were specifically instructed not to discuss their responses with one another between interviews. Indeed, their discussions during the joint interviews suggested that they had not discussed their individual answers between interviews.

As was already mentioned, 16 sets of mothers and daughters (one-third of dyads) agreed about the last tense situation in their relationship independently during the individual interviews. Yet, only one third of those dyads, or 11% ($n = 5$ dyads) gave that same response during the joint interview. As can be seen in Table 10.3, an additional 7% ($n = 3$) of dyads described situations that corresponded only to the mother's initial response and an additional 19% ($n = 9$) of dyads gave responses that corresponded only to the daughter's initial response (for a total of 29%). The remaining 63% of dyads described situations during the joint interview that did not correspond to either party's initial response. In other words, mothers and daughters were more likely to discuss a new issue than to bring up an issue they had previously discussed during their individual interviews ($\chi^2 = 18.68$, $df = 3$, $p < .0005$).

TABLE 10.3 Correspondence Between Mothers' and Daughters' Responses in Each Interview

	Mothers	Daughters
Individual interviews		
Individual responses the same	.33	.33
Individual responses differ	.67	.67
Joint interview		
Response same as individual	.07	.19
Response same as both individual	.10	.10
Response differs from both individual	.63	.63

Of course, it is possible that this lack of agreement across interviews simply reflects the fact that new problems came up between the interviews and these problems were discussed during the joint interviews. In a follow-up question, the interviewer asked mothers and daughters when the problematic situation had taken place. Mothers and daughters who gave new responses during the joint interview did not report new problems between the two interviews. Rather, the differences in their responses across the two interviews seemed to stem from their desire to protect the other party, to come up with a less upsetting situation, and to work toward compromise, rather than voicing grievances. Of particular note is that few mothers and daughters began the joint interview with the obvious opener, "What did you say in your last interview?"

Thus, mothers' and daughters' observed behavior suggests a mixture of directness and cooperation, marked by efforts to diffuse tensions through disclaimers and speaking to an outsider. The correspondence between their responses is a more tangential indicator of communication. Yet, this indicator, coupled with the more positive tone of the joint responses, suggests that mothers and daughters are careful about what they reveal in the other person's presence.

STORY COMPLETION TASK

One problem with self-report and observation methods lies in the inability to make comparisons across participants. Perhaps some mothers and daughters reported loyally accepting the tense situation because they were thinking about incidents involving unchangeable circumstances. Perhaps other mothers and daughters said that they tried to reconcile things because they felt that the problem could be easily resolved. It is not possible to say whether the former women would respond the same way that the latter did under similar circumstances. A story completion task allows researchers greater control in comparing how individuals think about different types of social problems.

The mothers and daughters in this study completed story stems provided in their questionnaire packets. Each story involved a situation in which an aging mother and an adult daughter have a misunderstanding. Participants described how the characters in the story deal with their dilemma. Under optimal circumstances, a researcher might wish to use six, eight, or ten story stems presented in different orders and controlling for a variety of factors such as the emotional salience of the situation (Acitelli, 1988; Blanchard-Fields et al., 1995). Given the number of tasks mothers and daughters completed in the present study, only two such stories were included. The first stem involved a daughter who intruded upon her mother, whereas the latter stem involved a mother who made demands on her daughter. Each story included both characters' point of view. Mothers and daughters wrote endings in response to the question, "What happened next? . . . " posed at the point in the story when the characters realized that they were irritated. Then, participants were asked to specifically describe how each character felt about the situation after that ending.

The first story involved an adult daughter, Linda, who repeatedly comes to visit her mother, Sarah. Linda is worried about her widowed mother who is still grieving the loss of her husband that took place 2 years previously. Although Linda finds it a hassle to stop in on her mother so often, she feels obligated to do so. On the other hand, Sarah resents her daughter's intrusiveness. Linda arrives unannounced. She uses her mother's things and eats her mother's food while she is there. Linda arrives at the mother's house one afternoon as the mother is ruminating about the situation. Participants were asked to complete the story.

The second story involved a daughter, Alice, who usually takes her mother to the grocery store on her afternoon off work. Her mother, Nancy, looks forward to the shopping trip. This week, Alice is tired. She is facing demands from work and her children and does not want to see her mother. Participants indicated what happened from the moment that Alice picked up the phone to call her mother.

These stories are limited in scope. The mothers in the stories were less healthy and less independent than the women who participated in this study. Yet, such scenarios might become more familiar to these mothers and daughter in the future as the older mother's health declines.

Although most participants completed the first story, nearly one third of mothers did not finish the second story. When asked why they had not completed that story, such mothers usually indicated that it had been a busy week or that they tired of completing questionnaires, rather than they did not resonate with the content of the second story. A few mothers completed the stories while the interviewer was there, and some even dictated their responses to her. In addition to the mothers who did not complete the stories, some mothers personalized their responses writing such things as, "My daughter would never come over announced" or "I do my own shopping without her." Such responses were difficult to use as assessments of behavior, and were thus excluded. Two independent raters coded the story completions with kappa's ranging from .88 to .95.

Behaviors in the Story Completion Task

As can be seen in Table 10.4, the majority of mothers and daughters described Linda and Sarah as at least partially communicating about their problems. Mothers and daughters alike indicated that when Linda arrived at Sarah's house, Sarah found a way of either directly expressing her dislike of Linda's intrusiveness or indirectly bringing the topic around to that subject. Yet, a third of mothers wrote story completions in which the characters did not discuss the problem at hand, and only half of participants had Sarah and Linda successfully resolve the situation.

A somewhat different pattern emerged with regard to the second story stem in which Alice did not wish to take her mother, Esther, on their weekly shopping trip. Most mothers and daughters had the characters at least partially discuss the situation. In this case,

TABLE 10.4 Proportions of Mothers and Daughters Whose Story Completions Fit Each Code

	Mothers	Daughters	McNemar's exact p
Characters' communication style			
Characters communicated openly	.37	.52	$p = .0446$
Characters only partially communicated	.32	.34	
Characters did not communicate	.32	.14	
Extraneous information included	.31	.27	$p = .8145$
Problem resolved	.52	.69	$p = .0963$

daughters wrote story completions in which Alice skirted around the key issue or Esther agreed to solutions that did not fully satisfy her. A third of daughters wrote stories in which Alice and Esther never discussed Alice's need for time to herself because Alice felt too guilty or the mother pushed too hard for the weekly shopping trip.

Mothers and daughters who wrote stories in which characters communicated openly were more likely to have the characters resolve their problems ($\chi^2 = 6.35$, $df = 40$, $p < .001$, for mothers, $\chi^2 = 24.70$, $df = 43$, $p < .001$, for daughters). Thus, the situations with partial or no communication often ended with no resolution to the problem. This is striking given that a story completion task with an unresolved problem implicitly requests a resolution. It was as though some mothers and daughters could not even imagine a way in which the characters might resolve their problems.

In some cases, participants created new information to help pull together a satisfactory ending to the story. In one story completion, Sarah (the mother in the first story) took off on a trip to Tahiti with a new lover, thus avoiding the problem of her daughter's frequent visits. In the second story, Alice's sister Terri suddenly appeared to take Mom shopping (there is no sister in the story stem) and offered that her own grown children would take over for Alice from now on. In yet another story completion, Alice's husband took the afternoon off and did all the shopping, cooked dinner, and ran Alice a hot bubble bath! Fantasies abounded. Even mothers and daughters who were more subtle sometimes introduced neighbors and friends to resolve problems so as not to leave the mother and daughter characters alone to deal with their difficulties.

In fact, the use of extraneous characters and situations appeared to parallel the observed behaviors during the joint interviews, when participants spoke to the interviewer. These new characters and situations seemed to tone down the problem in the initial stories and to offer the characters a means of feeling connected or empowered outside of their own relationship. Half of the mothers invented new characters to solve the problem in the second story, where Linda felt her mother was too demanding. In fact, many of these mothers wrote story completions that resolved the problem by taking it out of the daughter's hands and putting it back in the mother's (e.g., she decided to move to a retirement center where they did the shopping for her and her daughter visited each weekend). These stories again parallel other aspects of the mother/daughter relationship observed in this study. These mothers were determined to bring the stories back around to a more positive view of the relationship.

Characters' Feelings About the Situation

Table 10.5 shows participants' descriptions of the characters' feelings about the situation. In general, mothers and daughters alike felt that the characters would both feel satisfied with the way things turned out in the first story. In some cases, participants portrayed Linda as feeling somewhat taken aback or offended that her mother did not want her to visit so often. Later, however, Linda would be glad that her mother did not need her as much as she had thought (thus, Linda felt ambivalent). Few participants thought either character would be upset about the way things ended in the first story.

The second story showed a slightly different pattern. Again, few participants indicated that the characters would be upset in the end, but more mothers felt that the characters would experience some sort of negative feelings about the situation than had been the case in the first story. For mothers, the mother character, Esther, experienced disappointment that she could not see her daughter, Alice,

TABLE 10.5 Proportions of Story Completions Including Characters' Positive and Negative Affect

	Mothers	Daughters
Story completion #1: Linda comes to visit too often		
Sarah/mother character's affect		
Positive	.76	.62
Ambivalent	.15	.26
Negative	.10	.12
Linda/daughter character's affect		
Positive	.58	.35
Ambivalent	.26	.49
Negative	.16	.16
Story #2: Alice cannot take Esther shopping		
Esther/mother character's affect		
Positive	.24	.46
Ambivalent	.55	.29
Negative	.21	.25
Alice/daughter character's affect		
Positive	.34	.50
Ambivalent	.45	.21
Negative	.21	.29

more often, but was relieved that Alice would be getting more rest. Mothers thought Alice would regret her inability to see her mother as often, but would also feel good about her mother's acceptance of the situation.

Daughters described characters who felt worse about the situation in the second story than in the first story. The second story, of course, involved a dilemma in which the daughter does not want to meet the mother's needs. Alice is too tired and wants time to rest. The first story involved a daughter who was doing more than the mother needed. Again, the findings of the story completion parallel other findings in the study. It seems that exclusion (e.g., Alice's not wanting to be with her mother) is more tension-laden than intrusion (e.g., Linda's showing up too often).

Daughters portrayed the characters as having different feelings about the way things turned out depending upon the degree of communication in which they engaged over the dilemma. If characters communicated openly, daughters thought the mother character would feel better in the end ($\chi^2 = 21.47$, $p < .005$). Daughters wrote stories in which daughter characters felt ambivalent or lousy if they talked about the situation openly ($\chi^2 = 9.22$, $p < .06$). Mothers did not differentiate the characters' feelings based on how much they communicated.

In summary, mothers' and daughters' story completions varied depending upon the type of problem involved. It was easier to think about open conversations when the situation involved an overly solicitous daughter. In the situation involving a daughter who felt there were too many demands, participants were less likely to portray open conversations involving both parties. The daughters who participated in this study portrayed open communication as threatening to daughters in hypothetical situations, despite the fact that they themselves reported using it and also engaged in discussion of problems readily in both interviews. It is unclear why daughters wrote the types of endings that they did. The daughters' endings portrayed mothers who grew angry when their daughters asserted themselves and portrayed daughters who felt hurt in such situations. Daughters' beliefs about their right to tell their mothers how they feel and their beliefs about their mothers' reactions to such conversations warrant further investigation.

CONCLUSIONS

This study included multiple ways of examining mothers' and daughters' behaviors when they are annoyed with the other party. Of course, there are many other approaches to assessing mothers' and daughters' responses to annoyance that were not used in this study. For example, diary studies where individuals record feelings over the past day or "beeper" studies where they are paged at random intervals might be used to obtain more naturalistic data about feelings and behaviors. One dilemma with using such approaches is that the phenomena of interest appear to occur as infrequently as once a week or once a month. Thus, researchers might be required to accumulate excessive data in order to get a sufficient sample of aggravations and reactions. The use of event sampling (sometimes referred to as Rochester Diaries), in which participants record how they behaved when upset with the other party might allow researchers to sample the particular issue of interest, tensions between mothers and daughters. Yet, this approach also presents peculiar methodological difficulties. Asking women to record tensions only when they occur might be like saying, "Don't think of a pink elephant." If mothers and daughters are told the focus of the research, they might alter their behaviors so that these events occur more or less frequently. Given this bind, naturalistic time sampling approaches were not used here.

The multiple methods used in this study revealed that mothers and daughters claim to, and appear to engage in positive efforts to resolve difficulties quickly, while also protecting the other party. In some cases, mothers and daughters seemed to be resigned to the other party's foibles, and, in those cases, attempts to communicate about the problem may be perceived as futile. Mothers and daughters did report avoiding problems some of the time, and their behaviors during the joint interviews suggest that these reports are accurate. Few mother/daughter pairs discussed the same issue during the individual and the joint interviews. Moreover, mothers and daughters introduced questions for the interviewer in a manner that suggested they were trying to avoid tensions in their relationship. Their story completions showed a similar pattern, with new characters and situations introduced to diffuse the frustrations the mother and daughter characters faced.

Yet, recurrent intergenerational differences surfaced in mothers' and daughters' behaviors. Mothers were consistently positive in their self-reports, observed behaviors, and perceptions of their daughters' behaviors. Daughters' behaviors were more variable. They reported using active approaches to deal with problems, and appeared to be more active in the discussions than their mothers were. Yet, daughters also seemed protective of their mothers. Their story completions suggested ambivalence about expressing their negative feelings toward their mothers, particularly when those feelings pertained to a mother's need for love and attention from a middle-aged daughter.

NOTES

[1]Analyses involved the sign test, a nonparametric procedure comparing differences in ranked or ordinal data between matched pairs.

The sign test counts the positive and negative differences between each pair of variables, ignoring zero differences (Conover, 1980). As with McNemar's Test, it is possible to calculate the exact probability using the binominal distribution, rather than the chi square approximation, for instances where fewer than 25 differences are observed.

[2]Two independent raters coded the behaviors from the audiotapes. Inter-rater reliability was estimated using Cohen's kappa, which takes into account the likelihood of agreement by chance, kappa = .72 to .99 for different behaviors.

■ 11
Once a Mother, Always a Mother

There are times when she will make what my sisters and I refer to as "mother noises." And I sometimes take it as her criticizing me and I say, "Now, mother why are you making me feel bad? You make me feel like a child not like a 43-year-old adult." She can reduce me to feeling like a child even for just a minute. Then, you know, it might go back and forth on that. As I mentioned earlier, it passes and we don't hold a grudge.

—Lauren, 43-year-old daughter

The mother/daughter relationship begins when the daughter is born and ends when the mother dies. In the latter years of this relationship, daughters enter midlife and mothers enter old age, but mothers remain motherly and daughters remain filial. At the same time, each woman encounters changes that set a new tone for their relationship. The findings from this study suggest that mother/daughter ties in late life emerge from a relationship with a long history, but patterns are altered by the daughter's increased solicitude for the mother and the mother's increased investment in the family that will outlive her.

Aging mothers continue to perform the role they have always performed. They offer their daughters advice, they worry about their grandchildren, and they admire their daughters' achievements. Mothers view their daughters as part of a larger family, a family in which they, as mothers, are pivotal members. Daughters appreciate their mothers as mothers, even in later life. At the same time, daughters have a sense of themselves and their own families that is distinct and separate. They experience mixed emotions about this relationship. They resent their mother's efforts to be motherly, yet woe the day when she is no longer able to do so. As they enter late life, mothers hold to the past and may not keep pace with the changes their daughters are experiencing. Daughters gaze into the future and become preoccupied with what is to come, rather than what is occurring in the present.

The emotional patterns of the mother/daughter tie reflect this mosaic of continuity and change. Although mothers and daughters reported positive feelings about their relationships and one another, they also were upset with one another from time to time. Generational status, perceptions of tensions, the manner in which mothers and daughters communicate, and their larger family context appear to be related to feelings for the relationship and individual well-being itself. These issues are discussed in this chapter.

THE SOCIAL CONTEXT OF THE RELATIONSHIP

Mothers and daughters alike reported having many friends and relatives, but there were differences in the priority they attributed to their relationship. Mothers tended to view their relationships with their daughters within a larger social framework. Mothers included other family members in reports of the positive and negative interactions they had with their daughters. Daughters tended to focus less on outside individuals, and to center on the mother/daughter relationship itself when discussing its virtues and problems. For mothers, the relationship with the daughter appeared to be part of a larger whole. Indeed, a mother's rating of her daughter's importance was directly related to the size of the mother's family. If a mother had four children, she rated her daughter as being among the top six important people in her life rather than the top three people in her life. If the daughter was an only child, the mother rated her as the most important person in her life. For daughters, the relationship appeared to be an entity unto itself. Daughters did not base their ratings of their mothers' importance on the availability of other family members.

Differences in mothers' and daughters' value for their relationship are related to differences in their conception of the other party. Mothers viewed the daughter as "one of the kids." Mothers did not seem to distinguish their relationships with their daughters from other relationships. They described their daughters in the context of a larger kinship network. By contrast, daughters rated their husbands or partners as the most salient and important individuals in their lives. Daughters related to their mothers on an individual basis. They did not refer to other family members when they talked about their mothers. Daughters seemed to have a sense of their relationship as one that was dyadic and distinct. Mothers seemed to have a sense of their relationship as one that was part of a larger family.

This pattern was found with regard to mothers' and daughters' choices of whom they get along with best and whom they like to speak to when upset. Mothers generally preferred their offspring, and particularly their daughters for these functions. Mothers who did not name the target daughter as their confidant often named a different offspring as their confidant. Daughters preferred to confide in their spouses or partners. Their mothers and their children were not as central when it came to such emotional support.

These generational differences in the importance of the relationship may stem from differences in stage of life. The mothers were more likely to be widowed while their daughters were more likely to be married or to have lovers. Yet, differences in mothers' and daughters' relationship status do not fully account for mothers' preferences for their children. Only one third of those mothers who had a husband selected him as the person they get along with best or feel free to speak to when upset. Even mothers who had spouses tended to select their daughters as confidants. Nor did a mother's preference for her daughter appear to stem from an impoverished social network. Mothers and daughters alike listed a number of friends when they were asked to name important people in their lives. Mothers prefer their daughters because they prefer their daughters, not because they have no other choice.

Cohort differences in men's communication styles may also help account for daughters' selection of their husband as a confidant.

Middle-aged daughters are more likely to have husbands who freely discuss personal issues than are their mothers. Older men were socialized during a period when men were not encouraged to share emotional concerns. Moreover, marital ties are viewed as distinct partnerships today. When the older mothers and their husbands were growing up, marriages were less insular and more embedded in the context of other family ties. Yet, the generational differences observed here cannot be attributed solely to the type of marriage mothers and daughters have. Rather, these differences reflect complicated aspects of the aging mother and adult daughter relationship.

This generational disparity is not simply an extension of parents' investment in their offspring. Bengtson and Kuypers (1971) posited that the older generation views the younger generation as its legacy, and, thus, has a great investment in this relationship. The younger generation, on the other hand, is concerned with establishing independence, setting their own agenda, and viewing themselves as distinct from the older generation. As will be discussed, the situation described here involves a more complicated pattern. If the older generation were simply more invested in the younger generation, daughters would have listed their own offspring as the individuals they get along with best or feel most free to speak their minds to when upset. They tended to focus on their husbands instead.

The difference in salience of the daughter to the mother and the mother to the daughter reflects more fundamental differences in their conceptions of their relationship and their life contexts. Mothers view the relationship as embedded in the context of a larger family in which they, the mothers, retain a central role. Daughters view this relationship as more constricted and dyadic, interpreting their mothers' actions as targeted at them alone. In addition, as mothers age, their remaining ties to family are particularly important (Troll, 1988). Thus, aging mothers value their daughters more than their daughters value them, but they do so in a manner that places these daughters in the context of a larger array of meaningful social ties.

Outside Individuals in the Pleasant and Unpleasant Visits

Mothers and daughters think about their relationships in different ways. For mothers, pleasant and unpleasant visits with their daughters revolved around a larger constellation of family ties. Daughters tended to find visits with their mothers alone more emotionally salient than visits involving other family members. When mothers think about their daughters, they seem to consider other friends and relatives, as well. When daughters think about their mothers, they seem to think about their mothers.

Two thirds of the mothers described problems that focused on people in addition to the daughter whereas only one third of daughters did so. Mothers were also likely to refer to other family members when they talked about enjoyable visits with their daughters. Although some daughters included other family members in their descriptions of enjoyable visits, they did not consistently refer to outsiders in their discussions of their relationships with their mothers. Rather, the inclusion of other people in the daughters' descriptions of enjoyable visits appears to stem from ambivalence toward their mothers, as will be discussed in the next section.

Enjoyable Visits

Qualitative differences were found in discussions of enjoyable visits. When daughters brought up negative material while talking about the last time they had had an enjoyable visit with their mother, they focused on the mother. Daughters commented that they had enjoyed the visit because their mother had had more energy than usual or had not complained. When mothers included something negative in their discussion of enjoyable visits, these negative aspects centered on having the daughter help them through a hard experience. Mothers brought up negative issues pertaining to deaths of husbands and friends, sick children, difficult decisions. Their positive feelings did not center on the absence of one of the daughter's negative attributes, but were based simply on being together during an unavoidable and difficult experience. Again, for mothers, daughters were embedded in a large context. The daughter's presence was a positive, the situation was a negative. For daughters, the mother is the repository of emotion. When daughters talked about enjoying a visit because something negative was absent, they focused specifically on their mothers. The situation was positive because something negative about the mother was absent.

Mothers' consistent inclusion of outsiders in their relationships with their daughters may stem from their sense of themselves as a matriarch in this larger family. Mothers conceive of an entire family unit, of which the target daughter is a component. Discussions about the daughter by definition include discussion of other family members—the two units are inseparable. At the same time, the fact that daughters do not refer to other family members also reflects the idea that the mother plays a maternal role in her life, rather than simply the role of family member at large. Mothers hold a unique position in their daughters' lives. Mothers may not be as salient to daughters as daughters are to mothers, but daughters view their relationship with their mothers as important. When daughters answered questions about tense and enjoyable visits with their mothers, they offer focused responses, often presenting situations in which the mother still held the psychological role of parent. The filial role and the ambivalence accompanying it will be discussed in the next section

Understanding the aging mother's behavior in terms of her position as head of the family further undermines assumptions about role reversals in later life. As was discussed in the fourth chapter, the idea that daughters become mothers to their aging mothers has been largely discredited in recent years (Brody, 1990; Fingerman, 1997b; Seltzer, 1990). Furthermore, the findings presented here indicate that among well elderly, the role of "mother" dictates the way in which older mothers frame their relationships with offspring. Generational differences throughout this study revolved around the mother's perceptions of herself as chief executive of a family and the daughter's ambivalence toward that conception of the relationship.

Problematic Visits

Mothers' tendency to perceive this relationship in terms of a larger family context was particularly notable in the types of visits they described as enjoyable and as disagreeable. Even when mothers and daughters talked about the same types of problems, they did so in different ways. For example, when mothers talked about feeling excluded by their daughters, mothers referred to times when they felt left out of a family gathering, rather than a dyadic interaction.

Daughters talked about feeling like their mothers were inaccessible. For example, Allison, the daughter who was mentioned in chapter 5, felt excluded because her mother invited her over and then watched television while she was there. Bea, the mother who felt excluded by her daughter Wendy, was upset that Wendy would not allow her children to attend Mass with her mother. Bea was upset about being excluded from Wendy's family. Allison was upset about being excluded from her mother's attention.

Daughters As Segue to Other Relationships

The mothers' tendency to include outsiders in their scenarios, such as their daughters' children and spouses, parallel findings reported in the clinical literature. Bromberg (1987) found that middle-aged daughters attending a group therapy program for mothers and daughters reported that their mothers did not perceive them as individuals, but merely as the mothers of grandchildren. A comparable process may explain the findings in this study, but the mothers' conceptions of their daughters are more complicated than perceiving them simply as mothers of grandchildren. The mothers in this study did not constrain themselves to their daughters' children, rather, these mothers introduced their own spouses, their daughters' spouses, and their other offspring into their discussions. The mothers may not treat the daughters as isolated individuals, but nor are they merely mothers of grandchildren. The mothers view their daughters as segue to other relationships. The daughter is simultaneously an adult woman, one's own daughter, a father's daughter, a confidant, a sibling to other offspring, a little girl, the wife of a son-in-law, and a mother of grandchildren.

To the daughter, however, the mother is cast in a single social role. Daughters' ratings of their mothers' salience were not related to the daughters' social networks or familial structure. Rather, these ratings were more likely to be related to their mothers' social networks, as well. To the daughters, mothers remain mothers. However, daughters experience considerable ambivalence with regard to that constrained relationship.

POSITIVE AND NEGATIVE FEELINGS FOR THE RELATIONSHIP

In general, daughters had more negative feelings and perceived more problems in the relationship than did mothers. Of course, daughters also reported positive feelings for their mothers, rendering the portrait of the relationship complex. When asked to discuss interpersonal tension alone, all daughters responded, while over one third of the mothers either hesitated or did not respond. All daughters had some complaint, big or small, with their mothers. In addition, daughters were annoyed with their mothers in general. Whereas more mothers cited their daughters as preferred confidants, more daughters cited their mothers as the person who annoyed them most.

It is possible that mothers were merely conforming to social desirability demands by not discussing their daughters' faults with an interviewer. Mothers may feel an obligation to defend their daughters, regardless of their actual feelings. Yet, the generational differences in reports of tension are more complicated than a simple matter of mothers presenting themselves in the best light. Mothers were willing to join in conversations about problems during the joint interviews. Moreover, mothers were more effusive in their praise of the relationship than were daughters. Mothers appear to have more positive feelings for the relationship, while daughters appear to have more complex or ambivalent feelings.

Negative Aspects Embedded in the Relationship

Mothers and daughters viewed the negative aspects of their relationship in different ways. Daughters saw interpersonal tensions as embedded in the rhythm of the relationship itself. They were as likely to feel upset by a visit with their mothers as they were to feel happy with such a visit. Mothers viewed tensions as a foreign element. Furthermore, daughters claimed that the tense situation discussed during the joint interview was typical of other situations and was likely to recur. When mothers discussed a problem, they framed it as an issue that arises only as an anomaly. Even when mothers discussed negative visits they rated those visits as rare events that arose, as one mother put it, "once in a blue moon."

Daughters' reports of the frequency of tensions were related to their reports of the frequency of contact with their mothers. In other words, daughters who reported having the most frequent contact with their mothers were also the ones who reported having the most frequent experiences of tension. Negative encounters were a proportional aspect of the relationship. For daughters, negative visits are interwoven in the fabric that ties them to their mothers. The same was true for the daughters' positive visits. Negative events are so intrinsically linked to the daughters' concepts of the relationship, that nearly one third of the daughters cited the absence of their mothers' negative attributes as what made their enjoyable visit so pleasant. Daughters struggle in their efforts not to think about what annoys them. Indeed, daughters experience some sort of emotional reaction to their mothers, positive or negative, when they visit. Mothers' experience of tensions in the relationship did not involve an association with frequency of contact. Mothers basically enjoy their daughters.

Positive Feelings for the Relationship

Mothers were almost uniformly positive about their ties to their daughters. Mothers held their daughters' virtues in such high regard that they spontaneously praised their daughters when asked to discuss the last time they felt irritated or annoyed during a visit. Daughters also felt affection for their mothers, but mothers felt a stronger affinity for the relationship than did their daughters. The generational differences in positive feelings were more attenuated than the generational differences with regard to negative feelings.

There were few generational differences in mothers' and daughters' descriptions of enjoyable visits. Mothers and daughters alike derived pleasure from being with the other party, long conversations, and special outings. By midlife, daughters experience the same types of positive feelings for their mothers that their mothers feel for them. Generational differences appear to stem from a difference in the balance of negative feelings rather than the strength of positive feelings for this tie. Although mothers could acknowledge problems in their relationships with their daughters, they perceived their relationships as characteristically positive. By contrast, daughters perceived both positive and negative feelings as intrinsic to their relationship.

INTERPERSONAL TENSIONS

As was suggested throughout this book, the tensions mothers and daughters experience tell us a great deal about their relationships. There was variability in the types of problems that mothers and daughters described. Moreover, different types of problems had different consequences for the relationship. In general, when mothers and daughters felt intruded upon or excluded, their evaluations of the relationship on the whole were lower. By contrast, when mothers and daughters viewed the problem in terms of the other individual's unchangeable faults, they were more satisfied with their relationships.

Intrusion and Exclusion

This is not the first study to find that mothers and daughters struggle to define the parameters of their relationship in later life (e.g., Cohler, 1983, 1988; Talbott, 1990). It is interesting to note, however, that mothers and daughters in this study had different perspectives on problems arising from this issue. Daughters felt intruded upon in this relationship to a greater extent than did mothers. Furthermore, daughters tended to describe situations in which their mothers were critical or demanding. Mothers who accused their daughters of being intrusive tended to describe ways in which their daughters were overly solicitous. While both the mother and daughter experienced intrusion as infantalization, there was a qualitative distinction in their perceptions. Mothers described situations involving the daughters' concern. Although these mothers felt intruded upon, they did not cast the intruder as possessing malicious intent. Daughters experienced the intruder as oppressive, pushy, and domineering.

The slight variations in daughters' ratings of positive feelings for the relationship may be partially explained by variations in the types of problems that they perceived. Daughters who described a situation when their mother had been intrusive felt worse about themselves and their ties to their mothers. Their mothers also tended to feel worse about the relationship. It is possible that mothers are critical of their daughters and make demands upon them because they wish to change them. Their intrusiveness may be a misguided attempt to improve the relationship. Indeed, daughters who felt intruded upon often had mothers who felt excluded. There may be a dyadic pattern in which mothers and daughters get trapped in a dissatisfying relationship and cope with these feelings in ways that are harmful to both parties.

Mothers who felt intruded upon did not feel worse about their relationships with their daughters, but mothers who felt excluded seemed to fare poorly. Indeed, these mothers' descriptions of their relationships with their daughters were qualitatively different from other mothers' descriptions of their relationships. Mothers who felt excluded reported feelings of confusion, betrayal, disappointment, and isolation. In summary, mothers and daughters who described violations of the boundaries of the relationship were likely to feel worse about their relationships and themselves.

Habits and Traits

Mothers and daughters were equally likely to talk about irritations stemming from the other's habits or traits. Moreover, these reports were associated with strong regard for the relationship. When daughters described their mothers' faults as the root of tensions, both parties felt better about the relationships. Daughters who complain about their mothers' attributes may, paradoxically, accept their mothers as people to a greater extent than do daughters who complain about other issues. Daughters who discussed their mothers' habits showed an ability to discuss what they dislike about their mothers nonjudgmentally. They did not feel that they were under personal assault. The distinction may be one between thinking, "Here is what she did to me," versus, "Well, we all have our faults."

The daughters' tendency to view problems in terms of their mothers' faults also appears to reflect a dyadic pattern. Daughters who considered their mothers' attributes the source of tension were more likely to have mothers who could not remember tensions. These mothers and daughters may have better relationships. Their responses may stem from the fact that both mother and daughter find it difficult to remember a specific negative interaction between them. Of course, only six mother/daughter pairs fit the pattern where the mother denied tension and the daughter discussed the mother's habits. As such, further investigation is necessary with larger samples to understand more fully what happens in these relationships that allows such good feelings to arise.

Of course, all of these data stem from self-reports. Mothers and daughters who are willing to describe problems with intrusive relatives may simply be more willing to admit that they perceive those relationships negatively. Mothers and daughters who optimistically frame their partners' behaviors in terms of unchangeable faults may optimistically rate their relationships more highly. The actual relationships might not be as distinct as they appear to be. Yet, the patterns of results across this study appear to be more complicated than this explanation allows. In the next section, mothers' and daughters' behaviors are discussed.

COMMUNICATION STYLES

The generational and contextual differences in reported and observed communication styles in this study reveal a complex pattern. In general, mothers and daughters relied on constructive ways of communicating their feelings. Mothers and daughters shared a tendency to contextualize or digress from their discussions of tension throughout the study. Daughters, in particular, appeared to avoid expressing their sentiments to their mothers. On the whole, mothers may experience less tension than do daughters, but when they experience tension, they let their daughters know. Daughters stop and start in their communication of tension, speaking more openly than their mothers do, and yet, experiencing more tension than they discuss in her presence.

Self-Reported Communication Styles

Mothers and daughters seemed to have different ideas about what it means to communicate in different ways. Both generations reported engaging in communication that might be viewed as supportive. They claimed that they listened to the other's point of view or asked how she was feeling during the tense situation, and that these behaviors were also characteristic of the other party. Their observed behaviors were similar, but not identical to their self-reports.

There may be generational differences in claiming one does not openly discuss negative feelings about the other party. For mothers, not communicating seems to be linked to having no such tension to communicate. For daughters, not communicating seems to be linked to a desire to protect themselves, their mothers, and the relationship, rather than a reflection of their true underlying feelings.

Observed Behaviors

Mothers and daughters took indirect routes when journeying toward delicate topics in their relationship. In the individual and joint interviews, mothers and daughters introduced material that contextualized or distracted from their discussions of negative material. Mothers used praise to couch their negative feelings. For example, Mary who was described in chapter 5, discussed her irritation with her daughter's spending habits in positive terms, "Jean is such a giving person. She spends too much money on other people . . . "

Daughters introduced their mother's aging in a like manner, as a means of excusing their own negative feelings. By discussing the fact that their mothers were growing older, daughters attributed their mothers' faults to events beyond their mothers' control. For example, Janet apologized for her frustration with her mother, "She's getting older now and she's not as energetic as she used to be. She wasn't always like that . . . " Although mothers were more likely to praise their daughters and daughters were more likely to refer to their mother's aging in their descriptions of tensions, mothers and daughters alike used such issues to contextualize tensions in their relationships.

Joint Interview Behaviors

Mothers' and daughters' behaviors during the joint interviews revealed patterns of cooperation and engagement. Mothers and daughters tended to avoid confrontation. They asked one another questions, drew one another into the discussion, and listened attentively. They rarely rejected a comment made by the other.

There were methodological difficulties in the joint interviews stemming from the intricacies of conducting interviews in the women's homes. The interviewer remained in the room with the mother/daughter during their joint interviews. It would have been awkward for the interviewer to recluse herself to another room in these older women's homes. In over two thirds of the dyads, mothers or daughters turned to the interviewer with distracting questions or comments during their joint interviews. Some mothers or daughters were so persistent in their deviations that the interviewers responded to their comments, rather than maintaining silence or making some comment such as, "It's up to the two of you . . . " as dictated by the research protocol. This methodological difficulty is notable, because interviewers did not deviate from dictated silences or the protocol at any other point in the research battery. Neither mothers nor daughters appeared comfortable dealing with negative material in the others' presence. Their ability to include the interviewer in the discussion may be indicative of a conflict style not directly assessed in this study, namely, that of using outsiders to diffuse interpersonal tensions.

Such a pattern of communication would be in keeping with the mothers' treatment of the daughter as part of a larger family network. The inclusion of family members in discussion of tension might be explored in subsequent research on mother/daughter relationships across the life span. It is possible that including outsiders is not a tendency limited to later life relationships, but rather is an aspect of communication between mothers and daughters, and women in general, across the life span.

As will be discussed, the discomfort experienced by daughters when discussing tension during the joint interviews was a change from the ease with which they discussed negative aspects of the relationship individually. During the individual interviews, every daughter was able to come with a time when their mother had annoyed her. Daughters became less direct in their communication of interpersonal tension in their mothers' presence.

Avoidance of Communication

Mothers' and daughters' avoidant behaviors reveal unique insights into the nature of their relationships. Mothers and daughters reported that they rarely engaged in avoidant behaviors, but their observed behaviors indicated that they work hard to avoid confrontations. Whereas avoidant behavior has generally been considered the "wrong way" to handle relationship tensions, these behaviors seemed to be an effective strategy for mothers and daughters in this study. Contrary to ideas about conflict reported elsewhere (Lerner, 1985), mothers and daughters who used avoidant behaviors felt good about their relationships and about themselves. At the same time, there were differences in mothers' and daughters' use of such communication styles.

On the whole, daughters communicated their negative feelings more directly than their mothers did. Different uses of avoidance may stem from differences in feelings for the relationship. As was mentioned previously, daughters viewed tension as more integral to the relationship. Mothers held a diffusely positive view of their relationships with their daughters.

Although mothers might appear avoidant, their hesitation might result from an actual inability to remember something negative about the relationship. For example, mothers were less hesitant in the joint interview than they had been in the individual interview. This shift in behavior might be explained in two ways: (a) It was easier to think of an event in response to a question one has been asked in the previous 2 weeks, or (b) something about the daughter's presence contributed to ease of discussing interpersonal tensions. In other words, when mothers claim they cannot think of anything disagreeable about their daughters, their response might be genuine. They literally may not remember anything upsetting. With appropriate memory cues, they may readily come up with something irritating the daughter has done, be it ever so minor. Mothers' avoidant behaviors may not be avoidance at all, but rather, may be related to their overall positive beliefs about their relationships with their daughters.

When mothers had something negative to say about their daughters, they seemed to say it. Mothers' observed hesitation was not related to self-reported avoidance. Those mothers who did not provide an answer to the question about tensions during the individual interview claimed to use avoidance less often than those mothers who supplied an answer. Moreover, the nine mothers who could not come up with a tense situation during the individual interviews joined in the discussion about tensions during the joint interviews; some of these mothers even supplied the incident that mother and daughter discussed. These mothers reported that they rarely used destructive behaviors, but rather, that they used direct, constructive behaviors when upset with their daughters. They claimed that if they were upset with their daughters they told them, listened to them, and sought to resolve the problem. By their own reports, these mothers' failure to report an incident does not reflect a tendency to avoid discussing things that bother them. Rather, these mothers simply do not get annoyed with their daughters.

Daughters' use of avoidance appears to be more complicated and to reflect dynamics of their relationships with their mothers. Many daughters became more hesitant in their mothers' presence than they had been when they were interviewed alone. Yet, daughters' discourse about tensions still appeared to be more direct than their mothers' discourse. During the joint interviews, daughters were more likely to narrate the story of what happened. Of course, the events mothers and daughters selected tended to pertain to the daughter's life. Therefore, daughters may have provided information about the situation because they knew more about it than their mothers did. Nonetheless, differences in communication behaviors may reflect global differences in the relationship. Daughters' hesitation seems to stems from a complicated set of beliefs about the need to mask negative feelings and to protect their mothers. As their mothers approach the end of life, daughters shift away from confrontations that might have marred their relationship previously.

Avoidance: Well-Being

Although mothers and daughters did not report a preference for avoidant approaches to deal with their problems, their self-reported and observed use of avoidance were associated with their regard for the relationship and their emotional health. Mothers who hesitated to discuss problems during the individual interviews rated their relationships more highly and felt better about themselves. Their daughters also rated their relationships more highly. This paints a portrait of a mother who is globally positive about her tie to her daughter. She has difficulty thinking of negative events in her relationship with her daughter, feels good about the positive aspects of their relationship, believes her daughter feels strong regard for her, and reports being in fine spirits herself.

The implications of daughters' behaviors are more complicated. For daughters, well-being measures were associated with degree of avoidance, but in varying ways. Self-reported avoidance was related to depressed mood. Daughters who claimed to be more avoidant also reported that they were more depressed. By contrast, observed hesitation in the joint interview was related to lower depressed mood and higher perceptions of the mother's regard for them. In other words, daughters who claimed to hesitate generally felt worse, while daughters who actually did hesitate seemed to fare better! This pattern suggests that the meaning of daughters' avoidance in these two contexts is different.

Daughters generally became less direct in their discussion of problems in the relationship when asked to talk about these aspects in the mothers' presence. Their hesitation in this context appears to have a positive impact on the relationship. This lack of openness during the joint interviews may be part of a "show" put on for their mothers. Daughters who feign that there are no problems in the tie may be protecting their mothers. Such daughters do not wish to disillusion their mothers by announcing the difficulties they see with the relationship in a forthright manner. Daughters may avoid telling their mothers when they feel hurt, simply to avoid hurting their mothers.

When daughters report that they used indirect communication, their reasons for doing so may differ from the daughters who actually appeared more hesitant in the joint interviews. When daughters claim that they are being avoidant, they may do so because they do not feel that their mothers listen to them or understand them. Given mothers' and daughters' tendency to use nonconfrontational and avoidant communication when upset with the other, we have more to learn about how their communication fits into the context of the relationship.

CONCLUSIONS

Mothers and daughters love one another a great deal, but they come to their relationships with different perspectives. Even in late life, those perspectives remain distinct. While mothers generally felt more positive about their relationships with their daughters than daughters did, the findings in this study reveal a complicated portrait of emotions. The daughters were ambivalent about their mothers. They described negative feelings, yet also reported positive feelings for their mothers.

Mothers appear to be invested not only in their daughters as a legacy, but in maintaining their own position as matriarch in a familial network. Some daughters appear to resent the mothers' efforts to retain such a position, as indicated by their reports of intrusion. At the same time, daughters treat their mothers as mothers, respecting them, fearing them, protecting them, and not communicating their negative feelings to them. In keeping with the role of matriarch, mothers tended to perceive their daughters in a larger familial system. They generally perceived their relationships with their daughters in positive terms, and focused on other people in their discussions of negative aspects of the relationship.

Daughters presented more complicated feelings for their mothers. They expressed positive and negative feelings for their mothers when asked alone, yet did not communicate their negative feelings about their mothers in their presence. Daughters' failure to communicate negative feelings about the relationship may stem from their desire to protect the relationship, and to protect themselves from negative feelings following the confrontation.

Mothers' and daughters' behaviors feed into mothers' continuing perception that all is fine in the relationship. After all, daughters do not complain. Daughters, in turn, feed on their mothers' positive affect for the relationship and seek to maintain a more positive presentation of the relationship when in their mothers' presence. Although such a pattern might appear to be ripe for frustration, particularly for the daughter, the relationships presented in this study appear to be strong and high in positive regard. Although tense situations in other relationships may profit from direct forms of communication, the aging mother and daughter relationship may be a forum where avoidance of confrontation is beneficial. Older mothers and adult daughters may establish a sort of "demilitarized zone," in which they interact in safety by avoiding conflict-laden topics (Hagestad, 1981, 1987). Nearly a half century of accrued experience may allow them to detour the inevitable relationship pitfalls which they have learned, from experience, are irreconcilable for them.

Furthermore, the mothers and daughters in these relationships appeared to work together in the joint interview, as indicated by their asking one another questions and the mothers' engaging in the conversations to a greater degree than they had when asked alone. The pattern of interaction in these mother/daughter relationships may reflect a more "female" approach to relationships, in which the goal itself is harmony.

Limitations of the Study

The women who participated in the study described in this book represent a unique sample. These women tended to be healthier, more well-educated, and more successful than other women. Although this study suggests that the tensions mothers and daughters experience play a unique role in their lives, there are several limitations to the findings presented.

The predominantly European American composition of the sample limits the generalizability of this study. One might anticipate different tension and conflict patterns in cultures and ethnic groups with different mores and norms for familial relationships. The types of problems these women reported involved dominant themes of their culture, including issues of dependency versus autonomy, adult women's role in the family of origin, and perceptions of changes accompanying aging. The associations between intrusion/exclusion and well-being might be different in groups where familial connections are given different value. For example, adult daughters in another culture may value, rather than resent their mothers' comments about childrearing, and their feelings about the relationship may reflect such values.

At the same time, cross-culturally, women have been found to serve a central role in the family (Nydegger, 1983). Though the basic problems between mothers and daughters in different cultures may vary, the central themes may revolve around maintenance of family ties and succession in the role of matriarch. For example, in a culture where group cohesion is valued over individuation, adult daughters may experience tension over the ways in which their mothers maintain cohesion, perhaps even feeling that the mothers are not engaged enough in their daughters' lives.

In addition to limitations in understanding the specific types of problems that mothers and daughters reported, information about communication styles is also limited. Cohort differences may account for some of the generational differences found here. Women of the older generation may have been more reticent to discuss negative aspects of their lives with an interviewer. Yet, cohort differences do not explain all the paradoxes in interpersonal tension discussed here. For example, all analyses were conducted separately for mothers and daughters. The associations between tension and well-being were found within generations. There was also variation in behavior during the interviews; some older mothers were very direct in their complaints, some spoke up during joint interview, some did not. Being born before the Great Depression was not associated with a uniform response style.

Conclusion: Remaining Questions About Mothers and Daughters

Finally, this study introduces many new questions. While this study looked at tension between healthy aging mothers and adult daughters, it presents a labyrinthine puzzle. How do mothers and daughters travel from the types of relationships described in this book to those marked by caregiver stress described elsewhere? There is a cliché that marks the completion of a study with a single data collection point, namely the call for longitudinal designs. This study, too, poses specific questions about the nature of development in later life relationships. Do daughters who view their mothers as intrusive eventually take over as caregiver? What happens as the mother's health declines? Do daughters who complain about their mothers' habits while the mothers are healthy assume the role of caregiver more readily than those who are upset about their mothers' domineering, pushy ways? Moreover, do they become different types of caregivers? Although I have argued that the caregiver paradigm is not the only model for relationships between aging mothers and daughters, this model has dominated research on stress and tension. The findings of this book may be relevant to understanding the intricacies of mother/daughter relationships when daughters must assist their mothers in late life.

In addition, this study leaves many unanswered questions about the nature of family life. Mothers and daughters do not interact in a vacuum. Rather their relationships are embedded in the context of larger family systems (Fingerman & Bermann, in press). Many of the mothers who participated in this study had more than one daughter, but only one daughter was interviewed. Tensions between aging mothers and their adult daughters often centered on their differing beliefs about the parameters of the relationship. Daughters struggled with their efforts to balance their ties with their own family as an entity unto itself against their feelings for their mothers. Yet, we know little about how daughters' husbands and children fit into the mother/daughter tie. How do the daughter's children feel about their grandmother? How does the daughter's husband relate to his mother-in-law? Recent research suggests that the son-in-law may play a pivotal role in ties between mothers and daughters (Fingerman, 2000b). Future research should look at this issue from the son-in-law's perspective.

The daughters' irritations often involved their feelings about their mothers' aging, and implicitly, their position as incumbent heir to the family. The study does not provide information about the difficulties involved with the mothers' transition in the presence of several daughters. Presumably, mothers have different relationships with each daughter in adulthood, just as they did in childhood (Fingerman, Davey, & Jenkins-Tucker, 2000). Yet, it is unclear how these relationships change as mothers enter the final years of life. Does one daughter succeed her mother as matriarch in the larger family network? Does each daughter become head of her own independent realm? Or does the balance of power shift into a myriad of intertwined relationships? Future research might focus on the dynamics of the larger family system as the woman who may have served as its monarch abdicates her position (Fingerman & Bermann, in press).

Throughout this book, 48 older women and their adult daughters have presented their views on their relationships. Sara, a 42-year-old daughter, began her first interview by commenting, "I feel like I'm a good daughter and I feel like I have a really great mother. I never feel let down in our relationship. Am I supposed to be saying more things?" The mother/daughter tie has often been considered a repository for positive feelings and strong regard. Clearly, the women who participated in this study had such feelings for the other party. It is equally clear, however, that they had much more to say. Their complex emotions reveal a great deal about the mother/daughter tie at the end of life.

References

Acitelli, L. K. (1988). When spouses talk to each other about their relationship. *Journal of Social and Personal Relationships, 5,* 185–199.

Acitelli, L. K., & Antonucci, T. C. (1994). Gender differences in the link between marital support and satisfaction in older couples. *Journal of Personality and Social Psychology, 67,* 688–698.

Aldous, J. (1987). New views on the family life of the elderly and the near-elderly. *Journal of Marriage and the Family, 49,* 277–234.

Aldous, J., Klaus, E., & Klein, D. (1985). The understanding heart: Aging parents and their favorite children. *Child Development, 56,* 303–316.

Allen, K. R., & Walker, A. J. (1992a). Attentive love: A feminist perspective on the caregiving of adult daughters. *Family Relations, 41,* 284–289.

Allen, K. R., & Walker, A. J. (1992b). A feminist analysis of interviews with elderly mothers and their daughters. In J. F. Gilgun & D. Kerry (Eds.), *Qualitative methods in family research* (pp. 198–214). Newbury Park, CA: Sage.

Alexander, J. F. (1973). Defensive and supportive communication in family systems. *Journal of Marriage and the Family, 40,* 223–231.

Arnett, J. J. (1999). Adolescent storm and stress, reconsidered. *American Psychologist, 54,* 317–326.

Atkinson, M. P., Kivett, V. R., & Campbell, R. T. (1986). Intergenerational solidarity: An examination of a theoretical model. *Journal of Gerontology, 41,* 408–416.

Bahr, H. M., & Bahr, K. S. (1996). A paradigm of family transcendence. *Journal of Marriage and the Family, 58,* 541–555.

Barnett, R. C., Kibria, N., Baruch, G. K., & Pleck, J. H. (1991). Adult daughter-parent relationships and their associations with daughters' subjective well-being and psychological distress. *Journal of Marriage and the Family, 53,* 29–42.

Baruch, G., & Barnett, R. C. (1983). Adult daughters' relationships with their mothers, *Journal of Marriage and the Family, 45,* 601–606.

Bedford, V. H., & Blieszner, R. (1997). Personal relationships in later life families. In S. Duck (Ed.), *Handbook of personal relationships* (2nd ed., pp. 523–542). New York: Wiley.

Belenky, M. F., Clinchy, B. M., Goldberger, N. R., & Tarule, J. M. (1997). *Women's ways of knowing: The development of self, voice, and mind.* New York: Basic Books. (Original work published 1986)

Bengtson, V. L. (1970). The "generation gap": A review and typology of social-psychological perspectives. *Youth and Society, 2,* 7–31.

Bengtson, V. L., & Kuypers, J. A. (1971). Generational difference and the developmental stake. *Aging and Human Development, 2,* 249–260.

Bengtson, V. L., Olander, E. B., & Haddad, A. A. (1976). The "generation gap" and aging family members: Toward a conceptual model. In J. F. Gubrium (Ed.), *Time, roles, and self in old age* (pp. 237–263). New York: Human Sciences Press.

Bengtson, V., Rosenthal, C., & Burton, L. (1996). Paradoxes in families and aging. In R. H. Binstock & L. K. George (Eds.), *Handbook of aging and the social sciences* (4th ed., pp. 254–275). San Diego, CA: Academic Press.

Bengtson, V. L., & Schrader, S. S. (1982). Parent-child relations. In D. J. Mangen & W. A. Peterson (Eds.), *Social roles and social participation* (pp. 115–129). Minneapolis, MN: University of Minnesota Press.

Blanchard-Fields, F., Jahnke, H., & Camp, C. (1995). Age differences in problem solving style: The role of emotional salience. *Psychology and Aging, 10,* 173–180.

Blenkner, M. (1963). Social work and family relations in later life with some thoughts on filial maturity. In E. Shanas & G. F. Streib (Eds.), *Social structure and the family: Generational relations* (pp. 46–59). Englewood Cliffs, NJ: Prentice Hall.

Blieszner, R., & Adams, R. G. (1995, November). The causes and consequences of problems with friends in old age. In K. L. Fingerman (Chair), *Negative aspects of social relations in later life.* Symposium conducted at the meeting of the Gerontological Society of America, Los Angeles, CA.

Blieszner, R., Usita, P. M., & Mancini, J. A. (1996). Diversity and dynamics in late-life mother-daughter relationships. *Journal of Women & Aging, 8,* 5–24.

Booth, A., & Crouter, N. C. (Eds.) (1998). *Men in families: When do they get involved? What difference does it make?* Mahwah, NJ: Lawrence Erlbaum Associates.

Bowen, M. (1978). *Family therapy in clinical practice.* New York: Jason Aronson.

Bowlby, J. (1969). *Attachment and loss: Vol. 1. Attachment.* New York: Basic Books.

Boyd, C. J. (1989). Mothers and daughters: A discussion of theory and research. *Journal of Marriage and the Family, 51,* 291–301.

Bradbury, T. N., Cambell, S. M., & Fincham, F. D. (1995). Longitudinal and behavioral analysis of masculinity and femininity in marriage. *Journal of Personality and Social Psychology, 68,* 328–341.

Brody, E. M. (1990). Role reversal: An inaccurate and destructive concept. *Journal of Gerontological Social Work, 15,* 15–23.

Brody, E. M., Hoffman, C., Kleban, M. H., & Schoonover, C. B. (1989). Caregiving daughters and their local siblings: Perceptions, strains, and interactions. *Gerontologist, 29,* 529–538.

Bromberg, E. M. (1987). Mothers and daughters in later life: Rediscovery and renegotiation a group approach. *Journal of Gerontological Social Work, 11,* 7–24.

Brown, L. M., & Gilligan, C. (1993). Meeting at the crossroads: Women's psychology and girls' development. *Feminism & Psychology, 3,* 11–35.

Brown, P., & Levinson, S. (1987). *Politeness: Some universals in language usage.* Cambridge: Cambridge University Press.

Buchanan, C. M., Eccles, J. S., Flanagan, C., Midley, C., Feldlaufer, H., & Harold, R. D. (1990). Parents' and teachers' beliefs about adolescents: Effects of sex and experience. *Journal of Youth & Adolescence, 19,* 363–394.

Canary, D. J., & Cupach, W. R. (1988). Relational and episodic characteristics associated with conflict tactics. *Journal of Social and Personal Relationship, 5,* 305–325.

Canary, D. J., Cupach, W. R., & Messman, S. J. (1995). *Relationship conflict: Conflict in parent-child, friendship, and romantic relationships.* Thousand Oaks, CA: Sage.

Carstensen, L. L. (1992). Social and emotional patterns in adulthood: Support for socioemotional selectivity theory. *Psychology and Aging, 7,* 331–338.

Carstensen, L. L. (1995). Evidence for a life-span theory of socioemotional selectivity. *Current Directions in Psychological Science, 4,* 151–155.

Carstensen, L. L., Gross, J. J., & Fung, H. H. (1998). The social context of emotional experience. In K. W. Schaie & M. P. Lawton (Eds.), *Annual review of gerontology and geriatrics* (Vol. 17, pp. 325–352). New York: Springer Publishing Co.

Chodorow, N. (1994). *Femininities, masculinities, sexualities, Freud and beyond.* Lexington, KY: University Press of Kentucky.

Cicirelli, V. G. (1983a). Adult children's attachment and helping behavior to elderly parents: A path model. *Journal of Marriage and the Family, 45,* 815–825.

Cicirelli, V. G. (1983b). Personal strains and negative feelings in adult children's relationships with elderly parents. *Academic Psychology Bulletin, 5,* 31–36.

Cicirelli, V. G. (1988). A measure of filial anxiety regarding anticipated care of elderly parents. *Gerontologist, 28,* 478–482.

Climo, J. (1992). *Distant parents.* New Brunswick, NJ: Rutgers University Press.

Cohan, C. L., & Bradbury, T. N. (1997). Negative life events, marital interaction, and the longitudinal course of newlywed marriage. *Journal of Personality and Social Psychology, 73,* 114–128.

Cohler, B. J. (1983). Autonomy and interdependence in the family of adulthood: A psychological perspective. *Gerontologist, 23,* 33–39.

Cohler, B. J. (1988). The adult daughter-mother relationship: Perspectives from life-course family study and psychoanalysis. *Journal of Geriatric Psychiatry, 21,* 51–76.

Collins, W. A. (1990). Parent-child relationships in the transition to adolescence: Continuity and change in interaction, affect, and cognition. In R. Montemayor, G. R. Adams, & T. P. Gullotta (Eds.), *From childhood to adolescence: A transitional period?* (pp. 85–106). Newbury Park, CA: Sage.

Conger, R. D., & Ge, X. (1999). Conflict and cohesion in parent-adolescent relations: Changes in emotional expression from early to midadolescence. In M. J. Cox & J. Brooks-Gunn (Eds.), *Conflict and cohesion in families: Causes and consequences* (pp. 185–206). Mahwah, NJ: Lawrence Erlbaum.

Connidis, I. A., Rosenthal, C. J., & McMullin, J. A. (1996). The impact of family composition on providing help to older parents: A study of employed adults. *Research on Aging, 18,* 402–429.

Conover, W. J. (1980). *Practical nonparametric statistics* (2nd ed.). New York: Wiley.

Cupach, W. R. (1994). Social predicaments. In W. R. Cupach & B. H. Spitzberg (Eds.), *The dark side of interpersonal communication* (pp. 159–180). Hillsdale, NJ: Lawrence Erlbaum.

Cupach, W. R., & Metts, S. (1994). *Facework.* Thousand Oaks, CA: Sage.

Davey, A., & Eggebeen, D. J. (1998). Patterns of intergenerational exchange and mental health. *Journals of Gerontology: Psychological Sciences, 53,* P86–P95.

Di Leonardo, M. (1992). The female world of cards and holidays: Women, families, and the work of kinship. In B. Thorne & M. Yalom (Eds.), *Rethinking the family: Some feminist questions* (pp. 246–261). Boston, MA: Northeastern University Press.

Dilworth-Anderson, P., Williams, S. W., & Cooper, T. (1999). The contexts of experiencing emotional distress among caregivers to elderly African Americans. *Family Relations, 48,* 391–396.

Elder, G. H. (1998). The life course as developmental theory. *Child Development, 69,* 1–12.

Erikson, E. H. (1950). *Childhood and society.* New York: W. W. Norton.

Erikson, E. H., Erikson, J. M., & Kivnick, H. Q. (1986). *Vital involvement in old age: The experience of old age in our time.* New York: W. W. Norton.

Field, D. (July, 1989). Recollections of the personal past and psychological well-being in old age. In U. Lehr, *Biographical aspects of aging.* Invited symposium at the XIV International Congress of Gerontology, Acapulco, Mexico.

Field, D., Minkler, M., Falk, F. R., & Leino, E. V. (1993). The influence of health on family contacts and family feelings in advanced old age: A longitudinal study. *Journals of Gerontology, 48,* P18–P28.

Fine, M. A., Coleman, M., & Ganong, L. H. (1998). Consistency in perceptions of the step-parent role among step-parents, parents, and stepchildren. *Journal of Social and Personal Relationships, 15,* 810–828.

Fingerman, K. L. (1995). Aging mothers' and their adult daughters' perceptions of conflict behaviors. *Psychology and Aging, 10,* 639–650.

Fingerman, K. L. (1996). Sources of tension in the aging mother and adult daughter relationship. *Psychology and Aging, 11,* 591–606.

Fingerman, K. L. (1997a). Aging mothers' and their adult daughters' retrospective ratings of past conflict in their relationship. *Current Psychology, 16,* 131–154.

Fingerman, K. L. (1997b). Being more than a daughter: Middle-aged women's conceptions of their mothers. *Journal of Women and Aging, 9,* 55–72.

Fingerman, K. L. (1998a). The good, the bad, and the worrisome: Complexities in grandparents' relationships with individual grandchildren. *Family Relations, 47,* 403–414.

Fingerman, K. L. (1998b). Tight lips: Aging mothers' and their adult daughters' responses to interpersonal tensions in their relationship. *Personal Relationships, 5,* 121–138.

Fingerman, K. L. (2000a). "We had a nice little chat": Age and generational differences in mothers' and daughters' descriptions of enjoyable visits. *Journals of Gerontology: Psychological Sciences, 55,* P95–P106.

Fingerman, K. L. (2000b). The role of the middle generation in grandparents' relationships with grandchildren. Unpublished manuscript.

Fingerman, K. L., & Bermann, E. A. (in press). Applications of family systems to the study of adulthood. *International Journal of Aging and Human Development.*

Fingerman, K. L., & Birditt, K. S. (in press). Do age differences in close and problematic family networks reflect variation in living relatives? *Journals of Gerontology: Psychological Science.*

Fingerman, K. L., Davey, A., & Jenkins-Tucker, C. (2000). *Variation in adult siblings' memories of relationships with parents during childhood.* Unpublished manuscript.

Fingerman, K. L., Gallagher-Thompson, D., Lovett, S., & Rose, J. (1996). Internal resourcefulness, task demands, coping, and dysphoric affect amongst caregivers of the frail elderly. *International Journal of Aging and Human Development, 42,* 341–360.

Fingerman, K. L., & Griffiths, P. C. (1999). Season's greetings: Adults' social contact at the holiday season. *Psychology and Aging, 14,* 192–205.

Fingerman, K. L., & Perlmutter, M. (1995). Future time perspective across adulthood. *Journal of General Psychology, 122,* 95–112.

Fischer, L. R. (1981). Transitions in the mother-daughter relationship. *Journal of Marriage and the Family, 45,* 187–192.

Fischer, L. R. (1986). *Linked lives: Adult daughters and their mothers.* Newbury Park, CA: Sage.

Fleiss, J. L. (1981). *Statistical methods for rates and proportions* (2nd ed.). Wiley Series in Probability and Mathematics. New York: Wiley.

Folkman, S., & Lazarus, R. S. (1980). An analysis of coping in a middle-aged community sample. *Journal of Health & Social Behavior, 21,* 219–239.

Franklin, J. H. (1997). African American families: A historical note. In H. P. McAdoo (Ed.), *Black families* (3rd ed., pp. 5–8). Thousand Oaks, CA: Sage.

Freud, S. (1910). A special type of choice of object made by men. In S. Freud, *Standard edition of the collected works of Sigmund Freud, 11.* London, UK: Hogarth.

Ganong, L., & Coleman, M. (1999). *Changing families, changing responsibilities: Family obligations following divorce and remarriage.* Englewood, NJ: Lawrence Erlbaum.

Gilligan, C. (1982). *In a different voice: Psychological theory and women's development.* Cambridge, MA: Harvard University Press.

Gilligan, C., & Rogers, A. (1993). Reframing daughters and mothering: A paradigm shift in psychology. In J. van Mens-Verhults, K. Schrueurs, & L. Woertman (Eds.), *Daughtering and mothering: Female subjectivity reanalyzed* (pp. 125–134). London, UK: Routledge.

Goodnow, J. J. (1995). Parents' knowledge and expectations. In M. H. Bornstein (Ed.), *Handbook of parenting: Status and social conditions of parenting* (pp. 305–332). Mahway, NJ: Lawrence Erlbaum.

Gottman, J. M. (1979). *Marital interaction: Experimental investigations.* New York: Academic Press.

Gottman, J. M. (1993a). A theory of marital dissolution and stability. *Journal of Family Psychology, 7,* 57–75.

Gottman, J. M. (1993b). The roles of conflict engagement, escalation, and avoidance in marital interaction: A longitudinal view of five types of couples. *Journal of Clinical and Consulting Psychology, 61,* 6–15.

Gottman, J. M. (1998). Psychology and the study of the marital processes. *Annual Review of Psychology, 49,* 169–197.

Gottman, J. M., & Krokoff, L. J. (1989). Marital interaction and marital satisfaction: A longitudinal view. *Journal of Consulting and Clinical Psychology, 57,* 47–52.

Hagestad, G. O. (1981). Problems and promises in the social psychology of intergenerational relations. In R. Fogel, E. Hatfield, S. B. Kiesler, & E. Shanas (Eds.), *Stability and change in the family* (pp. 11–46). New York: Academic Press.

Hagestad, G. O. (1982). Parent and child: Generations in the family. In T. M. Field, A. Huston, H. C. Quay, L. Troll, & G. E. Finley (Eds.), *Review of human development* (pp. 485–499). New York: Wiley.

Hagestad, G. O. (1984). Multi-generational families, socialization, support, and strain. In V. Garms-Homolova, E. M. Hoerning, & D. Schaeffer (Eds.), *Intergenerational relationships* (pp. 105–114). Lewiston, NY: C. J. Hogrefe.

Hagestad, G. O. (1987). Parent-child relations in later life: Trends and gaps in past research. In J. B. Lancaster, J. Altmann, A. S. Rossi, & L. R. Sherrod (Eds.), *Parenting across the lifespan* (pp. 405–433). New York: Aldine de Gruyter.

Halpern, J. (1994). The sandwich generation: Conflict between adult children and their aging parents. In D. D. Cahn (Ed.), *Conflict in personal relationships* (pp. 143–160). Hillsdale, NJ: Lawrence Erlbaum.

Havighurst, R. J. (1972). *Developmental tasks and education* (3rd ed.). New York: McKay.

Heavey, C. L., Layne, C., & Christensen, A. (1993). Gender and conflict structure in marital interaction: A replication and extension. *Journal of Clinical and Consulting Psychology, 6,* 16–27.

Heider, F. (1958). *The psychology of interpersonal relations.* New York: Wiley.

Henwood, K. L. (1993). Women and later life: The discursive construction of identities within family relationships. *Journal of Aging Studies, 7,* 303–319.

Houser, B. B., & Berkman, S. L. (1984). Aging parent/mature child relationships. *Journal of Marriage and the Family, 46,* 295–299.

Johnson, C. L. (1988). Relationships among family members and friends in late life. In R. Milardo (Ed.), *Family and social networks* (pp. 168–189). Beverly Hills: Sage.

Jung, C. G. (1981/1931). Analytical psychology and weltanscauung. In *The structure of dynamics and the psyche: Volume 8 of the collected works of C. G. Jung.* R. F. C. Hull translator. Princeton, NJ: Princeton University Press. (Original work published 1931)

Kagan, J. (1996). Three pleasing ideas. *American Psychologist, 51,* 901–908.

Kastenbaum, R., & Aisenberg, R. (1972). *The psychology of death.* New York: Springer Publishing Co.

Kelly, E. L., & Conley, J. J. (1987). Personality and compatibility: A prospective analysis of martial stability and marital satisfaction. *Journal of Personality and Social Psychology, 52,* 27–40.

Kobrin, F., & Hendershot, G. (1977). Do family ties reduce mortality? Evidence from the United States 1996–1968. *Journal of Marriage and the Family, 39,* 737–745.

Kranichfeld, M. L. (1987). Rethinking family power. *Journal of Family Issues, 8,* 42–56.

Kurdek, L. A. (1993). Predicting marital dissolution: A 5-year prospective study of newlywed couples. *Journal of Personality and Social Psychology, 64,* 221–242.

Labouvie-Vief, G., Diehl, M., Chiodo, L. M., & Coyle, N. (1995). Representations of self and parents across the life span. *Journal of Adult Development, 2,* 207–222.

Lehr, U. (1984). The role of women in the family generation context. In V. Garms-Homolova, E. M. Hoerning, & D. Schaeffer (Eds.), *Intergenerational relationships* (pp. 125–132). Lewiston, NY: C. J. Hogrefe, Inc.

Lerner, H. G. (1985). *The dance of anger: A woman's guide to changing the patterns of intimate relationships.* New York: Harper & Row.

Levenson, R. W., Carstensen, L. L., & Gottman, J. M. (1993). Long-term marriage: Age, gender, and satisfaction. *Psychology and Aging, 8,* 301–313.

Lin, G., & Rogerson, P. A. (1995). Elderly parents and the geographic availability of their adult children. *Research on Aging, 17,* 303–331.

Luescher, K., & Pillemer, K. (1998). Intergenerational ambivalence: A new approach to the study of parent-child relations in later life. *Journal of Marriage and the Family, 60,* 413–425.

Mancini, J. A., & Blieszner, R., (1989). Aging parents and adult children: Research themes in intergenerational relations. *Journal of Marriage and the Family, 51,* 275–290.

Mangen, D. J. (1988). Measuring intergenerational family relations. In D. J. Mangen, V. L. Bengtson, & P. H. Landry (Eds.), *Measurement of intergenerational relations* (pp. 31–55). Newbury Park, CA: Sage.

Mares, M. L. (1995). The aging family. In M. A. Fitzpatrick & A. L. Vangelisti (Eds.), *Explaining family interaction* (pp. 344–374). Thousand Oaks, CA: Sage.

Morgan, D. L. (1989). Adjusting to widowhood. *Gerontologist, 29,* 101–107.

Moscovici, S. (1984). The phenomenon of social representations. In R. M. Farr & S. Moscovici (Eds.), *Social representations* (pp. 3–70). Cambridge, England: Cambridge University Press.

Mui, A. C. (1995). Caring for frail elderly parents: A comparison of adult sons and daughters. *Gerontologist, 35,* 86–93.

National Center for Health Statistics (2000). *Health and aging chart book from Health United States, 1999.* Hyattsville, MD: National Center for Health Statistics.

Neugarten, B. L. (1968). The awareness of middle-age. In B. L. Neugarten (Ed.), *Middle age and aging* (pp. 93–98). Chicago, IL: University of Chicago Press.

Nydegger, C. (1983). Family ties of the aged in cross-cultural perspective. *Gerontologist, 23,* 26–32.

Nydegger, C. N. (1991). The development of paternal and filial maturity. In K. A. Pillemer & K. McCartney (Eds.), *Parent-child relations throughout life* (pp. 93–112). Hillsdale, NJ: Lawrence Erlbaum Associates.

Nyedegger, C. N., & Mitteness, L. S. (1988). Etiquette and ritual in family conversation. *American Behavioral Scientist, 31,* 702–716.

Oggins, J., Veroff, J., & Leber, D. (1993). Perceptions of marital interaction among Black and White newlyweds. *Journal of Personality and Social Psychology, 65,* 494–511.

Paikoff, R. L., & Brooks-Gunn, J. (1991). Do parent-child relationships change during puberty? *Psychological Bulletin, 110,* 47–66.

Pasch, L. A., & Bradbury, T. N. (1998). Social support, conflict, and the development of marital dysfunction. *Journal of Consulting and Clinical Psychology, 66,* 219–230.

Pasch, L. A., Bradbury, T. N., & Davila, J. (1997). Gender negative affectivity, and observed social support behavior in marital interaction. *Personal Relationships, 4,* 361–378.

Pillemer, K., & Finkelhor, D. (1988). The prevalence of elder abuse: A random survey sample. *Gerontologist, 28,* 51–57.

Pillemer, K., & Suitor, J. J. (1991). Relationships with children and distress in the elderly. In K. Pillemer & K. McCartney (Eds.), *Parent-child relations throughout life* (pp. 163–179). Hillsdale, NJ: Lawrence Erlbaum.

Prinz, R. J., Foster, S., Kent, R. N., & O'Leary, K. D. (1979). Multivariate assessment of conflict in distressed and nondistressed mother-adolescent dyads. *Journal of Applied Behavior Analysis, 12,* 691–700.

Pruchno, R. A., Peters, N. D., & Burant, C. J. (1996). Child life events, parent-child disagreements, and parent well-being: Model development and testing. In C. D. Ryff & M. M. Seltzer (Eds.), *The parental experience in midlife* (pp. 561–606). Chicago, IL: University of Chicago Press.

Radloff, L. S. (1977). The CES-D Scale: A self-report depression scale for the general population. *Applied Psychological Measurement, 1,* 385–401.

Radloff, L. S., & Teri, L. (1986). Use of the center for epidemiological studies-depression scale with older adults. *Clinical Gerontologist, 5,* 119–135.

Reinhold, M. (1976). The generation gap in antiquity. In S. Bertman (Ed.), *The conflict of generations in ancient Greece and Rome* (pp. 15–54). Amsterdam: B. R. Gruner.

Roberts, R. E. L., Richards, L. N., & Bengtson, V. L. (1991). Intergenerational solidarity in families: Untangling the ties that bind. *Marriage and Family Review, 16,* 11–46.

Robertson, J. F. (1994). Grandparenting in an era of rapid change. In R. Blieszner & V. H. Bedford (Eds.), *Handbook of aging and the family* (pp. 243–260). Westport, CT: Greenwood Press.

Rook, K. S. (1984). The negative side of social interaction: Impact on psychological well-being, *Journal of Personality and Social Psychology, 46,* 1097–1108.

Rook, K. S. (1992). Detrimental aspects of social relationships: Taking Stock of an emerging literature. In H. O. F. Veiel & U. Baumann (Eds.), *The meaning and measurement of social support* (pp. 157–169). New York: Hemisphere.

Rosenthal, C. J. (1987). Generational succession: The passing on of family headship. *Journal of Comparative Family Studies, 18,* 61–77.

Rossi, A. S., & Rossi, P. H. (1990). *Of human bonding: Parent-child relations across the life course.* New York: Aldine de Gruyter.

Ruddick, S. (1989). *Maternal thinking: Toward a politics of peace.* Boston: Beacon.

Rusbult, C. E. (1980). Commitment and satisfaction in romantic associations: A test of the investment model. *Journal of Experimental and Social Psychology, 16,* 172–186.

Rusbult, C. E., Drigotas, S. M., & Verette, J. (1994). The investment model: An interdependence analysis of commitment processes and relationship maintenance phenomena. In D. J. Canary & L. Stafford (Eds.), *Communication and relational maintenance* (pp. 115–139). San Diego, CA: Academic Press.

Ryff, C. D., Lee, Y. H., Essex, M. J., & Schmutte, P. S. (1994). My children and me: Midlife evaluations of grown children and of self. *Psychology & Aging, 9,* 195–205.

Ryff, C. D., & Seltzer, M. M. (1996). The uncharted years of midlife parenting. In C. D. Ryff & M. M. Seltzer (Eds.), *The parental experience in midlife* (pp. 3–25). Chicago, IL: University of Chicago Press.

Sampson, E. E. (1988). The debate on individualism: Indigenous psychologies of the individual and their role in personal and societal functioning. *American Psychologist, 43,* 15–22.

Sampson, E. E. (1989). The challenge of social change for psychology: Globalization and psychology's theory of the person. *American Psychologist, 44,* 914–922.

Scharlach, A. E. (1987). Role strain in mother-daughter relationships in later life. *Gerontologist, 27,* 627–631.

Scheff, T. J. (1995). Conflict in family systems: The role of shame. In K. Fischer & J. Tangney (Eds.), *Self-conscious emotions.* New York: Guilford Press.

Seltzer, M. M. (1990). Role reversal: You don't go home again. *Journal of Gerontological Social Work, 15,* 5–14.

Shanas, E. (1979). Social myth as hypothesis: The case of the family relations of older people. *Gerontologist, 19,* 3–9.

Singh, G. K., Kochanek, K. D., & MacDorman, M. F. (1994). Report of final mortality statistics. *Monthly vital statistics, 45,* 19. Hyattsville, MD: National Center for Health Statistics.

Smith, J., & Goodnow, J. J. (1999). Unasked-for support and unsolicited advice: Age and quality of social experience. *Psychology and Aging, 14,* 108–121.

Speare, A., & Avery, R. (1993). Who helps whom in the elder parent-child family. *Journal of Gerontology, 48,* S64–S73.

Spitze, G., & Miner, S. (1992). Gender differences in adult-child contact among Black elderly parents. *Gerontologist, 32,* 213–217.

Steinman, L. A. (1979). Reactivated conflicts with aging parents. In P. K. Ragan (Ed.), *Aging parents* (pp. 126–143). Los Angeles, CA: University of Southern California Press.

Straus, M. A. (1979). Measuring intrafamily conflict and violence: The conflict tactics (CT) scales. *Journal of Marriage and the Family, 41,* 75–88.

Sudarkasa, N. (1997). African American families and family values. In H. P. McAdoo (Ed.), *Black families* (3rd ed.) (pp. 9–40). Thousand Oaks, CA: Sage.

Suitor, J. J. (1987). Mother-daughter relations when married daughters return to school: Effects of status similarity. *Journal of Marriage and the Family, 49,* 435–444.

Suitor, J. J., & Pillemer, K. (1987). The presence of adult children: A source of stress for elderly couple's marriages. *Journal of Marriage and the Family, 49,* 717–725.

Suitor, J. J., & Pillemer, K. (1988). Explaining intergenerational conflict when adult children and elderly parents live together. *Journal of Marriage and the Family, 50,* 1037–1047.

Suitor, J. J., & Pillemer, K. (1991). Family conflict when adult children and elderly parents share a home. In K. Pillemer & K. McCartney (Eds.), *Parent-child relations throughout life* (pp. 179–201). Hillsdale, NJ: Lawrence Erlbaum.

Suitor, J. J., Pillemer, K., Keeton, S., & Robison, J. (1996). Aged parents and aging children: Determinants of relationship quality. In R. Blieszner & V. H. Bedford (Eds.), *Handbook of aging and the family* (pp. 223–242). Westport, CT: Greenwood Press.

Sussman, M. B. (1985). The family life of old people. In R. H. Binstock & E. Shanas (Eds.), *Handbook of aging and the social sciences* (pp. 415–449). New York: Van Nostrand Reinhold Company.

Sweet, J., Bumpass, L., & Vauhgn, C. (1988). *The design and content of the National Survey of Families and Households.* Working Paper #1. Center for Demography and Ecology. Madison, WI: University of Wisconsin.

Talbott, M. M. (1990). The negative side of the relationship between older widows an their adult children: The mothers' perspective. *Gerontologist, 30,* 595–603.

Tavris, C. (1989). *Anger: The misunderstood emotion.* New York: Simon & Schuster.

Taylor, J. M., Gilligan, C., & Sullivan, A. M. (1995). *Between voice and silence: Women and girls, race and relationship.* Cambridge, MA: Harvard University Press.

Taylor, R. J., Jackson, J. S., & Chatters, L. M. (1997). *Family life in Black America.* Thousands Oaks, CA: Sage.

Thomas, S. P. (1993). *Anger and its manifestations in women.* New York: Springer Publishing Co.

Thompson, L., & Walker, A. J. (1982). The dyad as unit of analysis. Conceptual and methodological issues. *Journal of Marriage and the Family, 44,* 899–900.

Troll, L. E. (1971). The "generation gap" in later life. *Sociological Focus, 5,* 18–28.

Troll, L. E. (1988). New thoughts on old families. *Gerontologist, 28,* 586–591.

Troll, L. E. (1994a). Family-embedded vs. family deprived oldest-old: A study of contrasts. *International Journal of Aging and Human Development, 38,* 51–63.

Troll, L. E. (1994b). Attachments in later life. In B. Turner & L. E. Troll (Eds.), *Women growing older.* CA: Sage.

Troll, L. E. (1996). Modified-extended families over time: Discontinuity in parts, continuity in wholes. In V. Bengtson (Ed.), *Adulthood and aging:*

Research on continuities and discontinuities (pp. 246–268). New York: Springer Publishing Co.

Troll, L. E., Bengtson, V., & McFarland, D. (1979). Generations in the family. In W. R. Burr, R. Hill, F. I. Nye, & I. L. Reiss (Eds.), *Contemporary theories about the family: Vol 1, Research base theories* (pp. 127–161). New York: Free Press.

Troll, L., & Fingerman, K. L. (1996). Parent/child bonds in adulthood. In C. Malestesta-Magai & S. McFadden (Eds.), *Handbook of emotion, adult development and aging* (pp. 185–205). Orlando, FL: Academic Press.

Troll, L. E., & Smith, J. (1976). Attachment through the lifespan. *Human Development, 4,* 67–74.

Troll, L. E., & Stapley, J. (1985). Elders and the extended family system: Health, family salience, and affect. In J. A. Munnichs (Ed.), *Life span and change in a gerontological perspective* (pp. 211–238). New York: Academic Press.

Umberson, D. (1989). Relationships with children: Explaining parents' psychological well-being. *Journal of Marriage and the Family, 51,* 999–1012.

Umberson, D. (1992). Relationships between adult children and their parents: Psychological consequences for both generations. *Journal of Marriage and the Family, 54,* 664–674.

Umberson, D., & Gove, W. R. (1989). Parenthood and psychological well-being: Theory, measurement, and stage in the life course. *Journal of Family Issues, 10,* 440–462.

Usita, P. (1999, November). Older Japanese American mothers and their daughters. In D. Field (Chair), Intergenerational relationships. Symposium conducted at the annual meeting of the Gerontological Society of America, San Francisco, CA.

Uttal, D. H., & Perlmutter, M. A. (1989). Toward a broader conceptualization of development: The role of gains and losses across the life span. *Developmental Review, 9,* 101–132.

Veroff, J., Young, A., & Coon, H. (1997). The early years of marriage. In S. Duck (Ed.), *Handbook of personal relationships* (2nd ed.). London: Wiley.

Walker, A. J. (1994). You can't be a woman in your mother's house: Adult daughters and their mothers. In D. L. Sollie & L. A. Leslie (Eds.), *Gender, families and close relationships: Feminist research journeys* (pp. 74–96). Newbury Park, CA: Sage.

Walker, A. J., & Allen, K. R. (1991). Relationships between caregiving daughters and their elderly mothers. *Gerontologist, 31,* 389–396.

Walker, A. J., & Thompson, L. (1983). Intimacy and aid and contact among mothers and daughters. *Journal of Marriage and the Family, 45,* 841–848.

Walker, A. J., Thompson, L., & Morgan, C. S. (1987). Two generations of mothers and daughters: Role position and interdependence. *Psychology of Women Quarterly, 11,* 195–208.

Webster, P. S., & Herzog, R. A. (1995). Effects of parental divorce and memories of family problems on relationships between adult children and their parents. *Journal of Gerontology: Social Sciences, 50,* S24–S34.

Weishaus, S. S. (1978). Determinants of affect of middle-aged women towards their aging mothers. Unpublished doctoral dissertation, University of Southern California.

Weiss, R. L., & Heyman, R. E. (1990). Observation of marital interaction. In F. D. Fincham & T. N. Bradbury (Eds.), *The psychology of marriage: Basic issues and applications* (pp. 87–117). New York: Guilford Press.

Welsh, W. M., & Stewart, A. J. (1995). Relationships between women and their parents: Implications for midlife well-being. *Psychology and Aging, 10,* 181–190.

Whitbeck, L., Hoyt, D. R., & Huck, S. M. (1994). Early family relationships, intergenerational solidarity, and support provided to parents by their adult children. *Journal of Gerontology: Social Science, 49,* S85–S94.

Whitbeck, L. B., Simons, R. L., & Conger, R. S. (1991). The effects of early family relationships on contemporary relationships and assistance patterns between adult children and their parents. *Journal of Gerontology: Social Sciences, 46,* S330–337.

White, L., & Rogers, S. (in press). Economic circumstances and family outcomes: A review of the 90s. *Journal of Marriage and the Family.*

Wodak, R., & Schulz, M. (1986). *The language of love and guilt: Mother-daughter relationships from a cross-cultural perspective.* Amsterdam: John Benjamins.

Zarit, S. H., & Eggebeen, D. (1995). Parent–child relationships in adulthood and old age. In M. H. Bornstein (Ed.), *Handbook of parenting* (pp. 119–140). Mahwah, NJ: Lawrence Erlbaum.

■ Appendix A
Methodological Decisions

SAMPLE SELECTION

There were several methodological issues involved in establishing criteria for the participants. Research on familial relationships requires decisions about how to make comparisons between noncomparable units. It is impossible to control for age differences, relationships, generational position, number of offspring, and other variables across families. Therefore choices must be made in defining the sampling unit. An initial decision was made to look only at dyads here, and a second decision was made to examine relationships between women. Finally, a role relationship research design was selected, in which dyads consisting of mothers in a single cohort, those over the age of 70, and their adult daughters were asked to participate.

Research on intergenerational relationships is complicated by the fact that individuals can be assessed based on cohort, generation, or lineage, each of which introduce an array of methodological difficulties and confounds. Cohort-based designs involve the participation of individuals of a comparable age, who experienced historic events at a certain point in their individual development. Such historic events may have an impact on relationships (Elder, 1998). For example, individuals who are in their 50's today shared the experience of being adolescents during the 1960s, a time when parent/child relationships were notably turbulent. However, an individual's age or cohort alone is not sufficient for research on family relationships. An individual in her mid-40's might be the oldest living member of her family and a great-grandmother, or the youngest living member of her family and a grandchild.

Generational assessments involve the use of age-based and family relationship models, where individuals a certain age are interviewed because they occupy a given generational status. For example, 60-year-olds might be interviewed in their status as grandmothers. However, this approach may leave out individuals who hold a generational position but are not within the given age range. A 35-year-old woman and a 75-year-old woman may both be first time grandmothers (Hagestad, 1981, 1982), but would not both be included in a study using this approach to assessment.

The lineage approach has been contrasted to the cohort and generational approaches. In research utilizing a lineage approach, the observations of several individual family members form a familial unit of analysis (Mangen, 1988). Researchers can gather data from individuals who occupy parent, grandparent, or child roles. However, this approach presents difficulties of comparability across families with regard to such issues as number of members in any given generation and generational spacing. Although this approach makes conceptual sense for many research questions, the practicalities of recruiting volunteers renders such research designs prohibitive for most researchers.

At the same time, individuals provide limited data on issues that are embedded in the context of a relationship. In order to understand a given relationship, both members of the dyad should be interviewed. Some variables, such as power and conflict, can only be conceived at the dyadic level, not at the individual level (Thompson & Walker, 1982). Interpersonal tension, by definition, involves discrepancies in point of view. Therefore, both parties' perspectives must be examined. It is the disparity in individuals' perspectives on their relationship that provides meaningful information, not any individual's particular point of view.

Mangen (1988) presents an alternate research strategy to the generational and lineage approaches, involving a focus on role relationships:

> The researcher elects to focus on a limited number of role relationships in order to develop a manageable research problem. Observational procedures or questions can then be developed to evaluate the specific relationships from the perspective of each of the parties involved in that relationship, and measurement models appropriate to the data can be examined. (p. 35)

A role relationship approach was adopted in the current study. The unit of investigation involved dyads of mothers and daughters. Thus, greater insights into complexities of their relationships could be obtained.

Finally, research on parent/child ties at a given stage of life is further complicated by decisions about whose age to use to define the relationship, the parent's age or the child's age (Ryff & Seltzer, 1996). Some theorists have argued that family relationships are shaped by the developmental or life stage needs of the youngest members (Troll, Bengtson, & McFarland, 1979). Yet, in late life, the older member's health declines have been a central focus of research on parent/child ties (Zarit & Eggebeen, 1995). At the same time, age and developmental needs are not synonymous in late life (Uttal & Perlmutter, 1989). A 70-year-old woman may be healthy, active, and still employed or a 70-year-old woman may be widowed, sickly, and in need of assistance with daily tasks. Therefore, in this study, the mother's age and health status were used as the defining criteria for selection of mother/daughter pairs. Women over the age of 70 in good health who had at least one daughter residing nearby were asked to participate.

■ Appendix B
Interviews and Questionnaires

Participants answered the following questions in the individual interview, the take-home questionnaire or during the joint interviews. A version of the research protocols designed for daughters is presented here. Mothers' and daughters' protocols were identical, with the exception of the target of the questions (e.g., daughters answered questions about their mothers and mothers answered questions about their daughters).

INDIVIDUAL INTERVIEW

This interview took place in the mother's or daughter's home. Parts of the interview were tape recorded for later transcription. The interviewer provided specified instructions, follow-up questions, and introductory material not described here.

Section I: Family Background Information

A. *Information About Childhood Family*

1. How many sisters and brothers did you have growing up? (number)
2. How many do you still speak to on the telephone or visit at least once a month? (number)

3. Did your parents live together throughout your childhood? (yes/no)
4. Did anyone else serve as a mother figure to you growing up? (yes/no)

4a. If yes, who? (coded as: grandmother, aunt, stepmother, other relative (specify), other nonrelative (specify)

5. When you think about your relationship with your mother, what years were the happiest for you? (selected from: under age 5, ages 6 to 12, ages 13 to 17, ages 18 to 24, ages 25 to present)
6. Which of your parents did you get along with best growing up? (mother, father, neither, both)
7. I'd like to know a little about how you would rate the job your mother did in raising you and your siblings. Would you say that as a parent she was . . . (rating scale 1 = fair, 7 = superior)

B. *Tie to Father*

1. Is your father still alive? (yes/no)
2. If no, when did he die? (Then, go to next section)
3. If yes, how often do you see your father? (one time a week or more, one to three weeks, one time a month, one time few months, at least once a year, less than once a year)
4. How often do you visit with your father by phone, e-mail, or letter (one time a week or more, one to three weeks, one time a month, one time few months, at least once a year, less than once a year)?
5. Using this scale, can you please rate the quality of your current relationship with your father? (scale of 1 to 7, 1 = poor, 7 = outstanding, one item index)
6. How often do you have a disagreement, a difference of opinion, or a disagreeable visit with your father? (one time a week or more, one to three weeks, one time a month, one time few months, at least once a year, less than once a year)
7. What do you disagree about or get upset about at these times? (open-ended response)

C. *Own Family of Procreation*

1. Number of children of one's own (number)
2. Age, gender, residence of each child (in participant's home, in college, in own home)

3. How would you rate the job that you yourself have done as a mother? As mother would you say that you are . . . (fill in blank using scale where 1 = fair, 7 = superior)
4. Do you currently have a spouse or a serious partner? (with partner/without partner)
5. If married/with partner, How well do you get along with your partner in general? (Scale of 1 to 5, 1 = poorly, 5 = very well)
6. If married/with partner, How well does your mother get along with your (daughter's) partner in general? (Scale of 1 to 5, 1 = poorly, 5 = very well)
7. Is there anyone else is in your household or who plays an important role in your life that we should know about? (open ended)

D. Salience of Social Network Members

1. Out of all the important people in your life, whom do you get along with best? (Open-ended, coded response as: mother, sibling, friend, own child, father, other/specified)
2. Out of all the important people in your life, whom do you feel most free to confide in when you are upset? (Open-ended, coded response as: mother, sibling, friend, own child, father, other/specified)
3. Out of all the important people in your life, whom do you get annoyed with most often? (Open-ended, coded response as: mother, sibling, friend, own child, father, other/specified)
4. How important is your mother to you relative to other people in your life? (Coded choice: 1 = she is the most important person, 2 = she is among the 3 most important people, 3 = she is among the 6 most important people, 4 = she is among the 10 most important people, 5 = she is not among the 10 most important people)

Section II: First Assessment of Conflict

Mothers and daughters all have disagreements of one sort or another.

1. How often do you and your mother have a disagreement?

(once a week, once every one to three weeks, once a month, once every few months, once a year, less than one time per year)

2. When you are upset with your mother, how often do you avoid talking about what's wrong or pretend nothing is wrong (rating scale, 1 = almost never, 3 = sometimes, 5 = almost always)
3. Raise your voice or express your feelings in a way that could hurt her? (rating scale, 1 = almost never, 3 = sometimes, 5 = almost always)
4. Tell her what is wrong and what you'd like her to do? (rating scale, 1 = almost never, 3 = sometimes, 5 = almost always)
5. How do you usually feel after such a disagreement? (open-ended)

Section III: Center for Epidemiological Study of Depression Scale

Twenty-item scale assessing 4 dimensions of depressive symptoms in the general population. For additional information, see:

Radloff, L. S. (1977). The CES-D Scale: A self-report depression scale for the general population. *Applied Psychological Measurement, 1,* 385–401.

Radloff, L. S., & Teri, L. (1986). Use of the center for epidemiological studies-depression scale with older adults. *Clinical Gerontologist, 5,* 119–135.

Section IV: Contact and Interactions with Mother

1. When was the last time you saw your mother? (past 3 days, 3 to 7 days, 8 to 15 days, within the past month, more than 1 month ago)
2. How often do you usually see your mother? (nearly every day, 2 to 3 times a week, 1 time a week, once every 2 to 3 weeks, once a month or so, at family gathering/a few times a year)
3. When was the last time you spoke to your mother on the

telephone? (today, past 3 days, 3 to 7 days, the previous week, longer ago than the past week)

4. How often do you usually talk to her on the phone? (more than 1 time per day, one time per day, 2 to 3 times a week, 1 time a week, 2 to 3 times a month, once a month or less often)
5. How satisfied are you with the frequency of your contact with your mother? (rating scale 1= not very satisfied, 5 = very satisfied)
6. (If answered less than 4, on question) Would you like to see her more frequently or less frequently?
7. Emotional reactions to contact with mother.
   When you visit with your mother, how often do you feel each of the following? List of emotions rated on 3 point scale (rarely, sometimes, almost always): Happy, cared for, knowledgeable, hurt, nervous, grateful, resentful, appreciated, criticized, guilty, frustrated, capable, relaxed, sad, angry

Section V: Enjoyable Visit with Mother

1. I'd like to know a little about the things your mother does that make you happy. Think about the last time you had a particularly enjoyable visit with your mother. By visit I mean a time when you got together, talked on the phone, or went to the other's house. Tell me what happened and why you enjoyed the visit. (Open-ended, tape recorded, and transcribed. Follow-up question: Can you tell me a little more about what happened? Can you tell me a little more about why you enjoyed this visit?)
2. How did you feel at the time of this visit? (open ended, coded emotion)
3. Did your mother know how you felt (yes/no)

3a. If yes, how did she know? (open ended)

3b. If no, why didn't she know how you felt? (open ended)

4. How long ago did you have that visit? (past week, prior week, past month, one to three months ago, longer than 3 months ago)
5. How often do you have visits as pleasant as that one? (at least

1 time per week, once every 1 to 3 weeks, once a month, once every few months, once a year, less often than once a year)

Section VI: Difficult Visit with Mother

1. People we love and value can also be a source of irritation or annoyance at times. Now, I'd like to ask you tell me about the last time you felt irritated, hurt, or annoyed by a visit with your mother. Tell me what happened and why you were upset. (Open-ended, taperecorded, and transcribed. Follow-up question: Can you tell me a little more about what happened? Can you tell me a little more about what bothered you?)
2. How did you feel at the time of this visit? (open ended, coded emotion)
3. Did your mother know how you felt (yes/no)

3a. If yes, how did she know? (open ended)

3b. If no, why didn't she know how you felt? (open ended)

4. How long ago did you have that visit? (past week, prior week, past month, one to three months ago, longer than 3 months ago)
5. How often does this sort of thing happen? (at least 1 time per week, once every 1 to 3 weeks, once a month, once every few months, once a year, less often than once a year)
6. How did you feel about that disagreement after it was over? (Selected choice from: satisfied with what had happened in the end, unsatisfied with what had happened in the end, as though nothing had happened)
7. What other things does your mother do that bother you? (Open-ended, tape recorded, and transcribed. Follow-up question: Can you tell me a little more about what happened? Can you tell me a little more about what bothered you?)
8. How much would you say that your mother bothers you overall? (Rating scale, 1 = not much, 5 = a great deal)

Section VII: Past Difficulties with Mother

1. In this section, participants completed a bar graph using crayons to color in the bar graph numbered from 1 to 7 to

indicate the degree of difficulty they experienced at each specific stage of their relationship with their mother. (Daughter aged 6 to 12, aged 13 to 17, aged 18 to 24, aged 25 to present)

2. Interviewer notes the period that is colored in as most conflicted. Can you tell me a little about what you disagreed about or were upset about during that period? (Open-ended, taperecorded, and transcribed. Follow-up question: Can you tell me a little more about what happened? Can you tell me a little more about what bothered you?)
3. When you when you were those ages, and you were upset with your mother, how often did you avoid talking about what was wrong or pretend nothing is wrong? (rating scale, 1 = almost never, 3 = sometimes, 5 = almost always)
4. When you when you were those ages, and you were upset with your mother, how often did you raise your voice or express your feelings in a way that could hurt her? (rating scale, 1 = almost never, 3 = sometimes, 5 = almost always)
5. When you when you were those ages, and you were upset with your mother, how often did you tell her what was wrong and what you'd like her to do to make it better? (rating scale, 1 = almost never, 3 = sometimes, 5 = almost always)
6. How did you usually feel at those times? (open-ended)

Section VIII: Interview Conclusion

The interviewer assured the daughter of her confidentiality, asked the daughter not to discuss the interview with her mother, and confirmed the day and time of the joint interview. The daughter received a packet of questionnaires to complete prior to the next interview.

QUESTIONNAIRES

Women completed the questionnaires on their own during the interval between the individual and joint interviews. Instructions were provided for each section of the questionnaire. Interviewers assisted women with sections of the questionnaire that they had not completed on their own prior to the start of the joint interviews.

Section I: Background Information

1. Age, date of birth.
2. Marital status (married, remarried (marriage #), divorced, separated, single/never married, single/never married/with partner, widowed, other/specify).
3. How long has this been your current marital status? (reported in years)
4. Mother's marital status (married, divorced, widowed, other/specify).

4a. If mother is widowed, Taking all things into account, how has your relationship with your mother changed since she has been on her own? (1 = much worse, 3 = about the same, 5 = much better)

5. Own and spouse's achieved education levels
6. Have your ever worked for pay? (yes/no)
7. If yes, what is/was your main occupation? (open-ended, could offer multiple responses)
8. What is/was your spouse's occupation? (open-ended, could offer multiple responses)
9. What is your current work status? (employed full time, employed part time, retired, unemployed and seeking work, home maker, student, other/specify)
10. How stressful do you find your work or what you do on weekdays? (rating scale 1 = not at all stressful, 3 = somewhat stressful, 5 = very stressful)
11. How much leisure time (time to do what you want) do you have each week? (rating scale 1 = almost none, 3 = enough, 5 = too much)
12. What is your current religious affiliation? (open-ended, none included as a choice)

Section II: Health

1. List of current health problems (open-ended coded)
2. Approximately how many days in the past year were you incapacitated due to illness?
3. How many times in the past year did you see a medical doctor?

4. Does somebody help you get to the doctor? (yes/no)
4a. If yes, who? (open-ended)
5. How many days in the past year have you spent in the hospital?
6. How many prescription drugs do you presently take?
6a. List of prescription medications
7. Does somebody remind you to take your medicine? (yes/no)
7a. If yes, who reminds you? (open-ended)

Section III: Mother/Daughter Interdependency

A. *How often do you do each of the following for your mother?*
All responses were rated using 1 = many times a week, 2 = once a week, 3 = once every 2 to 3 weeks, 4 = once a month, 5 = a few times a year, 6 = less than once a year

1. Help take care of her when she is ill
2. Give her money/Loan her money
3. Offer her advice on how to deal with one of life's problems
4. Offer her advice on business or financial matters
5. Comfort her when she is upset about something
6. Run errands for her

B. *How often does your mother do each of the following for you?*
All responses were rated using 1 = many times a week, 2 = once a week, 3 = once every 2 to 3 weeks, 4 = once a month, 5 = a few times a year, 6 = less than once a year

1. Help take care of you when you are ill
2. Give you money/Loan you money
3. Offer you advice on how to deal with one of life's problems
4. Offer you advice on business or financial matters
5. Comfort you when you are upset about something
6. Run errands for you

Section IV: Story Completion

Participants completed the following story stems using lined space available for their responses. Responses were later transcribed into a computer and coded by independent raters.

1. Sarah is an elderly woman who has lived on her own since her husband died 2 years ago. Prior to his death, she saw her daughter Linda every couple of weeks. Over the past 2 years, Linda has begun to come over several times a week to get something to eat, use her mother's washing machine, or to borrow money. Sarah used to enjoy knowing that Linda might drop by. Recently, she has begun to wish Linda would call before she comes. Sarah also wishes Linda would ask before she uses or takes things from the house. Linda has been feeling increasingly responsible for her mother. She makes a point of stopping by to check on her mother several times a week. In fact, Sarah is expecting Linda to stop by any minute now . . .
   Please finish this story. What happens next? (Page with lined space provided)
   How does Sarah (the mother) feel about the way things turn out in the end?
   How does Linda (the daughter) feel about the way things turn out in the end?
2. Alice is a middle-aged woman with two children. She gets one afternoon a week off from her job and usually spends part of that time taking her mother, Esther, to the grocery store. Alice rarely has time to talk to her mother outside these weekly outings. Esther counts on these shopping trips with her daughter as a highlight in her week. Alice has been feeling increasingly tired recently. She would like to cancel her shopping trip with her mother this week. Alice calls her mother the morning of their usual shopping trip and . . .
   Please finish this story. What happens next? (Page with lined space provided)
   How does Esther (the mother) feel about the way things turn out in the end?
   How does Alice (the daughter) feel about the way things turn out in the end?

Section V: Relationship Quality

Participants completed the Positive Affect Index, providing information about their own and their mother's or daughter's feelings about the relationship. For additional information, see:

Bengtson, V. L. (1973) Positive affect index. In V. L. Bengtson & S.S. Schrader (1982) Parent-child relations. In D. J. Mangen & W. A. Peterson (Eds.), *Research Instruments in social gerontology: Vol. 1. Social roles and social participation* (p. 154). Minneapolis, MN: University of Minnesota Press.

JOINT INTERVIEW

The joint interviews took place in either the mother's or the daughter's home at a time of convenience to both parties. Analyses revealed no differences in the findings from these interviews as a function of whether the interview took place at the mother's or the daughter's house. These interviews included observed conversations between mothers and daughters and paper and pencil assessments completed individually by mother and daughter. Mother and daughter sat across the room from one another and completed these questionnaires without input from the other party.

Section I: Discussion of a Problematic Visit

The interviewer read the following instructions:
All families have disagreements or differences of opinion of one sort or another during the course of their daily lives. One person has an idea about how something should be done and the other person has a different idea about how it should be done. Or one person does something she feels is all right and the other person feels hurt about what has been done. This is particularly true between parents and children of all ages. I'd like you to think of a recent disagreement or difference of opinion you had. I'd like you both to agree on the same situation. You don't have to actually discuss the problem, just enough so that you both know you're talking about the same situation. Please describe a little about what happened and why one or both of you might have been upset. (Mother's and daughter's discussion was taperecorded, transcribed, and coded by independent raters).

Section II: Problematic Situation Follow-Up Questions

Mothers and daughters sat across the room from one another and completed the following questions on their own.

A. *Ratings of Behaviors During the Problematic Situation*
   Participants used the following scale to rate their own and their mother's or daughter's behaviors in this situation 1 = very true, 2 = somewhat true, 3 = not very true, 4 = not at all true

   1. Own Behaviors
      I calmly discussed the situation.
      I listened to her point of view
      I tried to find out what she was feeling
      I talked about nice things instead of the problem.
      I yelled at my mother.
      I suggested a new way to look at things
      I offended my mother
      I avoided my mother
      I brought up things that happened long ago
      I became very quiet
      I tried to make her laugh
      I didn't call her for awhile
      I wanted to compromise
      I had to have the last word
      I didn't know that anything was wrong at the time
   2. Mother's Behaviors
      My mother calmly discussed the situation.
      She listened to my point of view
      My mother tried to find out what I was feeling
      My mother talked about nice things instead
      My mother yelled at me
      My mother suggested a new way to look at things.
      My mother offended me
      My mother avoided me
      My mother brought up things that happened long ago
      My mother became very quiet
      She tried to make me laugh
      My mother didn't call me for awhile

My mother wanted to compromise
My mother had to have the last word
My mother didn't know that anything was wrong at the time

B. Feelings about Situation

1. How did you feel about the situation at the time that it happened? (open-ended response)
2. How did your mother feel about this situation at the time that it happened? (open-ended response)
3. Was this disagreement about something that is important to you? (yes/no)
4. Do you think the disagreement was completely settled, mostly settled, or do you think the problem will come up again? (Selected choice: completely settled, mostly settled, will come up again).
5. How typical was this situation of other disagreeable situations in your relationship? (Rating scale 1 = not at all typical, 5 = very typical)

Section III: Joint Problem Solving

This section of the joint interview focused on mothers' and daughters' approaches to solving problems together. There were two assessments of problem solving. Mothers and daughters first completed a check list, rating the degree to which they valued specific behaviors mothers and daughters might engage in as part of their relationship (e.g., Daughters should care for their mothers when they are ill and require assistance, no matter what they cost to them personally.) They then came together and rated the same checklists during a tape recorded discussion. Next, mothers and daughters received a picture of a woman and a girl and wrote a story on their own about the picture. They then came together and wrote a story collectively, based on that same picture. Their discussions were also tape recorded. Data from these problem solving tasks are not reported in this book, but rather, are reported elsewhere. For additional information about these tasks, see: Lefkowitz, E. S., & Fingerman,

K. L. (1944). *Conversational styles in the aging mother and adult daughter relationship* (unpublished manuscript).

Section IV: Final Assessment of Conflict

Mothers and daughters completed these questions independently, while seated across the room from one another.

1. How often do you and your mother have a disagreement? (once a week, once every one to three weeks, once a month, once every few months, once a year, less than one time per year)
2. When you are upset with your mother, how often do you avoid talking about what's wrong or pretend nothing is wrong (rating scale, 1 = almost never, 3 = sometimes, 5 = almost always)
3. Raise your voice or express your feelings in a way that could hurt her? (rating scale, 1 = almost never, 3 = sometimes, 5 = almost always)
4. Tell her what is wrong and what you'd like her to do? (rating scale, 1 = almost never, 3 = sometimes, 5 = almost always)
5. How do you usually feel after such a disagreement? (open-ended)

Section V: Interview Completion

Participants were debriefed through a discussion of their feelings about the study, their relationship, and an opportunity to ask the interviewer questions.

Index

Page numbers followed by "*t*" indicate a table, "*f*" indicates a figure.